CLEAN

AS A WHISTLE

CLEAN
AS A WHISTLE
HOUSEHOLD HINTS AND TIPS

GLORIA OXFORD

Published in 2013 by New Holland Publishers
London • Sydney • Cape Town • Auckland
www.newhollandpublishers.com • www.newholland.com.au

Garfield House 86–88 Edgware Road London W2 2EA United Kingdom
1/66 Gibbes Street Chatswood NSW 2067 Australia
Wembley Square First Floor Solan Road Gardens Cape Town 8001 South Africa
218 Lake Road Northcote Auckland New Zealand

A catalogue record of this book is available at the British Library and at the
National Library of Australia

ISBN: 9781742573601

10 9 8 7 6 5 4 3 2 1

Publisher: Fiona Schultz
Designer: Lorena Susak
Production director: Olga Dementiev
Printer: Toppan Leefung Printing Ltd, China

10 9 8 7 6 5 4 3 2 1

Cover image: iStock.

Follow New Holland Publishers on
Facebook: www.facebook.com/NewHollandPublishers

About the Author

Gloria Oxford was educated in the rudiments of home science when they were an integral part of the school curriculum.

Her early career was in statistics and market research, after which she spent five years with a top fashion magazine before joining a leading appliance manufacturer as advertising manager.

An inquiring mind and a love of puzzles make her an ideal trouble shooter and problem solver. This is clearly evidenced by consumer response to her magazine and newspaper columns, and her regular radio programs.

Gloria frequently reproduces problems that people write to her about, and then sets about finding a solution. She readily admits that this often involves considerable sleuthing and experimentation that can cause long delays in answering her enormous amount of mail.

An avid traveller, Gloria is constantly on the lookout for new ideas and hints to pass on to her readers and listeners.

Without being a fanatic, Gloria is environmentally aware, and encourages recycling in the home for saving money and the environment.

INTRODUCTION

After many years of writing columns, making television appearances, and taking part in talkback radio programs plus answering the thousands of letters I receive from all over the world, I have changed the format of this book to suit your needs.

The Hints, in the form of Household Help, are presented, at your request, room by room, to provide information and help you to organise the housework so that it does not become a burdensome chore.

I want you to enjoy your free time but, if you come home to chaos, enjoyment can quickly change to despair. I hope the information contained in these pages helps make life easier for you.

CONTENTS

OUTSIDE THE HOME

In the beginning, Man sallied forth from his cave with a club, grabbed a female by the hair, and dragged her back to do the cooking, cleaning, breeding and caring. Since then, everything has changed. Even the description of the cave has changed but, regardless of what it is named—house, home, apartment, flat, palace or chateau—one thing remains constant. The cave still needs to be cleaned and cared for.

The first introduction to your place of abode is the surrounding area, and if nothing else, it should be clean, tidy, and look as if someone cares.

The gate should be free of spider webs and dust. Paths should be swept regularly, and the front door clean. If the front door needs painting, don't delay - paint it.

ALUMINIUM WINDOW FRAMES

To clean aluminium window frames, make a paste with powdered whiting (available at hardware stores) and methylated spirits. Put some of the paste onto a cloth and polish the frames. Buff up with a soft, clean cloth. If the frames have caked-on dirt, use a brush, very hot water and wool wash before applying the whiting paste.

ANIMALS

When cats or dogs exercise their territorial claim by urinating on, in and around doorways, wash the claim away with hot water and a good disinfectant. Let it dry, then spray with one of the commercial deterrents, available from hardware stores and garden supply shops.

ANIMALS ON GARDENS

When animals choose one particular spot to urinate or defecate on the garden, apart from the smell, plants are likely to die. While there are commercial products which certainly act as a deterrent, it might be better to plant *Coleus caninus*, a small perennial which deters both cats and dogs. Use a bird and animal repellent, available from garden supply shops and some hardware stores. Respray Multicrop after rain or watering.

ANTS – IN THE GARDEN

An old recipe for keeping ants out of the garden is to mix 250 grams (½ lb) salt, with half a litre (1 pint) of water then mix in 5 kilograms (10 lbs) of sawdust or bran and about 10 cups of molasses. It makes a very crumbly mixture to spread around plants and shrubs, and is not dangerous to children and pets.

ANT – REPELLENT

I have had a great deal of success ridding my place of ants with diatomaceous earth. It is sold under different brand names for swimming pool filters. It is a powder and looks a bit messy when spread around but within two days the scurrying lines of ants slow to a crawl and after four days, disappear. They come back of course but with their numbers rapidly diminishing. As with talcum powder, don't breathe it in.

APHIDS

One of the best ways of keeping the aphid population to a minimum is to plant lots of garlic in the garden. It has the added advantage of producing an extra crop for kitchen use. Garlic chives have the same effect, so two or three clumps of them could also be added to the garden.

An effective natural spray for aphids is made by putting 1 tablespoon Epsom salt and 1 teaspoon Condy's crystals in a bucket of water and once every two weeks spray a little around the plant. A good idea is to save a pump spray from one of your household cleaners, wash it out,

fill with the Condy's spray and use it to spray around the plants. Alternatively, boil onions in water and when cold, sprinkle the strained water around the plants.

If a plague of aphids attacks washing on the line, a yellow plastic bucket, smeared with lanoline, and hung on the line will turn the aphids from the washing to the bucket. Aphids are attracted to yellow. They stick to the lanoline, making it a simple matter to rinse them away with hot water. Another way to rid the washing of aphids is to put the washing into a heavy green garbage bag, make it airtight and leave for several hours. The aphids suffocate and can easily be shaken from the clothes. Putting the washing into a tumble dryer also rids the clothing of aphids, but contain it in a pillowslip or the tumble dryer will be full of dead insects.

AZALEAS

If azaleas are to be planted in a cement tub, the container needs to be treated before planting. Put 125 grams ($^1/_3$ oz) of alum into the tub, then fill the tub with cold water and leave for three days to neutralise the lime in the cement.

BANANA SKINS

Don't throw the skins away. They are good food for staghorn ferns tucked in at the back of the plant. For potted maidenhair ferns, chop up banana skins and mix with the potting mix.

BEANS TO GROW

Seeds won't germinate if the ground is too cold, but if you want an early crop, sow them indoors in peat moss then plant out when the weather is warmer. In the springtime the seeds will need to be planted only about 2 cm below the surface, but as the hot sun penetrates the soil in summer, plant the seeds 3 cm down. Beans need plenty of water and fertiliser, and yield more if you keep picking when young and succulent.

BIRDS NESTING

Birds can be nuisances, particularly under the eaves of verandahs. To frighten the birds away from the nesting area, strips of aluminium foil can be tied on string and put up. The strips tinkle together as the birds flutter about. The combination of glittering tinsel and the noise will often scare the birds away. Chinese or Japanese "windsongs" can also be used as bird chasers or spray with a bird repellent. For bird droppings on the car, or other paintwork, get it off quickly, with plenty of hot soapy water. Bird droppings can damage paintwork.

BROOM HANDLE

Don't throw away that old broom. Remove the head and drive a 7.5 centimetre nail firmly into the end of the handle. Walk around the lawn pushing it into the grass. The holes will not be noticeable and will allow the water to penetrate instead of running off the top.

CANVAS MILDEW

Mildew on canvas should be scrubbed with two cups of salt dissolved in about half a bucket of water. If lemons are available put the juice of five or six lemons into the water with the salt. Moss, mildew and rust can all cause disintegration of the fabric which may not be noticeable until the fibres break, so proceed carefully.

CATS

Keep cats away from favourite plants by splashing a little kerosene or cloudy ammonia on a cloth and leaving it on the garden. Another tip that works well is chilli sauce. Sprinkle it around where cats like to go. One sniff and they'll quickly go somewhere else. Or, hose the cats with the garden hose; it won't hurt them but they will go elsewhere. Or, spray with a commercial product, available from nurseries and some hardware stores.

CONCRETE

To prepare concrete tubs for plants that may be allergic to lime, put in about 125 grams (4 oz) of alum and fill the tubs with water. Leave for about three days. Empty the tubs and wash them thoroughly before adding soil to plant azaleas, or other plants that don't tolerate lime.

Moss on concrete can be slippery and very dangerous. To kill moss, use 30 grams (1 oz) of sulphate of iron (available from hardware stores or nurserymen) to 4½ litres (152 fl oz) of water and scrub with a hard broom. Another way to rid paths of moss is to rub crushed butchers salt into the moss. Leave it until the moss dies then sweep with a stiff broom.

For rust on concrete use spirits of salts (obtainable from hardware shops or pharmacists). Cover the rust with spirits of salts, then with sawdust and leave about 12 hours. Use gloves to avoid burning your hands.

Strange but true! Kitty Litter will clean concrete. Dampen the concrete. Spread the litter, leave overnight then brush with a very hard yard broom.

To remove an oil spill on concrete, buy some chalk powder from a hardware store. The amount needed is dependent upon the size of the oil spill. Mix the chalk to a creamy paste with white spirits, or shellite (naptha). Spread the paste over the oil stain, cover it with plastic and leave for a week before brushing it on to a shovel and discarding it. If there is any residual staining, repeat the process. Finally, scrub the area with very hot water and disinfectent liquid. Use about two tablespoons of disinfectent liquid to a quarter bucket of water.

DOG FLEAS

There are a number of herbs that are said to repel fleas. Fennel can be planted around the dog's kennel if it is an outdoors dog. If the dog lives indoors, fennel can be rubbed into its coat. Pennyroyal rubbed into the skin of the dog, or used in pets bedding is also said to be a good repellent. Commercial products have been tested by experts who add herbal chemicals in amounts that are unlikely to harm your pets, so do take care to watch your dog's reaction to

the herbs you use. It is a good idea to check any herbal remedy with your vet before using it.

DOG PLANT

Coleus canis is a name used in nurseries for an unpleasant smelling, blue-flowered, succulent herb with a reputation for repelling dogs. The specific epithet *canis* is a misspelling as the species name should be *Coleus caninus*.

DOOR SCREENS

Sometimes impurities in the atmosphere eat into the finish of a security door. If the door is painted, repaint it, and once the paint is thoroughly dry, spray it regularly with a good silicone car polish. If the door has a metal finish, use a matching colour like a wax colour, available from car accessory shops. If you don't want to go to that expense, try a matching shoe polish.

EARWIGS

Earwigs come out at night and an easy way to get rid of them is to use folded newspaper or a cardboard box in the garden. Put the newspaper or box in the garden at night, the earwigs will swarm into the paper for their daily rest. When daylight comes, gather the paper or box and burn it, along with the earwigs. Another method is to put pieces of garden hose, about 20 centimetres long where earwigs gather. They will go into the hose and can be knocked out into the incinerator. Burn immediately or use boiling water to kill the insects.

FENNEL

This herb has an aniseed-type flavour and is ideal with fish, salad and spaghetti sauces.

FERNS

Potted ferns are most attractive indoor plants and are also an effective deterrent to flies. Place a hanging basket, or a pot, containing ferns near the door or window where flies come in. It may not stop a really determined fly, but the timid ones will go elsewhere.

GARDEN FURNITURE

White, plastic garden furniture is best cleaned with very hot water, a scrubbing brush and woollen mix. The plastic will not come back to its former, pristine white because heat, cold, rain and sun all cause changes in the plastic. Yellowing will certainly take place, and sometimes, the plastic will become brittle and crack. After cleaning, a softener should be applied. Any good, cream car polish is suitable. If at all possible, store plastic garden furniture indoors, or at least under cover, during the winter months when it is not in use.

GARDEN SPRAYS

• In a bucket of water, put 1 tablespoon of Epsom salt and 1 teaspoon of Condy's crystals

(obtainable from pharmacists). Use as a garden spray for plants, shrubs and vegetables. This spray is non-toxic.

- Garlic spray. Four hot peppers, four big onions, two bulbs of garlic. Crush the peppers, onions and garlic and cover with water, leave up to 24 hours. Strain, and add water to make up 4 litres (135 fl oz). This spray is non-toxic.
- The leaves of rhubarb can be used as a garden spray for vegetables. Roughly chop the leaves and put them into a large saucepan with enough water to more than cover them. Bring to the boil and keep simmering for about twenty minutes. Strain; allow to cool; then bottle. While this is a natural product, it is still highly toxic so it is important to wash vegetables thoroughly before use and use a non-cooking pot.

LIGHTS
For outdoor parties, try punching holes with a nail in an old fruit tin. Secure a candle in the tin. It gives a very soft light and prevents the candles from being snuffed out in the wind.

MASON BEES
Spread kerosene, or wipe with a kerosene saturated cloth, where mason bees are nesting.

POSSUMS
Use a pesticide for possums, such as a bird and animal repellent, particularly for roses and small plants. Follow the instructions on the packet. For fruit trees, light is an excellent possum deterrent, so why not rig the trees with fairy lights? Turn them on when the fruit begins to form and the possums are looking for a smorgasbord.

Tabasco sauce mixed with a water-glue then daubed over the trunk of the trees will also help to deter the possums.

In addition, spray the trees with lapsang souchong tea. Put 125 grams (4 oz) of tea into a bucket, cover the leaves with half a bucket of boiling water. Let it stand, with a cover to retain the aroma, until it is cold. Strain, and use as a spray. Lapsang souchong tea smells like creosote that is unpalatable to possums. It will be necessary to re-spray after rain.

SANDFLIES
A few dabs of citronella on the skin will help to keep sandflies at bay. If you are bitten, equal quantities of cold tea and methylated spirits will ease the itching almost immediately.

SEEDS
To successfully store seeds, it is important that the seeds reach maturity before they are picked from the plant. Spread the seeds to dry either in the sun or in a warm dry room. When thoroughly dry, dust lightly with a good powder fungicide, before storing. Don't store in containers where sweating is liable to occur.

SLUGS

To rid the garden of slugs without using chemicals, heat some cabbage leaves in the oven or microwave until soft, then coat the leaves with unsalted butter or clean dripping. Put the leaves in the garden where the slugs gather. Once the leaves are covered with slugs, they can be picked up and destroyed

SNAILS

An old-fashioned method of ridding the garden of snails is to mix lime, soot and bran together in equal quantities and sprinkle around the edges of the beds. Lime mixed with salt will also kill snails, but keep the lime away from azaleas.

UMBRELLA

Use a solution of salt and water to remove mould from a canvas umbrella. Scrub all over the umbrella using a soft brush with a solution of approximately two cups of salt to half a bucket of water. The umbrella should be open and it is best to scrub both sides. Leave open until dry.

VERANDAH – WOOD

Clear timber varnish will cover and weatherproof a timber verandah without altering the colour or grain of the wood. It may need two or even three coats, depending on how much use the verandah will get. Any coating will wear off with time but you should get a fairly long life from timber varnish.

WALLS - STAINED

Wasps, swallows and ivy, all leave discolouration on walls. First, try scrubbing with hot water and wool wash (see recipe). If that is not successful, it may be necessary to resort to liquid sugar soap, following the instructions on the bottle, but use at half strength because you only want to remove the stains. Check a small area first to evaluate the effect on the wall.

WASPS

Wasps nest almost anywhere. Spray at night when the wasps have retired. Cover your head with a scarf or see-through curtain. Spray quickly, then leave the area. Repeat the next night if necessary. Some local councils and government authorities have a wasp eradication program and it is a good idea to check this out first.

KITCHEN

When spring is in the air, it is time to think about doing a few of those rotten chores which most of us prefer to forget, such as cleaning the fridge, freezer, dishwasher, and microwave oven. The fridge is probably cleaned regularly but it is easy to miss the seals around the door. They are usually made of soft plastic, often with pleats or ridges that help the door to seal perfectly. Even the smooth seals gather dirt, moisture, and food spills, and if left without cleaning will eventually begin to disintegrate. When this happens, the efficiency of the fridge is affected. A strain is put upon the motor and the whole operation of the fridge becomes more costly. Clean those seals with hot water and dish washing liquid. Stubborn stains can be sprayed with an all purpose cleaner and use an old toothbrush to scrub the pleats and ridges. Dry the seals thoroughly with a thick towel after cleaning.

The freezer is the next job to tackle. Everything should be taken out, the freezer defrosted, cleaned and re-packed. Do this task the day before re-stocking the fridge for the week, thereby leaving plenty of shelf space in the fridge to put things from the freezer. They will stay frozen for the time it takes to clean and defrost the freezer and can be sorted as you put them back. When putting things back into the clean freezer, don't forget the old adage, "When in doubt, throw it out." It is not worth poisoning the family or friends for the sake of saving something you'd forgotten about anyway. The seal around the door of the freezer will not take as much effort to clean as the fridge seal because it is not in such continual use. Don't skip it because it looks okay. The cost of replacing worn out freezer seals is nothing compared with the cost of having to throw out everything from the freezer.

The seal around the oven door is bound to have attracted fat splatters, so wear gloves, use very hot water and any good detergent to clean it. For stubborn stains, spray with your favourite grease remover. For the microwave oven, follow the manufacturer's cleaning instructions. It is a good idea to leave the microwave oven door open occasionally to get rid of the build-up of cooking staleness. Cloudy ammonia is good for removing grease. Of all the seals to be cleaned in the kitchen, I think the automatic dishwasher is the worst job of all. Mainly because not only do you have to bend down to do the job, but invariably, you finish up with cuts all over your hands, trying to get into the corners. Wear gloves. Or, use a long-handled dish washing brush to clean the seals, then wrap a cloth over the brush to rinse and dry.

Attending to each and every one of the seals in the kitchen is an essential task but don't tackle them all on the same day.

COOKWARE

The best cookware is the cookware that suits your particular needs. Sets of different sizes will probably suit a family, but may not suit a person who cooks only for one or two people. Good quality stainless steel with a heavy copper bottom will suit both gas and electric cooking.

Aluminium cookware is good at the top of the range, particularly in designer colours. Cast iron cookware is popular but must be tempered before use. Also, it is heavy and becomes heavier with food in it. Before buying, check the weight. Check the handles - they must be firm and comfortable. Check that the base sits flat, and lastly, check the guarantee.

IN THE CLEANING CUPBOARD

Try not to overstock the cleaning cupboard but make sure the essentials for emergency cleaning are always at hand.

Here are ten things for the cleaning cupboard under the sink or in the laundry. With these, you will be able to cope with most stains, on the carpet, clothing or furniture.

- Powdered borax
- Methylated spirits
- Kerosene
- Mineral turpentine
- Ammonia
- household detergent
- Talcum powder
- Eucalyptus
- pen-off
- A solvent (shellite, acetone, white spirit or lacquer thinner)

OUT OF REACH

It is automatic to put things out of the reach of children, but for your own health's sake, put tea, coffee and other items which are used daily, just beyond your own reach. Once we have grown to adulthood, daily stretching is important for our bodies, as much of our lives are spent stooping, to children, ovens, cleaning, etc. Forget about putting things within easy reach, put the things most used on a shelf where it is necessary to stand on tiptoe and stretch up to get them.

OVEN – GENERAL

Always wipe the oven after each use and while it is still hot. It's a nuisance that takes a few minutes but will save hours of hard work in the future.

Even with continual wiping, the oven still needs regular cleaning. Heat the oven then turn it off and put a small bowl of cloudy ammonia on the middle shelf and a bowl of hot water on the bottom of the oven. Leave overnight and in the morning, sponge with hot, soapy water. If

the treatment is not satisfactory, wring out a cloth in hot water, sprinkle the cloth with cream of tartar and rub the inside of the oven. Very dirty ovens will need to be treated two or three times, and stubborn marks may need a commercial cleaner and steel wool. When using a commercial oven cleaner, read the instructions and follow them carefully. Mr. Muscles All Purpose Cleaner works well.

VEGETABLES

Green-topped vegetables—such as carrots, beetroots and turnips—keep better if the tops are removed before storing. Store them in a brown paper bag, not plastic. The paper absorbs some of the moisture while plastic can make them sweat and quickly deteriorate.

Leafy vegetables, such as lettuce and cabbage, are best wrapped in kitchen paper then put in a plastic bag. Keep in the vegetable drawer of the refrigerator.

Most vegetable stains can be removed by sponging with a solution of borax and warm water. Use 2 tablespoons of borax to 1 litre (2 pints) of water. Wring out a cloth in the solution and sponge from the outside edge of the stain to the centre.

WASHING DISHES

If you are machine-washing dishes, make sure the detergent you use is suitable, not only for the machine but also for the dishes.

Do not wash good china that has gold leaf on it in a dishwashing machine. Dark-coloured dinnerware becomes filmy with machine-washing. Put a little methylated spirits onto a soft cloth to rub the film off. Polish any smears away with a soft, dry cloth.

ANGELICA

The leaf of the herb angelica is used in salads. Stalks and stems can be crystallised for cake decoration. Chewing the stems is an old-fashioned remedy for flatulence.

APPLES

To freeze apples, place in a brine solution of 1 teaspoon salt to 1 cup water, for about 10 minutes, then blanch in boiling unsalted water for about 1½ minutes. No sugar is needed but the addition of lemon juice or ascorbic acid powder is a must.

To prevent sliced apples from going brown, squeeze lemon juice over them. If you don't like the taste of lemon juice, the apple slices can be kept in cold water with a pinch of salt until ready to be cooked.

APPLE – STAIN

Raw apples on clothing can leave a slight brown stain if not sponged off immediately with cold water on a damp cloth. If the stain is dry, dampen slightly then cover with powdered borax and leave for half an hour. If the material is suitable, run hot water through the borax. If not, use warm water.

APRICOTS

To freeze, peel and remove the stones. Always use perfect, unbruised fruit for freezing. Stew or blanch and leave to cool before freezing.

To dry apricots, make a solution with 8 litres (280 fl oz) cold water, 3 cups sugar and 200 grams (7 oz) sodium metabisulphite. Prepare the fruit by washing, slicing in half and removing the stones. Cut out and discard blemishes, or use perfect fruit. Put the fruit into a large container and cover them completely with the solution. Let stand overnight. Remove from the solution and put the fruit, cut side down, on a rack to dry. A warm garage, free of dust, is a good place to dry fruit. If it is to be left in the sun to dry, it should be under a mesh type canopy so that insects and dust do not spoil the fruit. The fruit needs to be turned every four days, or until dry.

To make sugarless apricot jam, stone and cut the fruit, removing any bruises and blemishes. Cover the fruit with water and bring to the boil. Boil hard to reduce the fluid content, then add 1 teaspoon gelatine for each cup of fruit. Without sugar, the gelatine is necessary for setting. This recipe will not have the keeping qualities of normal jam, so make it in small quantities, and store in the refrigerator.

ASPARAGUS

Freeze asparagus using only young spears with tight tips. Break off and discard the tough parts of the stalk; wash, then water blanch for two minutes. Do not use plastic bags for asparagus. A rigid container is best. When cooking asparagus, use a teaspoon of sugar to bring out the flavour. Salt toughens the delicate spears.

ASPIC

A jelly made from meat stock that has been sufficiently reduced by boiling to set firmly when cold. Gelatine may be added to the strained stock. Aspic should be served at room temperature.

AUBERGINE

More commonly known as eggplant, aubergine is often served with meat dishes, sliced and lightly fried in breadcrumbs. They can also be stuffed and served as a side or for a snack-type meal. This vegetable freezes well either sliced or as a puree.

AVOCADO

To ripen avocado fruit, wrap in dry newspaper or in a brown paper bag, and leave in a warm, dry place. An apple, wrapped with the avocado, helps to accelerate ripening. Once the fruit is sufficiently ripe, store in the vegetable section of the refrigerator.

BABY FOOD JARS

Re-sealable baby food jars are not suitable for preserving. The convenience factor of these jars is for the times when baby does not eat the entire contents at one sitting. Serve say, half the contents of the jar then re-seal for use at the next meal. It is not even recommended that uneaten food from baby's plate be returned to the jar because saliva from the spoon could contain bacteria.

BACON

A good way to keep bacon is to dampen a cloth with vinegar and wrap it around the sliced bacon then put into a plastic bag. If the bacon has been pre-packed, remove it from the plastic packet before wrapping in the cloth. Store in the refrigerator. Change the cloth every few days. White paper towel is just as suitable and a less tedious way to store bacon. There are varying opinions on whether to freeze bacon. It can be done, but is best in small amounts. Put dividers between each rasher and use within 4 weeks.

BACON COOKING TIPS

Dust bacon on both sides with a little plain flour before cooking or, remove the rind first, dust with flour, then fry or bake. The bacon rashers will not curl, and the flour stops the fat from splattering.

BAKING POWDER

Baking powder is a combination of sodium bicarbonate and cream of tartar. Unless a recipe states otherwise, always sift baking powder and other dry ingredients before adding any liquid. Because baking powder can become stale and lose its potency, it is always best to test before using it. Put a little into some cold water. If it fizzes well, the baking powder is fine to use. If not discard it and open a new tin.

BAY LEAVES

In dried form, bay leaves are readily available; an essential ingredient in bouquet garni and a very good additive to many casseroles and stews. The leaves can be used fresh or dried.

BEANS

There are many varieties of beans, all of which freeze well and are easily grown, even in small gardens.

- Broad beans are podded, like peas, before cooking but don't discard the pods. Use them for mulch in the garden.
- Dried beans can be a useful commodity to keep in the cupboard and you do not need to resort to the old-fashioned method of soaking them overnight before cooking. A much better way is to place them in a saucepan, cover with water and bring to the boil. Boil for two minutes, remove from the heat, and allow to stand in the water for one hour, then cook until tender.
- Bean sprouts make a quick, easy-to-grow, tasty vegetable. Special bean sprouters and suitable beans are available at health shops.
- To preserve green beans mix together 500 grams (16 oz) of salt and 250 grams (8 oz) of sugar. Top, tail, and string if necessary, 1 kilogram (32 oz) of fresh, clean, dry beans. Put the beans into an earthenware crock and spread the salt and sugar mixture evenly over them. Cover with a piece of net fabric and leave overnight. The salt and sugar will turn to a brine solution that should completely cover the beans. Now cover with two layers of net fabric and store in a cool place. Use as required by taking out sufficient beans for immediate use, wash them well in very cold water; then cook as usual.

BEETROOT – FREEZING

Cooked beetroot can be kept in the freezer, or the freezing compartment of the refrigerator. Choose firm, young, small beetroot, preferably free from cracks and blemishes. Cut off the tops, leaving just a little of the stem and, don't remove the root. Wash and boil until tender (about 30 minutes), then remove the skins and root. Small beetroot can be frozen whole. Large ones can be sliced or quartered. Pack in freezer bags or plastic containers.

BLINDS – BONDED

The kitchen usually has a build-up of grease and dust, which collects on blinds. Take the blinds down, cover with a mixture of 1 cup powdered borax, ½ cup of salt and 2 tablespoons of dry-cleaning fluid or shellite (naphtha). Rub the mixture over the blind with the palm of your hand, then brush down with a clean towel. Then, with a towel, dipped in fairly hot water, detergent and a dash of a liquid disinfectant, and wrung out until almost dry, sponge over any other spots. If the blind is too badly stained, reverse it so that the clean part from the top is at the bottom.

BLINDS – HOLLAND

Holland blinds, particularly those over the kitchen sink, often become watermarked or greasy. Watermarks are almost impossible to remove. If sponging with warm water and vinegar does not remove watermarks, invert the blind, putting the top to the bottom. For blinds that have become greasy, take them down and rub all over with warm bran. Let the bran sit on the blinds for an hour or so, brush it off, then sponge with warm soapy water.

BOTTLING

The lacquered lids becoming scratched often causes discolouration at the top of bottled fruit. Get new lids, or cover the fruit with cling film before sealing. Be sure that fruit is completely covered with liquid.

BREAD CRUMBS

Don't throw away left-over bread. Put slices in a slow oven to dry, then roll the hardened slices into crumbs. Store in an airtight jar. Stale bread can also be put in the food processor, then frozen and used in recipes that require fresh bread crumbs.

BURNT SAUCEPAN

Cover the bottom of the saucepan with oil, then put it on the stove to heat the oil. Stand over the stove while it is heating because the oil should not become smoking hot. Remove it from the heat, let it stand for about fifteen minutes, then tip the oil out and wash the saucepan. Any residual staining can be removed with a cleaning agent or paste while it is still hot, turn the saucepan upside down on the stainless steel bench top. The steam will loosen the burnt matter from the bottom of the saucepan, making it easier to clean. The handle of the saucepan should face into the sink so the pan sits flat and the steam is trapped inside.

BUTTERMILK

A good substitute for buttermilk is plain yoghurt, mixed with low-fat milk.

CAKES

Butter cakes have a tendency to dry, or brown on the bottom. They can be kept moist by putting a dish of water on the bottom of the oven while cooking.

For fruitcakes, two layers of brown paper are needed to line the tin. A layer of salt between the two bottom layers saves the cake from drying and burning. To prevent a fruitcake burning on top, add a layer of brown paper half way through cooking.

Cakes that are sticky when baking is complete are usually the result of the oven temperature being incorrect. Have the thermostat checked.

Your local gas or electricity service department will advise on the cheapest and easiest method for checking the thermostat.

CANDIED PEEL

The peel of citrus fruit can be used as an aromatic condiment. The strong flavour comes from the essential oil contained in the peel and is useful in many different dishes, both sweet and savoury. Chop the peel into thin strips, cover with cold water and slowly bring to boiling point. Drain off the water, add fresh water and repeat this three times. Weigh the peel and add an equal amount of sugar, with just enough boiling water to cover, and simmer until the peel is tender and clear. Cool, drain from the syrup, and spread it out to dry. Roll the strips in sugar, and if they are sticky after 24 hours, roll in sugar once more. See also Dried Peel.

CAST IRON

Cast iron should always be tempered before use. To do this, wipe over with a little oil, sprinkle the inside with salt and allow to heat for about five minutes. Let it cool for another five minutes, then wipe with paper towel to remove the salt and prevent rust. Before putting cast iron utensils away after use, always rub with a little oil. To stack cast iron pans, put paper towel between them to prevent scratching the surface.

CAULIFLOWER

To prevent the smell of cauliflower permeating the house while cooking, put a slice of bread in with the water. Better still, cook cauliflower in the microwave.

CHEESE

To keep cheese, wrap it in a cloth or put it in a screw-top glass jar and keep it in the refrigerator. To keep the cut edge from hardening, rub with a little butter. Another way of storing cheese is to keep it in a plastic container, in the refrigerator, with a couple of sugar lumps in the container. This keeps the cheese mould-free. Try using a potato peeler when slicing cheese for sandwiches. It is more economical and is easier to slice.

CHOKO

To serve as a vegetable, peel the chokos under running water, cut off the ends, halve and remove the seeds. Simmer in salted water until tender and serve with a white sauce or melted butter. Chokos can be frozen. If small they can be blanched whole, and unpeeled, for 2 minutes. Larger chokos should be peeled, cored and cut into quarters. Blanch in 4 cups water to 2 tablespoons lemon juice, for 3 minutes before freezing.

Choko bread, made the same as zucchini bread, is very good.

CHERRIES IN BRANDY

Remove the stalks and wash ¾ kilogram (24 oz) cherries. Put them in basin and add ½ kilogram (17½ oz) sugar. Pour 1 large bottle brandy over the cherries. Stir now and then until the sugar is dissolved; bottle and seal.

Leave for at least four weeks, though a year is better, before using.

The brandy syrup from the cherries can be poured over ice cream or used as a cordial by putting a little in the bottom of a tall glass with some ice. Fill the glass with soda water and add a sprig of mint.

CITRUS FRUIT

To peel citrus fruit quickly and easily, put fruit into hot water for five minutes before peeling. Citrus peel is a most useful flavouring. Peel very thinly, with a sharp knife or a potato peeler so that none of the pith is included. Put into a food processor and after processing store in plastic bags. Make sure the air is taken out of the bags and freeze for flavouring jams, cakes, etc. A pinch or two added to curry enhances the flavour.

To dry citrus peel, use a potato peeler to peel the fruit, cut it into thin slivers and dry in the oven at low temperature, or in the microwave on defrost for about 20 minutes, or until dry.

Store in airtight jars and use to decorate cakes, or in casseroles and stews.

CLOTTED CREAM

To make clotted cream, put the cream into a basin and put the basin into a pan of boiling water. Let the water simmer until the cream clots. Clotted cream must be done slowly and you must not stir it. When the cream has finished clotting it will still be slightly runny but it thickens as it becomes cold.

Another method that I find very satisfactory, if you have a microwave, is to just pop the cream into a bowl, leaving plenty of space at the top of the bowl. Don't overfill it. Put the microwave onto slow setting, such as defrost. Two cups of cream will take about 25 minutes to clot.

CONDENSED MILK

To make condensed milk, dissolve 1¾ cups of sugar in 1 cup of boiling water. Let it cool, then stir in, until smooth, two cups of full cream instant milk powder. Store in jars in the refrigerator.

COPPER

Bench tops covered with copper are usually surface coated and should only need to be washed with soap and water then buffed up with a soft, dry cloth. Use a commercial product to give a fine polish to the copper bench tops. Once polished, use another product to protect the surface and save all that hard work.

CRACKLING

For crisp crackling when baking pork, rub the rind with a little plain flour and seasoned salt prior to cooking. For the first 15 to 20 minutes cooking, turn the temperature to high. After the meat is cooked, put it in the top of the oven and turn the thermostat back to a high temperature again for a few minutes.

CROUTONS

Generally used as a garnish for soup, croutons are made by dicing about 3-day-old bread into small squares. Saute on all sides in sizzling hot butter until delicately brown and crisp.

CRUMBED

It is most frustrating to go to a lot of trouble to cook crumbed meat, fish, etc. only to find the crumbing parts company with the meat. This can be avoided by dusting the meat with flour before dipping in egg and breadcrumbs. Adding a few herbs to the crumb or flour and serving with a little lemon juice is a tasty trick that adds to the flavour.

CRYSTAL AND GLASS

Glass and crystal that develops a cloudy, or milky appearance, is usually a dishwasher induced problem. It does not happen with the first, second, or third time of washing. Glass or crystal can be washed in a dishwasher for years and come out looking more sparkling than when they were originally purchased. But over time, the mineral content of the water, combined with dish washing powder released under pressure, pounds the glass and crystal until it becomes frosted, or etched. Some tests have been done to reverse the condition with acid, but it is not a viable proposition at present. Precious glassware or crystal is best washed by hand in hot, soapy, water, rinsed in the same temperature water, then dried with a soft, clean, non-fluffy tea towel.

CUMQUAT MARMALADE

The word cumquat has the alternative spelling of kumquat so it is advisable to look under both letters when searching for a recipe. When harvesting the fruit, cut the cumquats from the tree with secateurs or scissors, leaving a small stalk. Wash the fruit in cold, salted water to remove or kill any insects or their eggs. Drain, and remove the stalks. Cut the fruit in half around the middle and flick out the pips. Then cut the fruit finely, and put it into a plastic or earthenware bowl. Add sufficient cold water to just cover the fruit and leave for about 12 hours. Now measure the mixture by cup and add a little over $^2/_3$ cup of sugar to each cup of the pulp. Put in a small nob of butter to prevent frothing and boil, or microwave until the mixture sets when tested with a metal spoon. I do small quantities in the microwave, by cooking on high until the mixture is at the boil, then I cook on simmer until it sets. It is no quicker than boiling on the stove, but the colour is much better.

To test with a metal spoon, dip the spoon into the boiling marmalade then hold it sideways over the cooking vessel. At first the mixture will run, or drip, from the centre, or lowest point, of the spoon. Cooking is complete when the mixture drips in three separate spots along the edge of the spoon. If you want to microwave, don't fill the cooking utensil to more than one-third.

CUPS

Tea and coffee can stain cups. The stain is easily removed by rubbing the inside quite firmly using

your fingers, with either plain salt, or a mixture of salt and lemon juice. If lemons are scarce, use salt and vinegar. Denture powder in water is also very good.

CUSTARD

If custard curdles during cooking, remove it from the saucepan, add a little cold water and whisk firmly. Finish cooking if necessary.

CUTLERY HANDLES

Cutlery handles made of ivory or bone should never be washed in hot water. Both will yellow with age, but hot water intensifies the yellow. If trying to whiten ivory or bone handles, first clean them with powdered whiting mixed to a paste with lemon juice. To whiten the handles, stand them in a glass of ½ water and ½ bleach for 12 hours. Then rub the handles with toothpaste. Dry and polish with talcum powder. Be careful not to let bleach solution cover the join where the handles meet the blade. It may weaken the adhesive.

CUTTING BOARD

Wooden cutting boards have a tendency to absorb flavours. They can be freshened by saturating a kitchen sponge with cold water and a little bleach. Rub the surface for a minute or so and then run hot water over it to get rid of the bleach smell or rub the board over with a lemon cut in half. White cutting boards can be cleaned with toothpaste. Always wash cutting boards in the dishwasher or in very hot water.

DAMP FOOD

Store sugar, flour, and such like in plastic containers with tight fitting lids. In tropical climates where the humidity is often very high, put a container of a damp absorbent product on the shelf where these things are stored. Both are available at hardware stores.

DICE

This means to cut into very small cubes, usually about 5 millimetres (¼ in) square.

DILL

Dill is frequently used in pickles and the seed was generally considered to aid digestion of cabbage, coleslaw, sauerkraut, cucumber, onions, etc. The pleasantly flavoured finely chopped leaves go with almost any food. The feathery leaf is good for plate decoration.

DISH CLOTHS

Brushes, cloths, and sponges that are used for washing dishes become smelly, dirty or slimy if they are not cared for on a continuing basis. Soak in Epsom salt or ½ water and ½ house-hold bleach. Rinse well. Clean brushes by putting them in the dishwasher with the cutlery.

DISHWASHER

When dishes from the dishwasher are not perfectly clean, the first thing to do is to check that it is not being overloaded, or stacked incorrectly. With years of use, bad stacking habits can develop and it is a good idea to go back to the instruction book and re-assess your methods. With that accomplished, and with the dishwasher empty, put 2 tablespoons of bicarbonate of soda, mixed with 2 teaspoons of citric acid, into the dispenser and put the machine through one full cycle. It may be necessary to repeat the treatment, and it is worth doing about once every six months, depending on how much use the machine gets.

DOG BISCUITS

Mix together 500 grams (16 oz) wholemeal flour, 200 grams (7 oz) minced meat, and 1 desertspoon salt. Add enough cold water to mix to a stiff dough. Roll out on a floured board and place on an oven slide. Mark into squares and prick with a fork. Bake in a slow oven until brown. If your dog is only a pup, add 1 tablespoon cod liver oil, as it is good for building bones.

DRIED FRUIT

A twist of lemon peel added to a jar of dried fruit not only keeps out weevils, but also helps to keep the fruit fresh and plump. Sixty seconds on high in the microwave oven brings dried fruit up to a soft, plump condition.

DRIED PEEL

Orange, lemon, mandarin, grapefruit and tangello can be dried and used for cake decoration, or to give a tangy aromatic flavour to casseroles or stew, or even sprinkled on pantry shelves to deter silverfish and weevils.

With a very sharp knife, or a potato peeler, remove the top layer of skin, avoiding as much pith as possible. Then slice the skins into very fine slivers, spread on a suitable dish, and put into the oven on a very low heat until dried. Or microwave on "defrost" for about 20 minutes. Store in airtight jars.

DUCK EGGS

When cooking with duck eggs, it is always good to remember that two duck eggs are equal to three hen eggs.

ENAMEL – COOKWARE

Enamel cookware becomes discoloured with use. To clean the inside of enamel pans, saucepans and kettles, put in enough bleach to just cover the base, then fill with cold water and allow to stand overnight. Wash in hot, soapy water and rinse thoroughly. Repeat, if necessary. Do not use steel wool on enamelware.

If the inside of a kettle is chipped and worn, always keep two marbles in it. As water is boiled, the movement of the marbles will prevent rust forming.

For enamelware with stainless steel rims, immerse completely in a bucket or trough with one part bleach to four parts water. Leave overnight, then wash in hot, soapy water, using an old toothbrush to clean around the stainless steel rims.

EXHAUST FANS

Light coloured plastic exhaust fans will discolour with time. It is sometimes possible to rejuvenate this type of plastic by washing it in a bleach solution. Use about one quarter bleach to three-quarters warm water. It is probably a good idea to wash the plastic in very hot, soapy water before using the bleach solution.

FLOUR, ALL PURPOSE

The term all purpose flour occurs in American recipes and is the same as plain flour.

FEIJOA

This is a very good fruit, ideal as a sweet or salad item. Once peeled, all the fruit, including the seeds, can be eaten. Peel thickly, and under running water to avoid sticky hands. To save the bother of peeling, cut the fruit in half, crossways, and scoop out the centre with a teaspoon – the same as passionfruit.

Feijoas are ideal for jam, jelly and chutney. For this purpose, the fruit does not need to be peeled, only topped and tailed, then sliced or chopped as the recipe requires.

FEIJOA CHUTNEY

Mix the following together in a pan.
  1 kg (36 oz) **diced feijoas**
  2 cups **raisins**
  3 cups **chopped dates**
  8 small **onions chopped**
  3 cups **brown sugar**
  1 tablespoon **ground ginger**
  1 tablespoon **curry powder**
  1 teaspoon **ground cloves**
  1 teaspoon **cayenne pepper**
  1 tablespoon **salt**
  5 cups **vinegar**
Bring to the boil, stirring constantly to prevent sticking. Boil for two hours. Pour into hot, sterilised jars; seal and label. Keep for six weeks before using.

FEIJOA JELLY

To make feijoa jelly, wash the fruit, top and tail each one, then cut into halves or quarters,

depending on the size of the feijoas. Put the chopped fruit into a pan and cover with cold water. Bring to the boil and simmer until the fruit is soft. Leave it to cool. Put a jelly bag, or fine curtain net, over a large bowl and empty the fruit into it. Now hang the jelly bag, with the bowl under it so the liquid drips into the bowl. Use a tie to squeeze the bag into a tight ball. Leave it to hang overnight. Now measure the liquid by cup, into a saucepan, and add 1 cup of sugar to each cup of juice. To every 6 cups of liquid add the juice and rind of 1 lemon. Put a knob of butter into the mixture, bring to the boil, stirring from time to time, and boil steadily until it tests for setting. The best way to test for setting is to use a metal tablespoon for stirring. When the spoon is held on its side, and two or three slow drips appear in a row along the edge and reluctantly leave the spoon, the jelly will set when poured into jars and allowed to get cold. Boiling time is about 45 minutes, depending on the quantity. Remove the lemon rind before pouring into hot, sterilised jars. Seal when cold.

FIGS

Figs can be dried in a cool oven, or out in the sun. It is best to dry figs whole, leaving a tiny bit of stalk on the fruit. First blanch the figs by immersing them in boiling water for about 4 minutes. Then quickly plunge the fruit into cold water for about 30 seconds. Remove the surface water by shaking the fruit in a dry towel. Then spread the fruit on trays for drying. For oven drying, the temperature should be no more than 55°C (110°F). Dry for about 2 hours then increase the oven heat to about 75°C (150°F). The oven door should be kept slightly open all the time, allowing the damp air to escape. When thoroughly dry, remove from the oven and leave overnight. If there is any sign of dampness next day, return the fruit to the oven until drying is complete.

To dry figs in the sun, they first need to be dipped in a bath of lye, which is 30 grams (1 oz) of caustic soda to 4½ litres (152 fl oz) of water. Dip in and out of boiling lye three times to the count of 3. Then lay the figs out in the sun to dry. Cover the drying figs with muslin to stop insects and flies enjoying them before you do.

FISH

When buying fish, get close enough to assure yourself the slight sea smell remains. The eyes should be clear, not cloudy. To remove the smell of fish, sprinkle dry mustard in the cooking utensils. In the fridge, dry mustard in a saucer takes the smell away.

FISH MARINADE

Marinating can be used to flavour, tenderise, or replace the need for cooking. If the fish is not to be cooked, it should be soaked overnight in the marinade. The acid has the same effect as heat on the fish, so no cooking is required. When cooking is preferred, the fish need soak in the marinade for only two hours. Here is a recipe I use for boneless fillets.

Into a plastic bowl put: juice of 3 **lemons**

juice of 1 **orange**
¼ cup **white wine**
1 tablespoon **onion chopped**
fish fillets
Make sure the fish is completely coated with the marinade, then cover and leave in the refrigerator until required. Drain off and discard the marinade. For a variation, add a tablespoon of chopped ginger to the marinade.

FRUIT CAKE – ALTERNATIVES

For a dry fruitcake, push a knitting needle down through the cake, almost to the bottom, in a number of places, then pour brandy or sherry down into the holes. Wrap it well in foil and let it sit for a while.

After the party is over and the family is sick of fruit cake, turn it into something else.

- **Steamed pudding:** Just crumble the cake, mix a beaten egg and half a cup of cold water through it, put into a greased basin and steam for about half an hour. Serve with custard sauce or ice cream.
- **Rum balls:** Combine 2½ cups of fruitcake crumbs, 1 teaspoon rum, 60 grams (2 oz) melted vegetable fat, 1 tablespoon cocoa, and mix well. Shape into small walnut-sized balls and roll in crushed nuts or coconut. Chill until needed.

FRUIT – TO RIPEN

Most fruit will ripen easily if put in a brown paper bag with an apple. If a pineapple is a little green, it can be ripened evenly by removing the leaves and standing it upside down in a brown paper bag.

GINGER

For crystallised ginger it is best to harvest the roots early, before they become fibrous. Wash the roots and remove the skin; cut into cubes, slices or strings. With just enough water to cover, boil until tender, then drain into a container and keep the water that has been drained off. Put the cooked ginger into a shallow dish and sprinkle with sugar. Cover and leave for two days. Put the ginger into a pan with the saved cooking water. Bring to the boil, stirring all the time until the syrup is completely absorbed by the ginger. Drain and cool. Sprinkle with sugar and spread on a cake rack to dry. Store in airtight containers.

GINGER BEER PLANT

Into a 500 ml (17 fl oz) jar put 1 teaspoon compressed yeast with 1 teaspoon sugar, 1 teaspoon ground ginger, and 1 cup warm water. Mix well, cover with muslin and leave for eight days, adding an extra teaspoon ginger and sugar each day.

To make the ginger beer put 1 litre (36 fl oz) of water and 1 kilogram (36 oz) of sugar into a large saucepan. Heat until it boils, stirring until sugar is dissolved. Remove from the heat and

stir in 6 litres (210 fl oz) of water and half a cup of strained lemon juice. Now strain the plant through two thicknesses of very fine muslin and stir the strained liquid into the saucepan. Pour through a funnel into eight clean bottles and cap with plastic seals. In about five days the ginger beer will be ready to drink. The sediment in the muslin (the plant) can now be divided in half. Put one half into the 500 ml (17 fl oz) jar, add 1 cup warm water, and 1 teaspoon each of sugar and ginger. Proceed as before for the next eight days. The other half of the plant can be discarded or given to a friend.

GINGER – CANDIED

The under-developed roots, which have not yet become fibrous, are probably the best for making candied ginger. Use a vegetable brush and plenty of cold, running water to clean the ginger and remove the outer skin. When it is clean, soak 500 grams of root ginger in cold water for one hour. Strain, then put the ginger into a saucepan, cover with more cold water, bring to the boil, and let it boil for ten minutes. Let it cool and repeat the par boiling and cooking in fresh water several times, then boil until the ginger is tender. This is more important with the May harvest when the roots are about 80% mature, and much more fibrous and the pungency of the ginger is much stronger.

Make a syrup with 500 grams of sugar and 1½ cups of boiling water. Drain the ginger, wipe it dry, then submerge it in the hot syrup and bring it to the boil. Let it cool for 24 hours. Drain off the syrup, boil it for 10 minutes then pour it over the root ginger and leave for 24 hours. Now heat the ginger in the syrup; boil for 5 minutes and leave for 2 or 3 days. The ginger should now be plump, clear and tender. Reheat the ginger and the syrup, boil for 5 minutes; then pack the ginger into hot, sterilised jars.

Continue boiling the syrup until slightly thickened, then pour the hot syrup over the ginger and seal the jars.

GINGER – FREEZE

To freeze the root of ginger, wash and drain, and wipe dry with paper towel. Do not peel, and do not blanch. Put the ginger into a freezer bag. To use, grate or slice the frozen piece. If left to thaw it will become soft and mushy.

GINGER MARMALADE

The underground stem, or rhizome, of the ginger plant, unlike fruit, contains no fructose or pectin, so necessary in jam making. For this reason, fruit containing the important setting qualities is added to make ginger jam. Ginger is regarded as a spice and is sought after throughout the world for its pungent flavour. Apples have very good setting qualities and readily take up the flavour of any spice. They also add the bulk that is needed for ginger jam. Only very immature rhizomes are free of fibre and are therefore best for making jam. The only other thing that may be worth trying is to use only ginger and a commercial jam setter.

GLASSES

If drinking glasses look smeary after washing, or if beer goes flat in them you must change the washing method. Use hot water and a good detergent in the sink. When the glasses have been thoroughly washed, make sure they are well rinsed with hot water and drain. Do not use a tea towel.

GRILL

Put cold water in the pan under the grill. It will greatly reduce the amount of smoke from grilling steak, chops, sausages etc. and is better for the kitchen paintwork as well as preventing the smoke detector from being activated.

HAM

Once a ham is cut, wrap it in a damp cloth. Change the cloth every few days. This should keep the ham fresh for at least three weeks. While a cloth dampened with water is sufficient, I prefer to add some vinegar to the water. About 1 tablespoon of vinegar to 2 litres (70 fl oz) of cold water.

HERBS - TO KEEP

Mint and parsley die off from time to time, so when plentiful, pick, wash, dry, chop, pat dry, pack in plastic bags and freeze. These herbs separate easily when frozen. Parsley can also be dried, either chopped or in whole sprigs, by boiling it quickly for about 2 minutes in a pot of water, then drying fairly quickly in the oven. Before using, it is a good idea to soak the parsley in warm water for a few minutes to freshen it. To dry mint, gather it on a clear, sunny day and dry it slowly in a very low oven. Crumble it when it is fairly dry and store in airtight jars. Herbs can also be dried successfully in a microwave oven on the defrost setting.

HERB VINEGAR

Any herbs can be used to make herb vinegar, and while the type of vinegar is not vital, the more subtle flavours are obtained by matching the herbs to the vinegar type. Basil, tarragon, rosemary, and marjoram are well suited to white or red wine vinegar. For mint or lemon balm, cider vinegar is good or, half malt vinegar and half white vinegar. These are guidelines. Try and taste. Alter to suit your palate is the best recipe. Gather the herbs on a dry day and before the plants come into flower.

Wash and dry the herbs, pack them into a glass jar, cover with the vinegar of your choice, seal with a screw-top or tight-fitting lid and keep on a sunny ledge for about two weeks. Shake the jar every day. Then strain and discard the herbs. Taste the vinegar. If it is not sufficiently flavoursome, repeat the process. When the herb vinegar is to your liking, put a fresh sprig of the appropriate herb into a sterilised bottle, add the vinegar, seal and label.

HONEY – TO MEASURE

To measure honey, treacle, or syrup, grease the cup or spoon first. It will pour more easily and will not be wasted by sticking to the surface of the measure.

ICE CUBES

Ice cubes freeze more quickly when the tray is filled with warm, not cold, water. To remove ice cubes cleanly, let cold tap water run over the bottom of the tray and they should come out easily.

ICING

Before icing a cake, brush over the top with white of egg. This prevents the icing from absorbing colour from the cake. To soften hard icing, very lightly brush with glycerine. Leave for two or three days. Avoid sticky icing by crushing a junket tablet into the icing when mixing.

JAM

Fruit for jam making is best gathered on a fine day, and should never be overripe. Wipe the fruit with a damp cloth. Partly cook fruit before adding the sugar. Bring fruit to the boil slowly to avoid burning. After sugar has been added, boil as rapidly as possible, stirring often to stop the jam catching. Fast boiling improves the colour and flavour of jam. To stop jam foaming while cooking, add a tablespoon of brandy or a knob of butter. This stops jam or jelly from scumming. To test jam, put a little on a saucer. The jam is ready when it cools and forms a skin on the top. Jam jars must be sterilised and thoroughly dry. Put the jam into warm jars to avoid breakages.

Homemade jam cannot always be stored under perfect conditions, and we often find mould on the surface. Just before covering and when the jam is quite cold, add a small teaspoon of vinegar to each pot then cover in the usual way.

If jam does not set, boil it with 2 tablespoons of fresh lemon juice for each kilogram (36 oz) of fruit used.

JAM – MULBERRY

Three different types of mulberry are grown. The most popular bears fruit which ripens to almost black. It is also the best variety for jam but the fruit should be fully ripe for jam making. First, wash and hull the berries, then soak overnight, 1 kilogram (36 oz) mulberries in half a cup of cold water. Put the fruit into a saucepan next day and bring it gently to the boil. Let it simmer for two minutes, then add one kilogram (36 oz) sugar, a knob of butter, and the thinly peeled rind of one small lemon. Bring it to the boil again and let it boil rapidly until the fruit becomes mushie and the mixture almost gels. Reduce the heat and simmer for 2 or 3 more minutes, until the jam sets when tested. Total cooking time should be about 20 to 30 minutes.

JARS – RECYCLE

Jars which are to be recycled should be thoroughly washed and dried. I like to put them into the oven, on a low temperature, to ensure perfect drying. Store jars without the lids on, and if they have contained strong-smelling foods, put a teaspoon of bicarbonate of soda into each jar. Plastic lids should be washed and dried, then stored in a plastic bag with a sprinkle of bicarbonate of soda. If either the lids or the jars still have a lingering odour when needed for re-use, put them

into the freezer for half an hour. Don't store metal lids in a plastic bag. Store them loose on an open tray for air circulation. Remove and discard paper seals. Remove, wash, and store any rubber seals in bicarbonate of soda.

JELLY

If jelly does not set it is due to either being overcooked, or the fruit is too ripe and therefore short of pectin. If this happens, use a commercial jam setter that can be purchased at supermarkets. The jelly may finish up slightly cloudy but at least it will not be wasted.

KETTLE

For discolouration inside a stainless steel kettle, fill to the top with cold water and add a tablespoon of denture powder. Let it stand overnight, then pour it out, rinse twice with very hot water. Regular treatment will stop discolouration build-up.

Or, put half a cup of vinegar into the electric jug, or kettle, then fill it with cold water. Bring the water to the boil. Let it stand for 10 minutes, then empty the jug. Repeat the treatment until the water is clear, then fill with cold water, bring it to the boil, empty, and repeat until the smell of vinegar is no longer noticeable.

Another way to clean a plastic, electric kettle, is to fill it to almost full, with cold water, then put in a tablespoon of denture powder, or, two Steradent tablets. Leave overnight, tip the mixture down the sink, rinse two or three times and repeat if necessary. Half a cup of bleach to a kettle full of water, also left overnight, is another method, but rinse three times in cold water and boil two lots of water in the kettle before using again to get rid of the chlorine taste.

For sediment in a kettle, put in a cup of vinegar and 1 litre (36 fl oz) of water. Bring to the boil, then rinse well. Add one or two marbles to the kettle. The constant moving of the marbles stops the build-up of sediment.

The outside of a copper kettle can be cleaned with Worcestershire sauce on a damp cloth. Buff up with a soft dry cloth. Another method is to use salt and lemon mixed to a paste and rubbed over the surface.

To clean the outside of a white plastic kettle, make a creamy paste with powdered whiting (available from hardware stores) and household bleach. Boil the jug, then empty it, so the plastic will be hot for cleaning. Now dip a kitchen wiper into the paste and rub all over the white plastic. When it is clean, rinse the plastic thoroughly with hot water and dry it with a clean, absorbent tea towel. Now re-surface the plastic by spraying it with car polish. Buff up with a soft, dry cloth. Leave for one day then spray again for a more lasting finish.

KITCHEN CHAIRS

Kitchen chairs of plastic or vinyl attract dirt, dust, grease, food, and ink marks. Scrub the chairs with very hot water and a good dish washing liquid. Wipe them dry with a thick towel. While

the plastic or vinyl is still hot, rub the ink marks with a pen remover on a soft cloth. When all the marks are removed and the surface absolutely dry, spray with a good silicone polish and buff up with a soft, dry cloth.

KIWIFRUIT CHUTNEY

Into a preserving pan put:

2 **onions chopped**

1 clove **crushed garlic**

¾ cup **brown sugar**

½ teasp **ground ginger**

2 **apples, peeled, chopped**

½ cup **raisins**

1 cup **brown vinegar**

½ teasp **allspice**

¼ teasp **ground cloves**

Boil gently for 30 minutes or until the mixture is soft and thickened. Then add 500 grams (17 oz) peeled, chopped kiwifruit. Cook for 20 minutes, or until chutney is thickened. Put into sterilised jars and seal when cold.

LEMON

For cordial, use a potato peeler to remove the rind from 6 lemons, then put the rind into a saucepan with 9 cups of water and 9 cups of sugar. Bring it to the boil and let it simmer for 5 minutes, stirring now and then to dissolve the sugar. Remove from the heat and add the juice of the 6 lemons. Stir in 1 tablespoon citric acid, 2 tablespoons tartaric acid, and 1 tablespoon Epsom salt. Leave to cool then strain and bottle. To store lemons, always cut a short stem and store in a dry cool place. Pack in sawdust or wrap in tissue. Rubbing with Vaseline helps to keep them. Don't store oranges and lemons together. There is less chance of mould if they are kept apart.

To get more juice from each lemon, plunge them into hot water for 4–5 minutes or in the oven for a couple of minutes, or microwave for 15 seconds. Freeze lemon juice in ice cube containers and, when solid, put the blocks into freezer bags.

In Grandma's day, lemon barley water was used to clear the kidneys and cleanse the skin of teenage acne. Boil a cup of barley in plenty of water, strain, and to the liquid add the juice of 12 lemons, 10 tablespoons of sugar and 1½ litres (3 pints) of boiling water. Put a little in a glass and top up with iced water or soda.

To make lemonade, boil 1 kilo (36 oz) of sugar, 500ml (17 fl oz) of strained lemon juice until the sugar is dissolved. Pour the syrup out, and when it is cold put into bottles, and cork closely. When wanted for use, put a tablespoon into a tumbler three parts full of cold water. Stir in about ¼ teaspoon of bicarbonate of soda (baking soda) and drink during effervescence.

LETTUCE

Don't store leafy greens in plastic bags without first wrapping them in paper towel. Store in the vegetable compartment of the refrigerator. They will stay fresh and crisp for weeks.

LIDS

To remove bottle tops or stubborn lids from jars, dampen a kitchen sponge, put it over the lid and then screw off. Or, run the hot tap over and around the lid.

MARINADE

Marinade usually has an acid liquid base, such as wine, plus the addition of herbs, spices, sauces etc. and maybe some oil. The marinade acts as a tenderiser, and improves the palatability of older meats. It also acts as a pickle, for a limited period, providing there is a high proportion of the added liquid, such as wine, beer, cider, vinegar or lemon juice. Yoghurt is a good marinade for hare or rabbit.

MARINATE

This means to immerse meat or fish and let it soak in a marinade, or keep it constantly moistened for a given period of time.

MARMALADE

Marmalade will often set hard if the fruit is not softened first by soaking in cold water for 12 hours before bringing to the boil and simmering until the rind softens. Sugar should not be added until the rind is soft. For marmalade that has set too firmly, put it back in the pan with extra hot water and stir continually over the heat until the jam is dissolved and the water mixed through. Try one jar first to check the quantity of water required.

Marmalade can be given extra flavour by using orange or grapefruit juice, or a mixture of both, instead of water in the recipe. Add a teaspoon of citric acid to give it more zing. This method is particularly good if you are using the skins from fruit that has been juiced.

MARSHMALLOWS

Boil 240 grams (8oz) sugar, 3 dessertspoons gelatine, ¼ level teaspoon cream of tartar in 1¼ cups hot water until the mixture forms a thread when a teaspoon is dropped into cold water. Stir and leave to cool. When cool add a dessertspoon of lemon juice and a pinch of salt and food colouring if desired. Beat until thick. Pour into a greased dish and leave for 24 hours. Cut into squares. Roll in a mixture of 3 parts icing sugar and 1 part cornflour. Store in a cool dry place. To toast, pop them on the end of a toasting fork, and lightly sear in the red-hot embers of a fire.

MICROWAVE OVEN CLEANING

It does not take a degree in engineering to use a microwave oven, but, it is necessary to understand

a few basic rules. Read the manual that comes with the oven. The inside of the oven may be metal or baked enamel so it is important to follow the cleaning method which is recommended for the brand of oven you have. Wipe the oven clean after each use and if additional cleaning is necessary, hot, soapy water will do no harm.

MILK

Milk boils over very quickly so don't turn your back on it. A spoon in the saucepan will prevent the boil-over and the smell of burnt milk. If the milk boils over on to an electric element, turn off the power immediately, then sprinkle liberally with salt. Leave it for a few minutes then wipe with a damp cloth. This way the milk is cleaned up quickly and the smell is completely obliterated.

After boiling milk, empty the saucepan, and while it is still hot, turn it upside down on the sink bench so that the steam is sealed in. This loosens the milk that sticks to the bottom and makes cleaning easy.

MINT

Sprinkle sugar on the leaves when chopping mint. It brings out the flavour.

MINT DRINK

Beat together:
  2 cups **plain yoghurt**
  4 cups **cold water**
  3 tablespoons **mint, finely chopped**
Serve in a glass, over crushed ice. A little sugar can be added, if desired, or a pinch of salt.

MINT SAUCE

Into a saucepan put: ½ cup mint, chopped, 1 tablespoon brown sugar. Leave for 30 minutes and then add 2 cups white wine vinegar.

Bring to the boil. Remove from the heat at once and let it stand for at least one day. This mint sauce can be stored in the fridge for a year and the more mature it is, the better it tastes.

MOCK CREAM

Mock cream can be very useful, particularly for those who are dieting. In a saucepan, heat 1 cup milk. Smoothly blend together and then add the following to the saucepan: 1 tablespoon cornflour and 2 tablespoons of cold milk. Stir to the boil then cook for 2 minutes, stirring all the time. Let it cool. Cream together then add 1 tablespoon butter with 1 tablespoon of caster sugar and a few drops of vanilla essence to the cooled milk mixture and beat.

MUSHROOMS

To freeze mushrooms, use only those that are fresh or undamaged.

Trim across the base of the stem, and wipe with a damp cloth. Wash only if very gritty under gently running cold water and make sure they are fully dry. Freeze on an open tray, and as soon as they are frozen hard, pack into freezer bags and seal.

NEVER-FAIL SPONGE

Beat 3 or 4 egg whites until stiff. Gradually add ½ cup caster sugar. Lightly beat and add egg yolks. Sift two or three times and fold into the egg mixture, ¾ cup custard powder, 1 tablespoon plain flour, 1 teaspoon bicarbonate of soda and ½ teaspoon cream of tartar. Bake in a greased 18 to 20 centimetre (7 or 8 inch) tin for 30 minutes at 180°C (350°F) temperature.

NON-STICK

Do not use harsh abrasives or scourers on non-stick surfaces. Metal implements such as spoons or knives can scratch and ruin the surface. Use only wooden or plastic spoons. Non-stick pans or saucepans should not be stored one inside the other. If something does catch on a non-stick surface, a little heated oil will generally remove it. Stains can be removed by wetting the surface, smother with cream of tartar and leave for 24 hours.

Neat bleach on a wet cloth is another alternative, or, one of the dishwashing machine powders smothered over a wet surface. Remember though, non-stick surfaces were not designed to take extreme temperatures, so if food is continually burnt in a pan or saucepan, the non-stick surface will cease to be non-stick.

ONIONS

You won't weep when peeling onions if you hold them under cold water to peel, or hold them upside down while peeling. Rubbing baking powder into your hands after peeling removes the odour. If you want to plump them up before cooking, plunge into hot water for 5 minutes, or put them into the microwave for 60 seconds. This improves the flavour. Chew a sprig of fresh parsley to take the smell of onions off the breath.

For onions that begin to sprout, don't throw them out. Put them in a pot containing a damp paper towel. Keep the paper damp and they will continue to sprout and you can cut off the green tops to use to flavour cooking.

ORANGE CORDIAL

Roughly cut 6 oranges (if they are very small, use 8) and soak overnight in 3 cups of cold water. Into a saucepan, put 3 cups cold water and 6 cups sugar. Bring to the boil, stirring to dissolve the sugar. Simmer gently for about 5 minutes then remove from the stove and add it to the soaked oranges. Stir in 50 grams tartaric acid, 25 grams citric acid and 25 grams Epsom salts. Stir to dissolve the acids, then strain and bottle. Put a little (depending on the strength desired) into a tumbler, add ice and water.

Important: Thoroughly sterilise bottles before use. Less than a quarter of a teaspoon of

sodium metabisulphite powder put into a bottle of water and left for 15 minutes is sufficient. Empty the bottles and leave to drain before pouring the cordial in.

ORANGES

To peel oranges, place into hot water for about five minutes, then peel, and the pith separates easily from the skin.

OREGANO

A spice which is very good used with poultry, fish, egg dishes, vegetables and sauces. The pungency of oregano is better when dried and this herb is a popular ingredient in many regional dishes of other countries such as pastas and pizzas from Italy.

OVEN

For people who are allergic to chemical cleaners, bicarbonate of soda (baking soda) mixed with cold water to the consistency of cream, then packed over the inside of a cold oven, left overnight and washed off next day with warm soapy water, is an excellent alternative.

To clean the glass on the oven door, rub with a damp cloth dipped in bicarbonate of soda (baking soda), then sponge with a clean cloth. If the glass develops a cloudy look, it is an indication that the seal on the double-glazing needs to be renewed.

OVEN – FAN FORCED

When cooking in a fan-forced oven, temperatures should be approximately 20 to 25°C (70 to 80°F) lower than for a conventional oven. The manufacturers will supply a chart to suit the model you have purchased.

OVEN – SELF-CLEANING

Self-cleaning ovens are manufactured with a special catalytic coating. The same coating is used on a self-cleaning throughout the world, so no matter what brand, or where it is manufactured, the cleaning instructions are the same. Follow the cleaning instructions that are provided with the oven. Caustic cleaners will kill the catalytic coating so do not use any commercial oven cleaners. Soap and water is the only cleaning agent recommended by manufacturers.

PAN-FRYING

Open pan-fraying can mean a lot of cleaning due to splattered fat. Before beginning to fry, sprinkle cooking salt over the top of the stove. It absorbs splatters and stops the fat from drying hard on the top of the stove.

PEANUT BUTTER

Put 250 grams (8 oz) of shelled, roasted, salted peanuts into a blender with 2 tablespoons

peanut oil and blend until the mixture is smooth and creamy. It only takes one or two minutes, depending on the blender being used. For crunchy style peanut butter, blend for only half a minute. The mixture will become firm on standing. This quantity makes about 1 cup of peanut butter. Unsalted peanuts can be used with the addition of ¾ of a teaspoon of salt. I prefer to use beer nuts for a more intense flavour.

PINEAPPLE

To ripen a slightly green pineapple, remove the green top leaves and store it upside down in a paper bag.

PLASTIC BOTTLES

After emptying plastic drink bottles, wash with detergent and bleach, rinse thoroughly, put the empty bottles into the freezer.

This treatment will keep the plastic drink bottles from smelling musty and prevent mould from forming on the inside.

PLASTIC CONTAINERS

Plastic containers should be washed thoroughly in plenty of hot water to which a little bleach has been added. Rinse, dry and put in the deep freeze for an hour or so before use. Many containers retain a smell after storing food in them. If this happens put them in the freezer overnight or put a tablespoon of dry mustard, or cream of tartar in the container. Leave for a few days.

PLASTIC PLATES

The only thing to be done with white plastic plates that show scratches, due to food being cut up on the plate, is to soak them in hot water with a little bleach. It won't get rid of the scratch marks, it simply cleans them so they are less noticeable. Scratches in plastic plates are a great resting place for bacteria and so plastic plates should always be washed in extremly hot water, or better still, replaced.

PLUMS

Precooked and frozen, plums will last for about twelve months in the freezer. They make an ideal stand-by for pies, or stewed fruit for breakfast. Prepare and stew the fruit for about half the normal time. Remove the stones.

To retain colour add a crushed vitamin C tablet to every 500 grams (17 oz) of fruit.

POACH

Where a recipe calls for food to be poached, cook in liquid by simmering only. Do not boil.

PORK

Roast pork is delicious, but should be kept moist while cooking. Put the pork onto a rack in the

baking dish and add enough cold water to cover the bottom of the baking dish. Do not baste while the meat is roasting. For crisp crackling, rub a little plain flour and salt into the sliced skin when the meat is cooked, then turn the oven to high for about 5 to 10 minutes.

POTATOES
Some potatoes go watery when boiled. Don't panic. If you want to mash them, add a little powdered milk with the butter and they will soon thicken.

Potato peelers should always be blue in colour. Blue does not resemble any fruit or vegetable and can easily be seen amongst the scraps and therefore not thrown out. Store potatoes in a cool dry place; never in a plastic bag. Potatoes are not so likely to turn green if kept in a tightly closed, brown paper bag that excludes light but allows "breathing".

POT ROAST
This is a method to cook a joint by first searing it on all sides, then adding one cup of stock, or water, and when the liquid is reduced, adding vegetables and cooking gently with the lid on. Ideal for cooking less tender cuts of meat.

POULTRY
Poultry or game is a good stand-by in the freezer, but be warned – it cannot be emphasised too often – thaw whole birds completely in the refrigerator. They are susceptible to bacterial growth that may not be destroyed in cooking, particularly if any part of the inside is still very cold or partly frozen.

PUMPKIN
Whole, undamaged pumpkins, with a little of the stalk left on, will keep in a cool place for many months. All types will freeze, but butternut freezes best. Peel, cut into serving-size pieces and water blanch for 3 minutes.

Once a pumpkin is cut, the edge will need to be sealed in order to preserve it. Remove the seeds, sprinkling the cut edge with plain flour, or cover very tightly with plastic wrap.

PUMPKIN SEED
I have not prepared cooked, salted, pumpkin seeds, but I quote from Virginia Hill's book, *Microwave Companion*, "The dried seeds of pumpkin can be used as a snack or garnish. Scoop the seeds from the pumpkin, rinse them well and pat dry. Spread them out on greaseproof paper on a Pyrex pie plate and cook, uncovered, on high (90-100%) for 4 to 5 minutes, stirring every minute or so to prevent burning. Sprinkle the seeds with cayenne pepper, cumin or curry powder and stand for 5 minutes."

PUREE
Whisk root vegetables, which have been boiled, steamed, or cooked in their jackets. Add a little

hot milk or cream, and melted butter. Whisk again until smooth and creamy. Add extra seasoning to taste.

Cooked, green-leaf vegetables should be very lightly chopped, then put through a sieve, before mixing with a little melted butter or cream. Add freshly ground pepper or a little nutmeg.

RAGOUT

Strictly speaking, a ragout is a rich, highly flavoured sauce made with mushrooms, truffles, sweetbreads, stewed vegetables, etc, and used as a garnish for starters or appetisers. Over the years ragout has come to mean a highly flavoured preparation of meat, fish poultry or game. In other words, stew.

RANGE HOOD

When a range hood is flued in, the filter is not really necessary. If the range hood is not flued in, the filter is most necessary but it needs to be replaced from time to time, depending upon the amount, and also the type, of use. In between times, if it becomes necessary, remove the filter and clean the metal mesh with any good surface spray.

RASPBERRIES – FREEZING

Of all the berry fruits, raspberries are the best to freeze because they retain both colour and flavour right through to the next season. Spread clean, dry berries onto a flat tray and freeze without covering. When frozen, pack the berries into freezer bags, expel the air and seal.

REFREEZING

Food that has been frozen then thawed should not be refrozen unless it is cooked first.

REFRIGERATOR

The refrigerator will stay fresh and sweet smelling if you wipe it out regularly with vanilla. It is also a good idea to keep a saucer of dry mustard or bicarbonate of soda (baking soda) on one of the shelves. When moving house pack the fridge with newspaper sprinkled with vanilla.

When defrosting, wipe the inside of the refrigerator with bleach. Use one-part bleach to four parts water. Vanilla is an alternative to bleach but it does not kill mould spores or bacteria.

REFRIGERATOR – EXTERIOR

First, wash the outside of the fridge with very hot water and any good washing-up detergent. Next, mix together one tablespoon of bicarbonate of soda (baking soda), a quarter cup of white vinegar, half a cup of cloudy ammonia and ten cups of water.

This mixture can be bottled and used for regular cleaning of the fridge or other enamelled surfaces.

To use, wring out a cloth in warm water, add a dash of the mixture to the cloth and wipe over the surfaces to be cleaned. Rinse the cleaner off and wipe with a dry cloth.

REFRIGERATOR – SMELLY

When the fridge or freezer develops an unpleasant smell that is hard to get rid of, take everything out and wash all surfaces with hot, soapy water. Pay attention to the seals around the door. The seals are made of a rubbery type of plastic, often with pleats or ridges. Use a brush to be sure that all the ridges are clean. Once everything is clean, wring out a cloth in hot water, add a dash of bleach to the cloth and wipe the surfaces. The smell of the bleach will dissipate quickly and not be a problem.

Before re-packing the fridge or freezer, put one tablespoon of dry mustard mixed with one tablespoon of bicarbonate of soda (baking soda), into a shallow dish and put it at the back of one of the shelves. Old ashtrays are good for this purpose. The mixture will go on absorbing smells for at least three months.

RHUBARB MARMALADE

Rhubarb makes very good marmalade, which is really the same as jam but more tangy. Cut up 2 kilograms (4 lb 6 oz) of rhubarb, and boil in ½ litre of water for 20 minutes. Now chop finely, 2 sweet oranges and 2 lemons, and put in with the rhubarb. Simmer until citrus fruit is transparent. Mince 500 grams (17 oz) of walnuts and add to cooked rhubarb with 3 kilograms (6 lb 10 oz) of brown sugar. Boil for about 1 hour or until it sets when tested.

RHUBARB RELISH

Mix 2 cups chopped rhubarb with 2 cups diced onion, 1 cup vinegar, 2 cups brown sugar, ½ teaspoon salt and cinnamon, ginger and cayenne to taste.

Put into an enamel or stainless steel saucepan, boil for 20 to 30 minutes, or until the consistency of jam; bottle and seal.

RICE

Short grain rice, sometimes known as sticky rice, is ideal for puddings or sweet dishes. When cooked the grains stick together. Try boiling in orange juice, topping with hot chocolate sauce and serving with ice cream for a quick dessert.

Long grain rice, cooks up to a light, fluffy texture. The grains separate well, making it ideal for savoury dishes such as curried chicken or fried rice.

Brown rice is darker and coarser, and has a slightly nutty flavour. It comes in both short and long grain varieties and takes longer to cook than white rice.

Wild rice is not really rice at all, but the seed of a wild grass that grows in North America. It is expensive and usually available only at speciality food shops.

To boil rice, use the ratio of 1 part dry rice to double the amount of cold water. Bring to the boil. Simmer until all the liquid is removed, then fluff up with a fork.

RICE PUDDING

Put a scant cup of rice into 1½ litres (2-3 pints) of milk into an ovenproof dish and let it stand

for about 8 hours. Then add a piece of butter, about half the size of an egg, ¾ cup sugar and a pinch of salt. Bake very slowly for about 1½ hours at a low temperature. After it has become hot enough to melt the butter, but not brown the top, stir it gently from the bottom, at the same time adding a handful of raisins. Now sprinkle a pinch of nutmeg over the top and continue baking until the top changes colour. This dish can be served with Golden Syrup or jam over the top of it or with ice cream.

RISSOLES

If you are going to the trouble of making rissoles, make a good quantity and freeze them. Such a good stand-by if you are in a hurry. A different recipe is 2 rashers of bacon chopped and gently fried with 1 chopped onion and a small knob chopped green ginger. Allow to cool then add it to 500 grams (17 oz) minced steak with salt and pepper to taste, a dessertspoon of soy sauce, 1 tablespoon powdered cloves, 1 small tin pineapple pieces, drained, and 2 slices crumbed white bread. Mix all together, measure out tablespoon lots, roll in flour and fry.

SAGE

A most aromatic herb, which is very good with any meat dish. Often used in savoury omelettes. Dried sage is a useful deterrent to insects in the linen or kitchen cupboards.

SAGO PLUM PUDDING

Soak overnight:

4 tablespoons **sago** in 1 cup **milk**

Next day add:

75 grams (2½ oz) **breadcrumbs**

1 tablespoon **melted butter**

½ teaspoon **bicarbonate** of **soda (baking soda)**

125 grams (4 oz) **sultanas**

125 grams (4 oz) **currants**

75 grams (2½ oz) **sugar**

Mix well then put into a greased basin. Cover the basin with greased paper and steam for 3 hours.

SALAD BOWLS

Wooden salad bowls should not be washed as a general rule. Wipe with kitchen paper before putting away. Occasionally, wash the salad bowl in warm soapy water. Dry thoroughly then wipe over with oil and vinegar.

SALAD DRESSING

2 teaspoons **dry mustard**

1 dessertspoon **butter**

1 tablespoon **sugar**
1 **egg**
¾ cup **milk**
2 dessertspoons **vinegar**
½ teaspoon **salt**

Put mustard, butter and sugar into a double saucepan. Stir until butter and sugar melt. Then add beaten egg and milk. Stir until well blended. Remove from the heat. Add vinegar and salt. Stir until mixture coats the spoon, like custard. Use a wooden spoon for stirring.

SALT

Humidity makes salt lumpy. Mix a little cornflour with the salt to make it free flowing, or put a couple of navy beans in the bottom of the shaker.

Over salting: For too much salt in a casserole or stew, peel a couple of potatoes and put into whatever you are cooking. They absorb the salt. Just before serving, remove the potatoes and throw them away.

Salt substitute: Herbs are a good substitute for salt in many dishes. Celery, summer savory, thyme and marjoram are all salt substitutes.

SAUCEPAN

A good general rule for a burnt saucepan is to add about an inch of oil. Bring it to the boil, tip the oil out immediately, then rub the pan with steel wool or cover the base with salt or bicarbonate of soda (baking soda) and a little water. Put on a low heat with the lid on, simmer for a few minutes and the burn should peel off. Another method is to put the saucepan outside, out of sight, and let the sun shine on the burnt surface. It takes about two weeks for the burn to flake off.

Treat enamel saucepans carefully as they can scratch. Put a tablespoon of bicarbonate of soda (baking soda) with a little vinegar into the saucepan. Bring to the boil and then rub with a soft cloth. Or, fill the saucepan with cold water and some bleach. Let it stand for an hour or so then wash in hot soapy water.

For stainless steel saucepans, put in a large unpeeled onion; cover with water, then bring to the boil and leave till it cools. When stainless steel saucepans become stained after cooking popcorn, barely cover the bottom with cold water, then sprinkle in about 2 tablespoons of denture powder. Leave overnight and repeat if necessary. Or, if you have no objection to using chemicals, cover the bottom of the pan with neat bleach. Leave overnight then wash in very hot, soapy water.

To remove burnt food from stainless steel saucepans turn upside down on the bench to seal in the steam and loosen the burnt food, making it easy to clean with a brush and hot, soapy water.

When boiling a pudding in any type of saucepan, prevent a black rim from forming by putting a few slices of lemon in the water.

Here are some extra tips for burnt saucepans.

- Put some vinegar in, bring to the boil, then simmer for ½ an hour with the lid on.
- Half fill with water and put in 1 or 2 cut up onions, skins and all. Boil for half an hour then leave until the next day; particularly good for aluminium.
- For milk, white sauce or scrambled eggs stuck to the bottom of the saucepan, turn it upside down on the bench, with the handle towards the sink so the heat is trapped inside. This method steams the residue loose and cleaning is easy.
- Put some ashes and a handful of washing soda in the saucepan, half-fill with water and boil with the lid on, then leave until it is cold.

SAUSAGES

Sausages that are to be cooked on a barbecue, in a pan, or grilled, are better to be partly boiled beforehand. Place them into a saucepan, cover with cold water, bring to the boil, then strain and leave to cool. They can be used immediately or frozen. With this method, sausages cook quickly and evenly, and with less splattering of fat.

SAUTE

Saute means to cook in an open pan in a small amount of butter, margarine or oil until brown. Heat slowly at first to evaporate moisture and prevent spattering.

SAVORY

Savory is a herb which grows from either a cutting or by seed. The finely chopped or dried leaves go with all kinds of cooked beans, either sprinkled over the beans or with a little melted butter, or in a cream.

The fresh or dried herb can be mixed with breadcrumbs for coating fish, or pork or veal fillets before frying. It is a good flavouring for seafood sauces and cocktails.

SCONES

The best scones are made with sour milk or sour cream. Not only are they lighter and more fluffy, but the flavour is deliciously improved. An expert scone maker I know gives these tips. Use plain flour and baking powder, not self-raising flour. Use 3 teaspoons baking powder to 2 cups flour.

Always use a knife to mix dough, and do not mix more than is necessary. Most importantly, sour the milk for mixing. If you don't have sour milk, mix a little lemon juice with the milk to sour it.

SHELVES

It is best to cover kitchen shelves with wipeable plastic, self-adhesive material. Wooden shelves that have become stained should be washed thoroughly with hot soapy water and wiped down with a solution of 1 part bleach to 4 parts water. Don't put things back onto the shelves until they are perfectly dry.

SINK

An efficient way to clean a blocked sink is to put a handful of washing soda or common salt down the sink. Then pour in half a cup of vinegar. Leave for about half an hour, then pour in boiling water.

Always keep a rubber plunger (from hardware stores or supermarkets) in the cupboards under the sink in case of a blockage.

SIPPETS

Used in soups, sippets are made from stale bread. Dice the bread and saute in hot butter until evenly browned and crisp.

SOUP FAT

The best way to remove fat from soup is to put the soup in the refrigerator until all the fat floats to the top and solidifies. Then it is easy to lift the fat from the soup and discard it. That method takes time, so if you are in a hurry, wrap some ice cubes in a paper towel and skim over the top. The fat will cling to the paper. It is necessary to change paper and ice cubes to skim over until all the fat has been absorbed.

SOURDOUGH

Sourdough paste is made with 3 tablespoons of flour mixed to a smooth consistency with unrefrigerated milk, then left uncovered for 2 or 3 days, or until it smells sour. To make sour bread, put 1¼ kilograms (2 lb 12 oz) of flour and 4 teaspoons of salt into a bowl. Make a well in the centre and add the sourdough paste, 115 grams (4oz) of melted margarine, ½ litre (17 fl oz) of warm milk and 15 grams (½ oz) of fresh creamed yeast. Mix the ingredients together and knead for about 15 minutes. Put the mixture into a bowl and cover with a damp cloth. Leave in a warm place to rise. It takes about 1 to 1½ hours, depending on the temperature. Remove from the bowl and knead the bread again for 1 minute only. Cut into portions and put into greased tins. Bake in a hot oven (220°C/430°F) for 30 minutes. Remove from the oven and brush with cream for a glossy finish. Put the loaves back into the oven for another 1½ hours at medium temperature (180°C/350°F).

STAINLESS STEEL

All stainless steel is not the same, so find the cleaner that is best suited to your stainless steel. Supermarkets and some hardware stores carry a products excellent for restoring the shine of stainless steel. Other products come as a fine cream cleanser in a tube. Methylated spirits mixed with a fine powder cleanser is very good for cleaning stainless steel

Sinks: Another method is to rub stainless steel with lemon peel, then wash with pure soapy water.

Clean stainless steel saucepans with a mixture of ⅓ cup brown vinegar, 3 cups hot water and 1 tablespoon dishwashing detergent.

STEEL WOOL

After using steel wool, put it into a plastic bag in the freezer compartment of the refrigerator. No rust and most economical.

STRAWBERRIES – TO FREEZE

Use clean fruit that needs to be wiped clean rather than washed. Hull the strawberries and put them onto a flat tray to freeze. Do not cover the fruit. When the fruit is frozen, pack them into plastic bags, seal and return to the freezer. The fruit is suitable for making desserts or jam and the flavour is fully retained for at least a year.

STRAWBERRIES – TO KEEP

Remove the strawberries from the punnet and wipe them gently with paper towel to remove any moisture or dirt. Don't remove the hulls. Line a flat dish with paper towel, put a layer of strawberries on the paper towel, then add another layer of strawberries and finish with paper towel. Now, lightly cover with aluminium foil and keep in the refrigerator. They will keep better, and for longer, using this method.

STRAWBERRIES – WITH PRE-DINNER DRINKS

If you are only eating strawberries as a dessert fruit, try something different. When the berries are fresh and large at the beginning of the season, wash, hull, and dry them, slice in half and pile on to the cut side, cream cheese mixed with freshly ground black pepper and a dash of chilli sauce. Arrange on a glass plate with rose petals and leaves, then serve with pre-dinner drinks, or with biscuits and cheese after dinner.

SULTANAS

Sultanas that need to be "plumped" up can be put in the microwave for about 60 seconds, depending on the quantity. The other method is to sprinkle them with cold water, cover with foil, then put them in a convection oven on low heat for about fifteen minutes.

TAMARILLO

The trees are decorative and grow to a height of about 4 metres (12 feet). The fruit is versatile and can be used for jam or chutney, as well as raw with cold meats, and as a fruit, either raw or cooked. The skin of the tamarillo is not pleasant to eat. Skin them by immersing the fruit in boiling water for a few minutes before peeling.

TAMARILLO JELLY

Pour boiling water over 1 kilogram (2 lb 4 oz) tamarillos and leave for 4 or 5 minutes. Tip off the water and pour cold water over. Peel. Roughly chop the peeled tamarillos and put in a saucepan with a thinly sliced lemon. Add 1 litre (36 fl oz) of water and boil for 35 minutes. Let the fruit

strain through a jelly bag overnight. Next day measure the liquid and bring to the boil. Add ¾ of a cup of sugar for every cup of liquid and boil hard for about 25 minutes. A small knob of butter or margarine added before boiling helps to prevent scumming. As soon as the jelly is set (established) by testing, remove from the heat and let it stand for a few minutes before pouring into hot, dry jars. Seal when cold.

TAMARILLO SAUCE

5 kilograms (11 lb) **tamarillos**
2 large **onions**
1 kilogram (2 lb 4 oz) **apples**
1 kilogram **brown sugar**
1 teaspoon **salt**
a little **black pepper**
1 teaspoon **allspice**
½ teaspoon **cayenne pepper**
2 litres (70 fl oz) **brown vinegar**
½ teaspoon **powdered cloves**
Boil all together for 4 hours then strain and bottle.

TANGELO

Tangelos are a crossbred mandarin with grapefruit. If you like the flavour of citrus fruit in cooking, don't waste the peel of the tangelo. Use a potato peeler to remove the skin, then with a sharp knife, cut it into fine slivers. Spread the slivers onto a plate and microwave on defrost for twenty minutes to dry out. During the summer months, the drying process can be done on a window ledge. Store in a screw-top jar and use in casseroles or curry dishes, sprinkle on roast duck or on pork about 10 minutes before the roast is taken from the oven.

TANGELO AND KIWIFRUIT MARMALADE

Using two kiwifruit to each tangelo, first slice the tangelos finely, remove any pips, and add 1½ cups of cold water to each cup of fruit and let it stand overnight. Next day, bring to the boil and simmer until the skin looks transparent. Remove from the heat, peel the kiwifruit, chop roughly and add it by cup measure, to the tangelo pulp. For each cup of kiwifruit, add half a cup of water. Now measure the whole mixture by cup into a large saucepan. For each cup of mixture, add a scant cup of sugar. Add the juice and rind of 1 lemon and a knob of butter. Bring to the boil, stirring constantly to dissolve the sugar, and keep boiling until the marmalade sets when tested. Remove the lemon rind before putting the mixture into jars.

TAPESTRIES

Woven tapestry wall hangings should not be washed. Use carpet stain remover, following the

instructions, or, make your own powder cleaner. Mix together 4 tablespoons of powdered borax, 4 tablespoons of salt and r tablespoons of shellite (naphtha). If necessary, increase the quantity to be sure there is sufficient to fully cover the tapestry with the powder. Roll the tapestry up and leave for at least 24 hours. Unroll and brush or vacuum off.

TEAK

To remove the build-up of oil from teak, clean with a soft, damp cloth, with a dash of brown vinegar on it. It may be necessary to repeat the treatment two or three times. Afterwards, sponge with a cloth, wrung out in warm soapy water and dry thoroughly. When oiling teak, use only teak oil, and remember, the oil must always be applied to the cloth first, and never directly onto the wood itself.

For a scratch on teak, a reader of my column suggests rubbing the scratch mark with a cork. The friction joins the scratch together.

TEFLON

The non-stick surface is fused onto utensils at the time of manufacture and the cost of renewing is often greater than that of replacing the articles. Care of non-stick cooking utensils is important. Avoid the use of harsh abrasives, steel wool, knives or metal spoons.

With time and continual use, non-stick surfaces will discolour. Treat regularly by putting 2 tablespoons of bicarbonate of soda (baking soda) into the pan or saucepan with 1 cup of water and boil for 15 minutes. Wash with dishwasher detergent, dry, then wipe with oil. For excessive staining, cover the surface with neat bleach, leave overnight, then wash in very hot water and detergent.

It is important to remember that "non-stick" works well with normal use. It was never intended for food to be burnt to a cinder.

THAW

When thawing meat, fish or chicken, make sure you do so in the refrigerator not on the kitchen bench. Thaw frozen vegetables by placing the packet in cold water, but most frozen vegetables can be plunged into boiling water to cook, or cooked from frozen, in the microwave.

THERMOS

For a stale smell, put in a tablespoon of bicarbonate of soda (baking soda); fill with water and leave overnight. To get rid of film on the inside, fill the thermos with warm water, add a couple of denture tablets or a tablespoon of denture powder and leave overnight. Next day give it a good shake with the cap on, then wash out with hot soapy water, and rinse.

THYME

This most versatile of all herbs can be used with meat in stuffings, tasty sauces, marinades and pâté. It gives a wonderful flavour to herb bread and many vegetables. Thyme is easy to grow, either in the garden or in pots. For drying, harvest the leafy branches just before they start to

flower and make sure you gather them on a dry day before midday. Hang in bunches in a shady, airy place, and when crisp dry, strip off the leaves and seal them in airtight containers. The flavour and aroma of thyme is more penetrating when dried.

TOMATOES

The oval-shaped tomatoes are the best variety to use for drying, because they are very meaty and contain few seeds. Choose tomatoes which are ripe but firm, unblemished and about the size of an egg. Slice the tomatoes in half, lengthwise. Or slice almost in half and open, butterfly style. Put the tomatoes into a large open pan and cover completely with a solution of 200 grams (7 oz) of sodium metabisulphite dissolved in 8 litres (280 fl oz) of cold water. Leave for about an hour, then lift the fruit onto sterilised racks, cut side down. Some of the metabisulphite solution can be used to sterilise the racks. They can be dried in the oven or in the sun. Spread on a tray to dry in the sun, or dry in the oven at about 65°C (150°F) with the door ajar. For sun drying, tomatoes should be contained under a mesh canopy so that insects do not spoil the fruit. Turn tomatoes every four days until dry.

To bottle: Use firm tomatoes. Blanch the fruit in boiling water for 3 minutes, then plunge into cold water and peel. Make a brine, using 1 dessertspoon of salt to 1 cup of water. Pour the hot brine over the fruit. Fill right to the top with boiling water and seal immediately.

For tomato paste: Use firm, ripe, tomatoes. Rough chop, and put them into a saucepan. Cover the tomatoes with water and add a teaspoon of salt, a bay leaf and a little basil. Boil to reduce the liquid to about half, put the mixture through a mincer, then through a sieve to remove the skin and seeds. To peel tomatoes, first plunge them into very hot water for about 2 minutes. Another method is to hold them over heat on a long toasting fork. For tomato sauce, chutney or relish stain, sponge with cold water then rub in a little glycerine. Leave for half an hour, then wash as normal.

TURKEY

Before cooking turkey it is best to know whether it is an old or young bird. An old bird has rough, reddish legs; a young turkey, smooth black legs. If the turkey is old, it is better to boil the bird, then finish off in the oven to give a roasted finish.

VANILLA POD

Some people think vanilla pods give a much better flavour than essence. Stir the pod into whatever is to be flavoured until the taste is satisfactory. Remove the pod and wash in two or three waters, then dry for future use. It will last for ages.

VEGETABLES, FROZEN

Frozen vegetables are more likely to retain their fresh flavour if you pour boiling water over them as soon as they are removed from the freezer. Quickly pour the boiling water away to remove

all traces of the frozen iced water from the vegetables. You will be amazed at the difference this makes to the flavour.

VINYL FLOOR

Vinyl floor covering which has an indented pattern is harder to care for than a smooth surface. Washing the floor with hot water and detergent removes the dirt from the surface, but the indentations are left with surplus water which always contains minute particles of grit. Over years of washing the floor, the grit builds up and solidifies. When this happens, the floor needs to be scrubbed with a firm brush, then wiped completely dry. Polish the floor, paying particular attention to the indentations. Then, make sure the floor is dried after every wash. Vinyl floors that have become stained and difficult to clean can be washed with one tablespoon of caustic soda in half a bucket of hot water. Use a squeegee mop so that you don't have to put your hands into the water. Wear gloves and dry the floor with a thick cloth to be sure it is dried quickly.

WALNUTS

Shelled walnuts will keep for well over 12 months in the freezer. Put them into a plastic container with a tight fitting lid. Take out as many as you need to use at any time, put the lid back on, then back into the freezer. The nuts retain their freshness and will be completely free of weevils.

To keep: Leave the walnuts in the shell and put them in an earthenware pot. Fill the pot almost to the top with walnuts, then cover with about 5 centimetres (2 inches) thickness of sawdust. Place in a cool spot.

To crack walnuts and keep them whole, soak overnight in salted water. Or, put them in a moderate oven for about 15 minutes. The shells will begin to open and the nuts can then be removed in one piece.

WATER BOTTLES

The easiest cleaning method is to put about a teaspoon of household bleach into the bottle, shake it around, then fill the bottle with cold water and leave overnight. Next day, empty the bottle, wash it with hot water and detergent, rinse in hot water then in cold, and stand it upside down to drain.

WEEVILS

The eggs of weevils can be contained in the sealed packets of flour, barley, cake mix etc. from the supermarket. They are not harmful but nobody wants to eat them. Screw-top lids don't worry them too much because they are small enough to find their way along the screw channels to invade the rest of your pantry. My pantry, once infested with them, has been completely free of the little beasts for more than three years now. You can do what I did. Take everything off the pantry shelves, spray over and under the edges of the shelves where they meet the wall, with a spray cleaner containing ammonia. Next, wipe the shelves with a cloth wrung out in very hot

water. Use a hair dryer, turned on "hot" to blast hot air into all the seams and cracks so that any eggs will be cooked and unable to hatch. Leave the pantry door open for the shelves to dry. Now check everything that has come out of the pantry. Flour, cornflour, etc., should be put through a sieve twice. All containers can have bay leaves taped to the inside of the lids. Lastly, bring to the boil 2 cups of vinegar, 1 tablespoon each of cloves, grated ginger, lemon rind and orange rind, plus 1 teaspoon of dried chilli and 2 bay leaves. Simmer for 15 minutes then remove from the heat and let it cool. Strain and discard the liquid. Put the strained spices into an open container and leave on a shelf in the pantry. If the pantry is large, divide the spices to leave it on two or three shelves. About once every six months, put 1 tablespoon of water over the spices, cover with plastic and microwave, on full, for 60 seconds. This will revive the pungent aroma of the spices and keep the weevils at bay. Keep walnuts, peanuts, etc, in a sealed container in the freezer.

BATHROOM

Bathrooms can be hard to keep clean as there is so much moisture in the air and lots of places for germs and bacteria to grow.

Here's a recipe for a bathroom cleaner for tiles, mirrors and glass showers screens. to help keep your bathroom sparkling and clean. Into a 750 ml (26 fl oz) bottle, with a child-proof screw-top, mix together a ¼ cup each of methylated spirits and kerosene. Add ½ cup of fabric softener, 1 teaspoon eucalyptus oil and 2 cups cold water. Wring out a cloth in hot or cold water, and add a dash of the mixtures to clean all bathroom surfaces. Buff up with a soft, dry cloth. Don't forget to label the bottle, and shake before using.

BATH

Condy's crystals, baby oil or bore water can stain the bath. Fill the bath with water, add a large bottle of household bleach and leave overnight. For most baths this is only about 1 part bleach to 120 parts water. White Lily or Kleen-Up are good bath cleaners. Another method is to mix a paste of salt and vinegar, put some of the paste onto a soft cloth and rub over the bath's surface. A weekly application of kerosene on a soft cloth helps to prevent stains occurring. For dark-coloured baths, polish with methylated spirits on a soft cloth.

Fibreglass baths need special care. Do not use abrasives. Clean the bath regularly with kerosene on a soft cloth.

BATH - BABY

Baby-minding grandparents can 'make do' at bath time by putting a plastic clothes basket into the ordinary bath with the baby in the basket. Both baby and minder will feel more secure.

BATH – CALCIUM

Put white vinegar onto a cloth and rub the stains. Where the calcium is stuck on and stubbornly refuses to move, pour the vinegar directly onto the calcium, leave it for ½ an hour then rub.

BATH MAT – RUBBER

A rubber mat in the bath prevents nasty falls but they need constant attention to keep mildew at bay. The best treatment is to scrub the mat, on both sides, with a weak bleach solution of about 1 part bleach to 6 parts water. Then wring out a cloth in the bleach solution and wipe the bottom of the bath. Hang the mat to dry after each use.

BATH – MOULD

When there is a continuing problem with mould under the sealant, it is time to look for the cause. It is possible the dampness that allows mould to grow is coming from under the bath. Removing the sealant and flushing the crack between the bath and the wall with undiluted bleach will solve the problem on a temporary basis. Once that has been done, if the mould returns, get a professional to check the cause. Don't re-seal until the cause of the mould has been removed.

BATH OIL

To make bath oil it is best to use sunflower oil and although any fresh herbs can be mixed together for a pleasing perfumed bath, I think that either lavender or rosemary is more acceptable to most females. Men would probably find mixed herbs more to their liking.

Fill a glass jar with 500 millilitres (17 fl oz) of sunflower oil, then add as much fresh lavender, or herbs, as the jar can accommodate. Seal with a lid, or aluminium foil and leave the jar in a warm place, such as a sunny window ledge, for three or four days. Strain, then repeat the

procedure three or four times with fresh herbs. Bottle, label and add a sprig of lavender to each bottle.

BATH SALTS

Bath salts can be made with 1 kilogram (1 lb 4 oz) of washing soda crystals, 2 teaspoons of essential oil, such as lavender, and 6 or 7 drops sandalwood oil. Sandalwood oil does not perfume the salts, but helps to retain the perfume. The washing soda crystals are white, but can be coloured with food colouring, available from most health food stores and supermarkets. One or 2 tablespoons of bath salts added to the bath water softens and perfumes. Packed in small jars and tied with a pretty ribbon, homemade bath salts make a great personal gift.

BATHROOM CEILING

Mould on the ceiling of the bathroom or shower recess is due to lack of ventilation. One of the commercial products can be used, following the instructions on the bottle, or, scrub the ceiling with liquid sugar soap. A solution of ½ water and ½ household bleach can be used if the mould is severe. These are harsh treatments and precautions should be taken when using them. Wear gloves; cover the face and nostrils; and be sure the doors and windows are wide open to allow the air to circulate. Mould must be removed before repainting, and use a paint which contains a mould inhibitor.

BATH RUST STAINS

Dripping taps usually cause rust stains on a bath and hand basin. Before removing the stains, remove the cause of the stains. Most handymen can change a washer, the usual cause of dripping taps. To remove the stain, make a paste with cream of tartar and ammonia. Put the paste on to a cloth and rub over the stained area. Wear a scarf tied over the nose and mouth because ammonia fumes are very pungent. When the stains are removed, rub the surface of the bath and basin with kerosene on a soft cloth.

BATH SCUM

Wring out a cloth in hot water, add a dash of kerosene to the cloth, then dip the cloth in a saucer of dry salt. Rub around the scum line on the bath and when it is removed, polish the area where the scum line forms, with some wax paste. Don't polish the base of the bath because it may be too slippery to stand on.

BUBBLE BATH

For a bubble bath, mix together, ¼ cup of any good oil (almond or olive oil is best), 1 cup of shampoo and 100 drops of essential oil. Before using, turn the bottle upside down two or three times, to mix the contents. To use, run the tap very hard, while gradually trickling half to a ¼ cup of the mixture to the water. Then agitate the water with both hands to maximise the bubbles.

DRY SHAMPOO

To make a dry shampoo, mix together 3 parts talcum powder with 1 part salt. Sprinkle the hair with the powder. Softly spread it through with the fingers, then rub vigorously with a clean, dry towel. Brush well and towel again. It's second best to wet shampooing but for many people whose hair quickly becomes greasy, it can be very useful.

ENAMEL BATH

If a white enamel bath has become discoloured, use chlorine bleach. Fill the bath with cold water and add 1 full bottle of bleach. Leave overnight if possible.

SHOWER

Clear plastic curtains can be kept clean and free from mildew, by washing them in warm water and about 1 cup of bleach. Depending on the amount of cleaning needed, it may be necessary to add 1 teaspoon of detergent to the water with the bleach. Use dishwashing detergent and rinse in clear, warm water.

SHOWER CLEANER

For a shower recess with a glass screen, one method of cleaning is to mix together ¼ cup brown vinegar with ½ a cup of salt. Rub over the scummed area with a cloth dipped in the mixture. Once the scum is removed, rinse to get rid of the vinegar and salt. Use neat methylated spirits on a soft cloth to shine the glass. A mesh bag, the type that oranges and onions come in, can be rolled into a ball and used to shift scum build-up or, better still, use Gloria's Window Cleaner (see recipe for Window Cleaner – Gloria's), which is good for tiles, mirrors and glass.

SHOWER CURTAIN

The hemline of a nylon shower curtain accumulates soap. This can be removed with a paste made of salt and lemon juice. Rub firmly and then wash in lukewarm water. For a plastic curtain, wring out a cloth in hot water, then add methylated spirits to the cloth and wipe over. Without taking the curtain down, let the bottom soak for a few hours in a bucket of hot water and nappy soaking powder. Turn the shower on to rinse.

SHOWER MOULD

Using an old toothbrush for the corners should be sufficient to keep the around the shower clean. If mould appears under the silicone, it is because moisture is also under the seal. The remedy is to remove all the silicone and ensure the area is both mould, and moisture free, before re-sealing. This is really a job for a professional who will be well aware of the problems created by moisture and mould under silicone sealants in a bathroom. Be sure to get a guarantee in writing before committing the work to be done.

LAUNDRY

Dry cleaning is a modern trade that grew out of laundries. Our grandmothers washed just about everything, either boiled up in the copper for household linen, or gently hand washed, for clothing. Linen clothing was usually starched after washing because it goes limp and creases easily. The problem with today's clothing is that we often do not know what all the parts are made from. The stiffener in the lapels of a jacket or the thread with which it is sewn might be non-washable. It is important to check the labels for cleaning instructions. Some labels spell out the care needed, others may be labelled with the international textile care code, as shown below.

	1 = dot cool, 2 = dots warm, 3 = dots hot *or* iron at degree setting		Hand wash only
	Machine wash at this temperature		Do not bleach
	Bleach can be used		Do not iron
	Do not wash		Do not tumble dry
	Dry clean		Improved with tumble drying
	Dry clean with care		Do not dry clean
	Dry clean in white spirit or solvent 113, needs special care		Dry clean in perchlorethylene white spirit, solvent 113 or 11
	Hang to dry		Drip dry

COLOUR FADING

There are many reasons why colours either run or fade in the wash:
- The water is too hot.
- Detergent is used instead of mild soap.
- A detergent containing a bleaching agent is used.
- Too much detergent is used.
- Machine washing is used instead of hand washing.
- Not enough rinsing, leaving detergent in the fabric.

Once colours have run or faded, reversing the process is difficult and often impossible. Before buying any garment, read the care instructions. It's no good buying a "hand wash only" garment if you're a person who never has time to hand wash.

Garments can sometimes be restored by dyeing. Use a good quality dye and follow the instructions carefully. Make sure the material is compatible with the dye being used. Any badly faded out patch will dye lighter than the rest of the garment and it might be necessary to use a dye stripper first to even the all-over colour. Any garment made with different colours or fabrics will very likely take on different tones despite the dye being even. The effect will not be the same as the original but can still look very attractive.

FABRIC – VISCOSE

Viscose is made of cellulose from wood pulp and cotton waste, and needs very careful handling. If you choose to wash a garment containing viscose, use lukewarm water and drip-dry. Iron on low heat with a cloth between the iron and the fabric.

IRONING

There are some do's and don'ts. Don't iron more than is absolutely necessary. Fold sheets, towels and flat articles as soon as they are dry and they will not need to be ironed. Do have a good ironing board that is comfortable for your use. Don't have a highly coloured cover. Heat and steam can transfer some of the colour to the articles being ironed. Do use hot water to dampen articles to be ironed. Hot water penetrates better than cold. Do stand on a soft thick rug to prevent your feet and legs from tiring. Do put silk things into a plastic bag in the freezer for half an hour before ironing. Do use a damp cloth over the knee area of trousers where stretching occurs. Always start ironing trousers at the knee and steam the stretched area into shape before pressing.

POCKETS

Before washing, turn pockets inside out and scrub along the seam with a nailbrush. This gets rid of any accumulated dirt.

WASHING

It is better to wash multicoloured clothes by hand, in lukewarm water, with either ¼ cup of vinegar or a handful of salt in both the wash and the rinse water. Rinse in cold water. Measure out the required amount of detergent, then put half of it back. Overdoing the cleaning agent can eventually break down colour. In the washing machine, wash whites and coloureds separately if at all possible and never add soap or detergent to dry clothes or linen. Detergent added to fabric that is not completely covered with water is likely to leave clothes or linen with blotchy white or yellow patches. Do not use bleach on anything except pure cotton or pure linen. Drip-dry on plastic hangers; metal can cause rust spots. Before loading the washing machine, check all pockets for things like pens, crayons and tissues. Any stray items can discolour other items or clog the machine.

SPIN DRYER

Do not over-dry clothing. Over-drying can result in a breakdown of fibres and cause clothes to wear out quickly. It is normal for elastic in socks, bras, trousers, etc. to remain slightly damp on removal from the dryer, but don't put them away damp. Leave for a while to air and become thoroughly dry.

ACRYLIC

White acrylic knits become yellow over time. The yellowing often occurs on the outside of the garment while the inside remains pristine white. Try soaking the garment, overnight, in a bucket of lukewarm water with 1 tablespoon of citric acid, 2 tablespoons cream of tartar, and 1 dessertspoon of dissolved pure soap flakes. Next day rinse well in two lots of clean lukewarm water and turn it inside out to dry. Repeat if necessary, and always turn acrylic knits inside out before putting them away.

AGE STAINS

Age stains on fabric are usually either rust or mould caused by long periods of undisturbed storage. Grandma's lovely old white linen or crochet is often affected. If you are certain that white fabric is pure cotton or linen, soak in a mild bleach solution. Use one part bleach to four parts water. Leave for a couple of hours, then wash in hot, soapy water.

APRICOT STAINS

Apricot stains on clothing can be readily rinsed away with cold water if the stain is fresh. For an apricot stain that has dried on clothing, dampen the stain with warm water, cover with powdered borax, then let the hot tap run through the borax. The stain will be removed and the garment can then be washed in the normal way.

BABY CLOTHES

Baby clothes that are not being used can become yellow and develop brown spots. Soak the clothes overnight in a bucket of water with a handful of nappy-soaking powder. Use cold water for soaking; wash the next day in fairly hot water.

For woollens, use lukewarm water and wool wash. Soak for 1 hour only and use the same temperature water for washing and rinsing.

Age or mould stains that cannot be removed with normal washing can be treated by covering the marks with a paste made by mixing cream of tartar with water. Leave to dry then brush off. Or mix lemon juice and salt to a paste and cover the stains. Leave to dry and brush off.

As a last resort, and only if nothing else works, sponge the marks with a solution of 2 tablespoons denture powder dissolved in ½ litre (17 fl oz) of cold water. Wash in lukewarm water with a little nappy soaking powder. Rust stains should be treated with a rust remover.

BANANA SAP

Banana sap stains, no matter how old, will be obliterated completely if you first dampen the stain, then smother with denture powder. Let it stand for about an hour, then pour hot water over it. Any residual stain can be removed by soaking the garment overnight in nappy soaking powder, then washing in the normal way.

BASEBALL AND SOFTBALL PANTS

Baseball pants are subject to grass and dirt stains because of the slides towards base, often made at full stretch along the ground. This also ensures the grass and dirt stains become thoroughly ingrained into the weave, or knit, of the fabric. Use one of the commercial eucalyptus wool detergents as a stain remover. Apply it straight from the bottle to the stain. Leave for about ten minutes, then wash in the normal manner.

BATTERY ACID

Torch battery acid on fabric can often be removed with a mixture of washing soda and water, or bicarbonate of soda (baking soda) and water. Mix to a paste and, for best results, leave on the stain until the paste is quite dry. Remove the paste and sponge over if necessary. As a last resort, a weak solution of bleach can be used, but not on synthetic fabrics. Use no more than 1 part bleach to 6 parts water.

BAUXITE DUST

Fine red dust gets into everything. The only successful way I have found for removing the fine dust is to soak the clothes in cold water to which borax has been added. About 2 tablespoons of powdered borax to 1 litre (36 fl oz) of water. Soak overnight, then wash the clothes in hot soapy water with 2 tablespoons of methylated spirits and 1 teaspoon of eucalyptus oil. Care will be needed with coloureds. Check to see that the methylated spirits will not cause colour to run.

BED LINEN – MUSTY

To get rid of the musty smell from the bed linen, use a few drops of commercial odour neutraliser in the wash water and a little fabric conditioner concentrate in the rinse water. If possible, dry outside rather than in the dryer.

BEER

Sponge beer-stained clothes with warm water and borax, using 2 tablespoons of powdered borax to 1 litre (36 fl oz) of warm water. Rinse in clear water before hanging out to dry.

BLOOD STAINS

Dampen the bloodstains, cover them with salt, then leave for about 2 hours before letting cold water from the tap run through the salt and the stains. Next, wash the garment quickly, rinse in cold water, spin dry and hang inside out to dry.

BLOOD UNDIES

When accidents occur it is not always convenient to change underwear before blood has dried. As soon as possible, soak the undies in enough cold water to cover them and mix in a handful of salt. It won't hurt to leave them overnight but don't leave them soaking for days on end.

Tip the salt water out and wash the garments in water as hot as the fabric will allow, using pure soap flakes in preference to detergent. Rinse well. On some fabrics, a more effective treatment is to soak the garments overnight in cold water with a little cloudy ammonia.

CASHMERE

Cashmere is a very fine wool and should always be washed by hand. Use warm water and wool wash. Always try to wash woollens on a fine day but dry away from direct sunlight. Turn inside-out to dry.

CHEF'S UNIFORM

Try soaking the uniforms overnight in cold water, with laundry powder. Next day, wash in hot water with any good detergent and about 2 tablespoons of a household detergent.

CHENILLE

Chenille is a fabric that often sheds fluff. Wash bedspreads, one at a time, in the washing machine. Add 2 tablespoons of pure soap flakes dissolved in hot water. Tumble dry with two or three clean tennis balls in the drier.

CHRISTENING GOWN – YELLOWED

For a christening gown made of synthetic fabric that has yellowed, make your own soaker.

In a 750 millilitre (24 fl oz) screw-top bottle, put ¼ cup of methylated spirits, ¼ cup washing-up liquid, 1 tablespoon ammonia, 1 teaspoon eucalyptus oil, 1 tablespoon citric acid and enough cold water to fill the bottle. Label the bottle. Add about ¼ cup of the mixture to half a bucket of cold water and soak the christening gown overnight. Next day, wash as usual and hang the garment inside out to dry.

COLOURFAST

A very old-fashioned method used to set colour in garments is to put a handful of bran into a saucepan and cover it with about 1 litre (36 fl oz) of cold water. Simmer for half an hour, strain, add sufficient cold water to bring the temperature to lukewarm, then wash the garment in it.

COLOUR IN SILK

Silk is a fabric that readily accepts dye but just as readily lets go of it, so this is why silk should always be washed in tepid water and rinsed in water of the same temperature. Add about ¼ cup of white vinegar to the rinse water. Use pure soap, such as pure soap flakes rather than detergent, and dissolve the flakes in hot water before adding to the tepid wash water. Even better, wash silk in special silk washing liquid.

When wearing silk that imparts colour to your underwear, wear underwear of the same, or, a darker colour. If the colour only comes out under the arms, it is no doubt due to heat,

perspiration, deodorant, or a combination of all three. It is worth putting under-arm protectors into the garment.

COLOUR RUN

Garments that are made partly with light-coloured fabric, and partly with dark-coloured fabric, should be hand washed, then dried very quickly, taking some effort to keep the colours apart until drying is complete. If a mistake is made and colour is transferred from the dark to the light fabric, dampen the stained area and sprinkle it with a mixture of half cream of tartar and half citric acid. Leave it for an hour, then sponge with warm water, taking care not to wet the dark fabric.

When dye from another garment runs into a white cotton garment, soak it overnight in 1 part bleach to 6 parts cold water. Next day wash the garment in very hot water with any good detergent and a little washing powder. If the garment is not pure cotton, soak it overnight in cold water and 1 tablespoon of citric acid. Wash in warm water next day with a little detergent and detergent powder. Adding salt or vinegar to the wash and the rinse water helps to prevent the colour running. Cold water is better than hot water, and use pure soap, such as pure soap flakes, rather than detergent because, if the colour is not set fast, hot water and detergent may cause colour to run. If you are not buying colourfast fabrics, dry cleaning is the safest method of cleaning.

FABRIC – INDIAN

In India some of the fabric and clothing is produced at cottage industry level. In the main, vegetable dyes are used, and the fabrics are hand printed. The result is wonderful, vibrant colours and very creative patterns. The trouble is, the colour often runs. Wash the garments in cold water. Do not use any detergent but rub a little laundry soap on only the soiled parts of the garment, such as cuffs and collars. Rinse in cold water in to which ½ cup of salt has been added to each 2 litres (70 fl oz) of water. Spin-dry in the washing machine to get rid of as much water as possible, then dry outside as quickly as you can. It won't stop the vegetable dye from discolouring the water but it will help to delay the dull look due to colour loss.

FABRIC SMELL

Sometimes the finish used by overseas fabric manufacturers to set colour will cause a smell. Black, and very bright colours, are more likely to be affected because the deeper colours often need more finish, but even light colours can be affected. Try putting a few drops of commercial odour remover in the wash and the rinse water. If the smell persists, when the garment is dry, spray with odour remover or odour neutraliser.

FABRIC SOFTENER

A tablespoon of vinegar can be used in the final rinse instead of fabric softener.

FABRIC – SYNTHETIC – IRONING

Clothing made with synthetic fibres is best ironed under a damp tea towel, then put on a hanger to become completely dry. If the iron, even a steam iron, is placed directly onto the garment, it is likely to fuse the fibre and leave a mark that cannot be removed. Sometimes the mark can be made less noticeable by gently rubbing the area with steel wool. Dark fabrics can sometimes be improved by rubbing with a cloth dipped in brown vinegar.

FABRIC WHITE

Once upon a time you could guarantee that white terry towelling was pure cotton, in which case soaking for an hour or so in a solution of 1 part bleach to 6 parts water, was sufficient to make it look as pure as the driven snow. The advance of science has given us synthetics and mixtures of synthetic with pure fibre. It makes washing, drying and ironing a lot easier but cleaning is often harder. Bleach usually yellows synthetics, so if you are not sure of the fibre, soak the garment overnight in half a bucket of warm water with 1 tablespoon of pure soap flakes (dissolved first in hot water) and 2 teaspoons citric acid powder. Put the lot in the washing machine next day and wash with water as hot as the fabric will bear.

FACE WASHERS

Face washers become stiff no matter how much rinsing they are given after each use, because soap builds up in the weave of the cloth. Soak face washers overnight, covered in plenty of cold water and 2 tablespoons powdered borax. Next day, wash them in very hot water with hardly any detergent, rinse in lots of cold water with a couple of teaspoons of salt.

FLANNELETTE SHEETS

Add 2 tablespoons of borax to the wash to soften flannelette sheets and stop them from pilling. Another method is to wash a few times, each time using the tumble dryer to dry them. Two or three clean tennis balls in the drier will help to keep pilling at bay. Rough skin on the heels of the feet will cause pilling, so rub hardened skin with pumice and apply a cream softener to the feet.

FLUFF

Some clothing, particularly synthetic fibre, attracts fluff. If possible, wash the clothing and put a good brand name fabric softener in the rinse water. Another method is to spray evenly over the outside of the garment with a commercial anti-static product.

GREASE ON CLOTHING

Put the garment flat and smother with talcum powder. Leave the talcum powder for at least an hour and then remove. Now cover with powder again and put a couple of layers of paper towel under the greasy mark and more paper towel over the top of the powder. Now hold an iron, as hot as the fabric will bear, over the top of the paper. Do not press down heavily onto

the fabric. The heat will draw the grease up into the powder and you will be able to shake it off. Lightly sponge any residual mark with eucalyptus, or wash as usual but add about a tablespoon of household detergent to the wash water.

GREASY OVERALLS

Greasy overalls can be difficult to wash. One way is to add 1 tablespoon of bicarbonate of soda (baking soda) to the washing powder, or put a handful of salt in the washing machine. Or use ½ cup sugar in very hot water and washing powder, not detergent. Or soak overnight in a bucket of hot water with ½ cup methylated spirits and ½ cup kerosene. Next day, throw the lot into washing machine and wash with wool wash and hot water.

HAIR RIBBONS

To clean hair ribbons, wash in warm soapy water, rinse and wind the washed ribbons around a bottle filled with warm water. The ribbons will dry in no time and will not need ironing. Hair ribbons sometimes fray quickly. Carefully singe the ends with a naked flame.

IRON – CLEANING

To clean the plastic film from the base of a non-coated electric iron, heat the iron and turn off the power. Then rub with dry steel wool and a little vinegar. If a rust spot forms on the plate, rub with fine wet and dry sandpaper, or sprinkle salt over a piece of foil and rub the iron over it two or three times.

For a Teflon or coated iron, rub with a little olive oil while the iron is still warm, then with methylated sprits. Make sure no oil remains to be transferred to the garments.

For the inside of a steam iron, fill the iron with equal parts of water and brown vinegar. Heat the iron, pour out and repeat a couple of times. When clean, fill with cold water and give a few good bursts of steam before pouring the water away so the iron is ready for use again.

IRONING AID

For a spray starch, mix together, 1 tablespoon of starch and ½ teaspoon of powdered borax. Gradually add 300 millilitres (10 fl oz) of warm water and mix until smooth. Put it into a bottle with a spray top. Shake the bottle, spray the clothes and iron as usual. This type of spray starch is good for cotton uniforms, shirts and table linen.

LINEN AND COTTON – CREASING

Linen and cotton are notorious for creasing, and garments made with these fibres usually need ironing after every wear. When ironing, spray with a good brand of spray starch and steam iron.

MAKE-UP

Make-up marks around a neckline, particularly on a dark-coloured garment, can often be removed by rubbing with stale breadcrumbs. The breadcrumbs need to be at least two days old.

Cosmetics and make-up around the collars of garments can be removed with a soft cloth dipped in a little warm water to which has been added some cloudy ammonia, or sponge with a cloth wrung out in warm water and wool wash.

MILK FORMULA STAINS

For milk formula stains on flannelette and Viyella baby clothes, try making a paste with equal parts of borax and cream of tartar with water. Spread the paste over the stained area and leave it to dry. On mothers' clothes, the best method is to soak the garment in 2 tablespoons of borax to 1 litre (2 pints) of warm water, for about an hour, then wash as usual.

MOHAIR

Mohair should always be washed by hand in lukewarm water with wool wash and dried away from direct heat. Turn inside out to dry. When it is dry, shake well to revive the fluffy hair, or brush with a soft bristle brush. If the fluffy hair is shedding, spray the garment with commercial water repellent, or even a light spray with hair spray. Check first to see that the treatment will not flatten the garment too much. Putting it in a plastic bag in the freezer for an hour before use helps to stop the garment from shedding hair.

MUD STAINS

Mud on fabric should be allowed to dry. When it is dry, brush it from the cloth or rub the cloth between fingers and thumb to get rid of the mud sediment. if the mud leaves a residual stain, try sponging it with wool wash in warm water. It is necessary to test on an inside seam to be sure the sponging does not leave a watermark.

NAPPIES

To soften babies nappies, soak for a few hours in warm water and borax. Use about 2 tablespoons of Borax to 1 litre (2 pints) of water. After soaking the nappies, wash in wool wash. In areas where there is an excess of iron, copper or bauxite in the water supply, it is wise to place a filter over the tap. Rinse thoroughly.

When nappies become stained with a greasy ointment, soak them overnight in warm water with about ¼ cup of nappy soaking powder, and about ¼ cup mineral turpentine to 1 bucket of water. That will get rid of the stain, but wash the nappies again in hot water and pure soap flakes to get rid of the mineral turpentine, because babies' bottoms have sensitive skin.

NAPPY WHITENER

This recipe is also good for white socks to prevent discolouration

Into a large bottle (750ml) with a screw cap, mix ¼ cup each of methylated spirits and dishwashing detergent. Add 1 tablespoon cloudy ammonia, 1 teaspoon eucalyptus, 1 tablespoon citric acid and fill to the top with cold water. Soak the nappies overnight in a bucket of warm

water with ½ cup of the mixture. Next day, hand-rub the nappies and give them a bit of a pounding, as if you were doing the washing on a rock in the river. Then soak them for another 24 hours in hot water with 1 dessertspoon of citric acid, then wash in the normal manner. Soaking, and washing, with a couple of tablespoons of powdered borax will keep the nappies soft.

NYLON

To prevent nylon from yellowing, soak in warm water to which has been added 1 dessertspoon of bicarbonate of soda (baking soda), then wash in the normal manner.

Another method is to soak white nylon overnight in a bucket of lukewarm water with 1 cup of dishwashing machine liquid. Empty the bucket into the washing machine next day and wash as usual. Do not use hot water for nylon: it sets creases caused by washing. Also, never tumble dry – drip dry only.

NYLON – BABY CLOTHES

Nylon baby clothes that have yellowed with age can often be brightened. Soak them for about four hours in half a bucket of warm water with ½ cup of cream of tartar. Rinse well, gently squeeze out excess water, turn inside out, and dry away from direct sunlight. Do not put nylon garments in the tumble drier. it may be necessary to repeat the treatment two or three times.

OIL – GENERAL

Oil marks should not be treated with either hot, or cold, water. It is much better to smother the stain with lots of talcum powder, then cover the talc with a layer of paper towel and hold a hot iron over the paper. This treatment needs patience because it is necessary to heat the paper first, allowing enough time to heat the powder and then the oil. When the oil is sufficiently warmed, it will be drawn up into the powder. Do not press down with the iron because that will push the oil further into the fabric and it will eventually rise to the surface once more. It may take one or two treatments. When the oil is removed, brush or vacuum the powder off then sponge the stain, from the outside edge to the centre, with a wool wash.

Sometimes, with an oil mark on clothing, I simply smother the stain with talcum powder, loosely roll the garment, then leave it overnight in a warm place, such as the laundry. Any residual mark can be sponged with warm water and a little household detergent.

PERSPIRATION ODOUR

Strong perspiration odours on fabrics other than silk can be steamed over a basin containing hot water and 2 tablespoons cloudy ammonia.

PERSPIRATION ODOUR – T-SHIRTS

Dissolve a tablespoon of pure soap flakes in a litre of hot water. Let it cool, then add about 10 drops of commercial odour neutraliser. Use the mixture as if it were a pre-stain remover and

wash the T-shirts in the normal way. If the perspiration odour has been there for some time and has heavily impregnated the fabric, repeat the treatment two or three times and add more commerical odour neutraliser.

PERSPIRATION - SHIRTS

Make a paste, to the consistency of runny cream, with equal parts of cream of tartar, powdered borax and citric acid, mixed with glycerine. Cover the discoloured area with the mixture and leave overnight, then wash as usual. It may take two or three treatments.

PERSPIRATION – SILK

Try making a paste with cream of tartar and glycerine. Cover the stains, leave overnight, then rinse off with pure soap flakes dissolved in lukewarm water, or use a product formulated specially for washing silk. Follow the instructions on the bottle.

PERSPIRATION STAIN

Some people perspire more than others and therefore need to take extra precautions to keep garments fresh and free from underarm staining. Try different deodorants to find one that suits your particular body. Buy garments that do not fit tightly under the arms. If necessary, pin or velcro protectors to the under-arm seam. They can easily be removed and washed after each wear. For perspiration stains on light-coloured garments, make a paste with equal parts of cream of tartar and citric acid mixed with cold water. Cover the stain, leave for a few hours, then shake the paste off and sponge the area with mild soap and warm water.

For dark-coloured fabrics, wring out a cloth in cold water, add a dash of white vinegar to the cloth and sponge the stain. Use warm water and mild soap to sponge the vinegar away. The combination of perspiration and deodorant will often remove colour from dark clothing. If that happens, use a matching felt-tip pen to colour the bleached under-arm, then spray the coloured-in area with a waterproof spray.

PILLOWS

Pillows filled with unwashable material can be lightly sponged with a cloth dipped in warm water and borax, or cleaned with talcum powder. Feather pillows can be washed in the same manner as a feather quilt, in the washing machine, with wool wash then tumble dry with a couple of clean tennis balls in the dryer. The tennis balls thoroughly spread the feathers and the pillows come out soft and fluffy.

Pillows which have seen their days indoors can be of continued use outdoors. Make a bright cover from waterproof fabrics and use on outdoor furniture.

PILLOWSLIPS

For perspiration stains on pillowslips, soak them overnight in half a bucket of cold water with a

tablespoon each of cream of tartar and citric acid. Next day, empty the bucket into the washing machine and wash as usual.

POLYESTER

There is no reason why polyester or viscose cannot be washed. Nor should a mixture of the two fibres be a bar to washing. Polyester is usually finished with a resin to prevent creasing. With time, or with hot water, the resin will wash out and the fabric will lose some of its crispness. I think the same will happen with continual dry cleaning, which simply means that nothing lasts forever. Both polyester and viscose need very careful handling and should always be washed by hand, in tepid water, and drip-dried. With strong colours, wash the garments on their own because the colour might run. Remember, if you take the risk and go against the manufacture's instructions, you have no claim.

POLYESTER – SCORCHED

Heat and polyester simply don't mix and an iron that is hot enough to scorch will probably cause permanent damage. The one thing worth trying is toothpaste. Use a toothpaste which contains cream of tartar or bicarbonate of soda (baking soda). Spread the toothpaste over the scorch mark, then leave it for two or three hours. Sponge the toothpaste off with warm water and repeat if the mark looks like fading.

RASPBERRY

Because it is such a dense colour, raspberry stain can be difficult to remove. On washable materials, first wash with soapy water, and then rub lemon juice over the stain. Leave for about an hour before washing. Or try a few drops of a pen remover drizzled onto the stain, left for a few minutes, then washed with warm soapy water.

SCHOOL SOCKS

White school socks have a better chance of staying white if they are soaked regularly in lukewarm water with about 2 tablespoons of cream of tartar. It is a good idea to leave them soaking overnight. Then wash in hot soapy water and add a dash of kerosene to the wash.

SEMEN STAINS

On sheets, first soak in cold water with about 2 tablespoons borax, then wash as usual. If the sheets are put straight into the wash without soaking, the water will set the stain. On the mattress, sponge with cold water and borax using 1 tablespoon borax to 1 litre (2 pints) water, then sponge over with warm water and wool wash.

SHEEPSKINS

Some sheep or lamb skins, particularly those used for invalids and babies, can be washed. Usually

washing instructions come with the article, but if you don't have the care instructions hand wash in warm water with wool wash. If the skin is not washable, rub brown vinegar into the back of the skin to prevent hardening. Then scrub the wool side with a rough towel wrung out in 1 tablespoon of wool wash to half a bucket of warm water. Do this in sections to prevent saturation, and as you go, rub each washed section with a dry cloth.

SHEETS – HARD

Try washing the sheets with about 2 tablespoons of washing soda. It is sold in supermarkets, some hardware stores, and specialty soap shops. Another method is to put 2 tablespoons of powdered borax into the wash water and two tablespoons of Epsom salts in the rinse water.

SHIRT CARE

The majority of shirts today are made from "easy care" fabrics, but they do in fact require some care. The care usually needs to be taken when the shirts are washed. Hand wash, then rinse in the same temperature water. Put on a hanger to drip-dry, making sure the garment hangs straight. Stretch the collar and cuffs so they sit correctly with no wrinkles. If possible, check and maybe stretch the collar again when the shirt is half dry.

"Easy care" shirts all develop creases when packed in a suitcase but these disappear very quickly if they are removed from the case and hung on hangers as soon as you arrive at your destination.

Pure silk and pure cotton look fantastic but they are not easy to care for. Look for labels that are "hand wash, drip dry, do not iron". Check that the fabric breathes so that body odour does not become a problem.

SILK

When washing silk, use a gentle detergent formulated for protein fibres such as silk and wool.

SINGLET OR SLEEVELESS SHIRT

If singlets are made from pure cotton, bleach can be used to whiten them. If, on the other hand, singlets are made of synthetic fibre, or even a mixture of synthetic and cotton, it is a mistake to put them into any bleach mixture. Try soaking them in half a bucket of warm water with 2 tablespoons of cream of tartar. Leave them to soak for about four hours, then wash in hot water with a strong laundry soaking powder.

SOFT DRINK

On clothes, sponge off a soft drink stain with a mixture of warm water and borax. Use 1 tablespoon of Borax to ½ litre (1 pint) of water. Another method is to dampen the stain and cover with denture powder. Leave to dry then sponge over with warm water and a nappy soaking powder.

SOY SAUCE

Dampen the stain, then smother it with denture powder, leaving it for about 15 minutes. Drizzle a little pen remover over the residual mark to remove it completely.

SUNSCREEN LOTION

Sunscreen lotion usually washes out of garments with normal washing, but with some people, their own body oils and acids react with the lotion, causing yellowing where the lotion rubs onto a garment. Soak the garments overnight in half a bucket of warm water with 2 tablespoons tartaric acid. Then wash in water as hot as the fabric will take, with pure soap flakes.

TEA TOWELS

For tea towels that will not absorb water, soak overnight in a bucket of water and ½ cup Epsom salts. Don't rinse. Hang in the air to dry. A good boiling occasionally, in a pan on the stove, with soapy water is a good idea. For tea towels that have become very discoloured, soak them in cold water with 1 tablespoon of borax to every ½ litre of water before boiling. Or, soak in nappy soaking powder and cold water before washing. A weak bleach solution is also good. Ironed tea towels are less likely to leave fluff on glasses.

TERYLENE CURTAINS

Stop terylene curtains from yellowing by pre-soaking in a tub-full of warm water and ½ cup of bicarbonate of soda (baking soda). Wash and rinse curtains in water of the same temperature. Sharp changes of temperature causes creasing. After rinsing, drip-dry and re-hang before they are quite dry. Another good idea to avoid the creasing is to add 1 tablespoon of plain gelatin, dissolved in hot water, to the final rinse. Do not tumble dry terylene curtains.

TIES

Ties can be washed, using all the precautions needed for the fabric from which they are made. Test for colourfastness on the end of the tie that is tucked out of sight when it is worn. Always wash in lukewarm water with pure soap and rinse in the same temperature water. Dry the ties by putting a towel on the ironing board and laying the ties flat along the length of the board. Because ties are cut on the cross of the fabric and also lined, ironing is where the most care is needed. Iron both sides of the tie under a damp cloth, pressing very lightly.

TOWELS

Bath towels and tea towels can be softened and made more absorbent by soaking overnight in a solution of water and powdered Borax. Use 1 tablespoon of borax to about 1 litre (2 pints) of water. Put them in the tumble drier with one or two clean tennis balls to dry. It may take two or three treatments. Another method is to soak the towels overnight in a bucket of warm water with half a cup of Epsom salts. Hang to dry without rinsing.

TOWELS – BEACH

No matter how often they are washed, beach towels get a build-up of salt and sand. About twice every season it is essential to put them in a tub of very hot water and soak them for 24 hours. Put them outside to dry on a very windy day. Then soak them for another 24 hours in hot water and a ¼ cup of powdered borax. Put them into the washing machine with another ¼ cup of powdered borax and wash as usual. Add a good fabric softener to the rinse. Dry in a tumble dryer with two or three clean tennis balls.

TOWELS – MASSAGE OILS

Towels will not become impregnated with oil if they are soaked overnight in hot water with ½ cup of household detergent. Next day, toss them into the washing machine and wash as usual.

TRACK SUIT

Fleecy-lined track-suit fabric is less likely to transfer colour or pilling to other garments if all garments are rinsed in a good quality fabric softener. The generic fabric softeners are good for most washing, but a really thick one is needed for this problem so don't be tempted to economise. Also, spray the inside of the tracksuit with hairspray.

T-SHIRT MILDEW

Providing the white cotton T-shirt really is pure cotton, mildew can be removed by soaking it overnight in a solution of bleach and cold water. Use approximately 1 part bleach to 4 parts water. Wash next day in very hot water with any good detergent and 1 tablespoon of laundry powder. Turn the garment inside out to dry in the sun.

T-SHIRT – OIL

When anything that contains oil is spilt on fabric, it is important to remove the oil before applying a stain remover. To do this, simply smother the stain with talcum powder, pulling knitted fabric in all directions to spread the powder behind the knit. Leave it in a warm spot so the oil is absorbed into powder.

T-SHIRT – BLACK

Black is a colour that does not wear well in strong sunlight. A good idea would be to lightly dye black T-shirts at the end of summer each year. Done regularly, before the burnt, rusty look appears, the dye will take evenly. There is always a risk of colour from any garment, whether it is dyed commercially or at home, being transferred to under-garments.

With some people it may never happen, but others, due to perspiration and body enzymes, set up a reaction which causes colour to break down. The best thing is to wear dark underclothes with dark outer clothes and light underclothes with white and delicate colours.

T-SHIRT – GENERAL

Knitted garments, such as T-shirts, will probably hold their shape for a few washes, while they are still reasonably new. Once the newness wears off, the elasticity of the knit lessens, and the garments will stretch, sometimes sideways and sometimes lengthways. To stop this happening, roll each garment in a towel before putting it in the washing machine. To correct the problem, when washing and rinsing are complete, remove the garment and stretch it to the correct shape before drying. Or, after it is dry, iron it under a wet tea towel, stretching it back into shape as you iron. The only other answer is to hand wash all knitted fabrics.

UNDERWEAR – STAINED

Soaking underwear in warm water and nappy soaking powder is often sufficient to remove yellowing and any other stains. After soaking, wash in water as hot as the fabric will tolerate.

Another method is to make your own mixture. Here is my recipe that produces very good results. Into a 750 millilitre (26 fl oz) bottle put 1 dessertspoon of citric add, 1 tablespoon powdered borax, 2 tablespoons ammonia, 1 tablespoon antispectic disinfectant, ¼ cup methylated spirits and ¼ cup dishwasher liquid concentrate. Fill the bottle to the top with cold water and shake gently to dissolve the crystals. Use about two tablespoons of the mixture in half a bucket of warm water to soak the garments overnight. Rub the stained areas between your hands to gently separate the knit, or the weave, of the fabric. Rinse well.

Bras, like all garments worn next to the skin, should be washed after each wear. Sometimes you come home tired and really can't be bothered, but rinsing your undies out the minute you take them off is a very good habit to get into. You'll feel better, smell fresher, and won't be ashamed to have the undies seen. Try soaking grubby bras in cold water and nappy soaking powder. Leave to soak overnight and before washing them in hot water, hand rub the under-arm area.

WASHING MACHINE

To clean the machine put 2 tablespoons of Epsom salts into warm water in the machine and run through a full cycle. Do this regularly and the washing machine will remain clean. If you don't have Epsom salts, use 2 cups of vinegar. Tricleanium, available from hardware stores, is also good for removing smells and the build-up soap or grease.

WOOL CARE

With the use of the wool wash, washing woollens is not a problem. The no-rinse method saves a lot of effort. If you can not drag yourself from the old "wash and rinse" method, then rinse heavy garments, which take longer to dry, can be rolled in a towel after washing, then put in the washing machine to spin dry on slow cycle. Always use the same temperature for washing and rinsing woollens. For very dirty woollens, wash in two lots of water. Always turn garments inside out to dry. Do not tumble dry, or woollens will become matted. Do not dry woollens in the sun. Direct sunlight can burn and discolour the wool.

WOOLLENS – SHRUNK

Try dissolving 90 grams (3 oz) Epsom salts in boiling water. Allow to cool, then soak the garment in the solution for about half an hour. After soaking, squeeze out the excess water, lay the garment flat on a towel and stretch it into its correct shape. When almost dry, iron under a damp cloth.

£IVI.NG

ANIMAL – UPHOLSTERY

Cats or dogs often lie beside a favourite upholstered chair or couch, rubbing against it for comfort. The dirt and oils from the coat of the animal eventually leaves a very noticeable dirty patch. The best method of cleaning is to sponge the soiled area with warm water and wool wash.

ANIMAL STAINS ON CARPET

Excreta and vomit: Remove solid matter with a spatula or piece of cardboard. Do this carefully to avoid pushing any of the solids into the carpet. After removal of solids, use paper towels, or any old cloth to mop up moisture. Then sponge with a cloth wrung out in a warm water and wool wash . Use about 1 tablespoon of wool wash to 2 litres (4 pints) of warm water. Try not to wet the carpet too much and work from the outside edge of the stain to the centre. If the stain is stubborn, mix 1 tablespoon denture powder in a small bowl of water and sponge over, using a clean cloth. Another method for a stubborn stain is to make a paste with water and nappy soaking powder. Cover the stain with the paste, leave to dry, then vacuum off. The removal of any stubborn stain is likely to remove colour. If the carpet is light in colour, generally walking across the cleaned area is usually enough to blend the cleaning mark into the rest of the carpet. For dark carpets, test any cleaning method on an inconspicuous area first.

Urine: Mop up quickly to prevent as much moisture as possible from soaking into the carpet. The composition of urine can differ so that the same method of treating the stain may not always be successful. Normally urine is acid, so first sponge with a solution of 1 tablespoon cloudy ammonia to 1 litre (2 pints) warm water. If that is not successful it may be because the urine is alkaline. In which case, sponging with equal quantities of white vinegar and warm water will probably remove the stain. After cleaning is complete, cover the damp area with powdered borax and a few drops or spray of a commerical odour neutraliser to remove odour. When dry, vacuum the borax from the carpet. For dog or cat urine stains that have dried, wring out a cloth in lukewarm water, put a splash of white vinegar on the cloth and sponge the stain, working from

the outside edge of the stain to the centre. Then sponge with lukewarm water and wool wash to remove the vinegar. Take care not to get the carpet too wet. Mop up with a thick, dry towel. Stomping up and down on the towel is a good way to dry the carpet.

BLINDS

Venetian blinds are best cleaned with plenty of hot water and any good detergent. It is better to take them down for cleaning, particularly if you can get them outside on the lawn and hose them after cleaning. If they cannot be taken down, make sure you put down plenty of paper or towels to catch any drips.

BLINDS – VERTICAL

Most verticals are made from fabric that can be cleaned of mould with a bleach solution. Use about 4 parts water to 1 part bleach, and a soft nailbrush to scrub both sides. This treatment will kill the mould spores that have lodged between the weave of the fabric and also remove the stain. Test first to be sure the treatment will not harm the fabric and be sure to rinse in clean water to remove all traces of the bleach solution.

BOOKS – MAINTENANCE

The ideal storage place for books, particularly old books, is in a completely controlled atmosphere. While this is not possible in the average home, it does not mean that great care cannot be taken to preserve precious books for future generations. One hundred and fifty years ago paper was not treated as it is today so there is every possibility that the paper will become slightly brown as time goes by.

The best bookshelves are made of steel with a smooth baked enamel finish. If wooden shelves are to be used, they need to be sealed with two or three coats of polyurethane sealant which must be given at least one week to ensure hardening before putting books on the shelves.

Don't pack books so tightly that they become difficult to remove. On the other hand, loose packing might allow dust to fall between the pages. Use bookends if the books are likely to fall slantwise, thereby putting a strain on the bindings. Large, or thick, heavy books are probably best stored flat rather than upright, but do not pack too many on top of each other. If bookshelves are not backed put them against an inside, not an outside, wall. Dust regularly and check for any problems, such as mildew. Have precious books valued and be sure they are insured against theft, fire and water damage. Consult your local library for further information.

BOOKS – WET

To dry wet books, and keep the pages from wrinkling, put paper towels and talcum powder on both sides of every wet page. Close the book and put a heavy book of the same size on top. Leave overnight. For mildew on book covers, wipe over with a cloth wrung out in very hot water and a little neat antiseptic disinfectant added to the cloth. Dry with a soft cloth.

CANDLE WAX

Put tablecloths in a plastic bag, then into the freezer. Leave it overnight so the wax is frozen hard, then rub it with both hands to crumble the wax off. Any residual mark can be sponged away with a little eucalyptus oil before the cloths are washed. Candle wax should not be difficult to remove from brass candlesticks. Soak the candlesticks in boiling water and, while they are still under water, use a brush to remove the wax. Use a long-handled dishwashing brush to protect your hands from the very hot water. Once the wax has been removed, and providing there is not a sealant over the brass, polish with metal polish and then with a sealer to finish.

Candle wax can be removed from vinyl by adding a little kerosene to very hot water, then scrubbing with a firm brush. Any residual stain can be removed with kerosene on a dry cloth. Another method is to put ice blocks on the wax so it becomes hard and brittle, then use a spatula to lift the wax from the vinyl. Any residual staining can be sponged with kerosene. Candle wax can be removed from a glass tabletop with kerosene on a soft cloth. Don't try scraping it off with a knife because it is likely to scratch the glass.

CARPET

Keep a container of powdered borax in the cupboard. If red wine is spilt on the carpet, drop kitchen paper or an old towel onto the spill. Don't rub, just gently pat, allowing the paper to absorb the excess moisture. Immediately put the paper into a bucket that you have carried to the spill. Don't carry it to the waste bin, dripping further problems as you go. Now smother the red wine spill with masses of borax powder. Leave overnight, remove the borax and repeat if necessary. You can also use borax to remove orange cordial when the stain is still wet. When most of the stain is removed, treat the residual mark with a drizzle of pen remover, then sponge lightly with warm water and a little wool wash.

Water-based or acrylic paints can be removed with cold water, but only when the stain is still fresh. Once dry, water-based paint stains are almost impossible to remove. It is worth trying acetone, used in the same manner as turpentine on oil paint, but test first to see how the acetone effects the fabric. Depending on the carpet, it may be possible to shave the stain from the pile. This would, of course, leave an uneven area which may look better than the paint stain. The only other remedy is to cover the stain with a mat.

Once colour has been bleached out of the carpet, it cannot be brought back. Contact a commercial carpet dyeing company for a quote to either match the colour of the carpet or recolour the carpet completely. It is not much more expensive than shampooing the carpet and is better than trying to do it yourself. The only other answer is to have the bleached areas cut out and replaced with matching carpet. After they has been walked on a few times the patches will not be noticed.

For candle wax on the carpet, put some ice cubes into a plastic bag, seal the bag, then let it sit on the candle wax. The wax will become hard and brittle after about 10 minutes. Then use a plastic spatula to lift the wax from the carpet. Don't use a knife because it could damage the carpet. Any

residual mark can be removed by putting eucalyptus oil onto a cloth and dabbing the stain.

It takes time and patience to get rid of carpet beetle. Spraying with a suitable commercial spray can eradicate live beetle grubs. The trouble lies with the fact that the spray does not always kill the eggs, so it is necessary to either spray continually, or cook the eggs so they cannot hatch. The eggs are usually laid in corners and along the edges where the carpet meets the wall. A hair dryer turned on "hot" can be used along the carpet where the eggs are hiding.

Or use a steam iron. Put a damp towel between the carpet and the iron to prevent damage to the carpet. I prefer the steam iron method because I think it will cook more eggs. However, no matter how thoroughly the job is done, the eggs are so small that some will always escape, so it takes months of repetitive treatment to completely rid the carpet of these pests. Remember it only takes one leftover egg to hatch to produce a completely new colony.

For Blu Tack on the carpet, wring out a cloth until almost dry, in hot water. Put the cloth over the Blu Tack to warm, and soften it slightly. While it is warming, soften some fresh Blu Tack by rolling it in the palms of your hands. Remove the cloth and roll the fresh Blu Tack over the old. Any residual stain can be sponged with eucalyptus oil or acetone.

CARPET – CAR

A reader recently told me that she cured the smelly problem of milk spilt in the car, and then gone sour, by removing the carpet and washing it with vinegar. Once the carpet was dry, she brushed it thoroughly to remove any milk flakes. It seems like a good idea, but don't forget to wash the floor of the car with any good detergent and a little disinfectant.

CARPET – CAT URINE

On a mat or carpet that can be rolled up, mix together two 2 of powdered borax, 2 cups of salt and 2 cups of shellite (naphtha). Sprinkle the slightly damp powder all over the top of the carpet, paying particular attention to the area that smells the most. Now, spray over the powder with commerical odour neutraliser and roll the carpet up. Leave it rolled for about a week before unrolling and brushing the powder off. It may be necessary to repeat the treatment two or three times.

When cats or dogs urinate on the carpet, it often goes through to the backing of the carpet and the underfelt. Colour is then pulled up to the surface of the carpet and it is difficult to remove. Here is a treatment that I have given to many people who now swear by it. In a 750 millilitre (26 fl oz) screw-top bottle, mix together ¼ cup of methylated spirits, ¼ cup of dish washing liquid, 1 tablespoon ammonia, 1 teaspoon eucalyptus oil, 1 teaspoon citric acid, and 2 cups of cold water. Label the bottle. Put 2 tablespoons of the mixture into 1 litre of warm water, wring a cloth out in it, and sponge the urine stain, working from the outside edge of the stain towards the centre.

CARPET CAT WORMING FORMULA

Put acetone onto a clean cloth and dab the cat worming formula from the carpet. Work from the outside edge of the stain towards the centre. Once the stain is removed, sponge the acetone off the carpet with a little warm water and wool wash.

CARPET – CHEWING GUM

For chewing gum on the carpet, put some ice cubes in a plastic bag, then put the bag of ice cubes over the chewing gum. Leave it until the gum is hard and brittle, then use a plastic spatula to scrabble the hardened gum from the carpet. Do not use a knife for fear of damaging the carpet fibres. Any residual staining can be sponged with eucalyptus oil.

CARPET – CIGARETTE BURNS

On synthetic carpet, cigarette burns melt the fibre and there is no way to reverse the problem. Minor marks on the surface might be improved by covering them with a paste made with bicarbonate of soda (baking soda) and water. Leave to dry then vacuum off, or cut out the area that is burnt and inset another piece of carpet. If the burn is too deep on wool carpet, there may be little you can do. Try lightly rubbing the burn with dry steel wool.

CARPET CLEANER – LIQUID

Into a 750 millilitre (26 fl oz) bottle with a screw-top, put a quarter cup of methylated spirits, a quarter cup of Morning Fresh dishwashing liquid, one tablespoon of ammonia and one dessertspoon of citric acid, and enough cold water to fill the bottle. Put a quarter cup of this mixture into two litres of warm water, wring out a rough towel in the liquid and sponge the carpet. For very soiled areas, it may be necessary to use a soft brush. Be light handed with the brush to avoid furring the wool. When cleaning is complete, cover with a clean towel and stamp on it to remove as much moisture as possible.

CARPET CLEANER – POWDER

A good, all purpose powder cleaner for carpets, or furniture upholstered with fabric, is to mix together four tablespoons powdered borax, four tablespoons salt, and four tablespoons of either shellite (naphtha) [from hardware stores or supermarkets], or dry cleaning fluid. Store the powder in a glass jar with a screw-top lid. To use it, sprinkle some on the stain, scrabble it in a little with your fingers, then leave overnight before brushing or vacuuming off.

CARPET – CORDIAL

Try dampening the stain then covering it with denture powder. Leave for ten minutes, then sponge with nappy-soaking powder and warm water. Another thing worth trying is pen remover.

Drizzle a few drops of pen remover onto the stain, leave for ten minutes, then sponge with 1 tablespoon borax dissolved in 1 cup of warm water.

CARPET – CURRY STAIN

Dampen the curry stain with cold water, then smother it with denture powder. Leave it for ten minutes before sponging the powder off. Don't get the carpet too wet. If any stain remains, cover it with bicarbonate of soda (baking soda) and leave to dry. Brush or vacuum off.

CARPET – DRIED STAINS

If you do not notice a stain until it is dry, rub in some glycerine, leave overnight and the next day sponge lightly with a mixture made from 1 tablespoon of borax to 1 ½ cups of warm water. Keep mopping up so as not to get the carpet too wet.

CARPET – DRIED VOMIT

Dampen the vomit stain then cover it with denture powder. Leave it for about an hour before brushing or vacuuming it off. Any residual stain can be sponged with warm water and a little nappy-soaking powder. Don't get the carpet too wet and work from the outside edge of the stain towards the centre. When the sponging is complete, cover the damp area with lots of powdered borax; leave for at least 24 hours before vacuuming off.

CARPET – FLOODED

When a carpet has been saturated with water it is not enough to simply mop up the water from the top of the carpet then let it dry. The carpet must be lifted to allow the underfelt and the floor to dry. If necessary, put layers of newspaper both under and over the underfelt, a thick towel over the carpet, then stamp on it to expel the water. When the newspaper is saturated, replace it and perform another Indian war dance on the carpet. Keep doing that until the newspaper does not saturate. Sprinkle powdered borax under the underfelt but leave the carpet with a plastic container, or the like, under the carpet to keep it off the floor until the carpet and the underfelt are completely dry. If mildew has grown under the carpet, rotting it and causing bad odour, lift the carpet. Rotting underfelt may need to be replaced. Any dampness will have to be dried out. Mix a cup of powdered borax with 1 tablespoon of antiseptic disinfectant, sprinkle it under and over the underfelt.

Leave the carpet lifted until the floor and carpet are completely dry before replacing the underfelt and re-setting the carpet. For slight staining of the carpet, spray with carpet stain remover. Follow the instructions on the container.

CARPET – FRUIT STAINS

Mix 1 tablespoon borax to 1½ cups of water. Use a clean cloth wrung out in the mixture to sponge the stain. Try not to get the carpet too wet.

CARPET – FURNITURE INDENTATIONS

When heavy furniture has indented carpet, wring out a thick towel in cold water, put it over the indentations then hold a hot iron over it. Don't press down heavily. When the carpet fibre is warm and steamy, it will be possible to gently push the pile back to its original height.

CARPET GREASE

Sprinkle a grease stain with talcum powder. Cover the talcum powder with a paper towel and hold a hot iron over the top of the paper. Do not press down hard. What you are trying to do is to draw the grease up into the powder. Pressing down could push the grease further into the carpet. You may need to repeat this process two or three times.

CARPET – INK

For ink to be removed from the carpet, it is useful to know the type of ink. Old-fashioned fountain pen ink can usually be removed by sponging the stain with milk. Some red ballpoint pen inks can be removed with methylated spirits. Most ballpoint pen inks will disappear completely with the application of pen remover in conjunction with powdered borax. Drizzle pen remover over the stain, then cover it with plenty of borax powder. Most of the stain will be absorbed into the powder and any residual stain can be sponged with warm water and any good detergent.

CARPET – KEROSENE

The kerosene spill on the carpet should be sponged, working from the outside edge of the stain towards the centre, with warm water and wool wash. For this stain it is better to make your own wool wash rather than use the commercial variety. Mix together, 4 cups of pure soap flakes, 1 cup of methylated spirits, and 50 millilitres (2 fl oz) eucalyptus oil. Store it in a glass jar with a firm-fitting lid. Use about 1 teaspoon of the mixture to 2 litres (70 fl oz) of water. Wring out a cloth in the mixture to sponge the carpet.

CARPET – KITCHEN

Scrubbing with wool wash can easily clean washable kitchen carpet. You can use the commercial product that is readily available in supermarkets. Put about 1 tablespoon of wool wash into half a bucket of warm water and use a firm brush to scrub the carpet. Use a clean towel to remove excess moisture after scrubbing the carpet.

CARPET – LIPSTICK

Put a little glycerine onto a cloth and dab the lipstick stain. As the cloth becomes soiled with lipstick, colour keep changing the cloth to a clean spot to avoid re-colouring the carpet. Any residual stain can be removed by drizzling a little pen remover onto the stain. Blot it off immediately with a clean cloth and finally, sponge the area, very lightly, with warm water and a little wool wash.

CARPET – MOTOR GREASE

A heavy blob of motor grease on the carpet can probably be removed with a powder. Mix together 4 tablespoons of powdered borax, 4 tablespoons of salt and 4 tablespoons of shellite (naphtha). Because of the shellite (naphtha), it is a slightly damp powder. Pack the mixture over the stain and leave for about 24 hours. Brush off. Repeat, if necessary. Any residual stain can be sponged with warm water and wool wash, or, warm water with a dash of household detergent.

CARPET – NAIL POLISH

Try acetone or white spirit, available at hardware stores. Test some on an inconspicuous area of the carpet first, because it may not be suitable for the carpet. Put the acetone onto a clean cloth and apply to the carpet, working from the outside edge of the stain towards the centre.

CARPET – OIL STAIN

First, smother the oil stain with lots of talcum powder. Cover the talc with two layers of paper towelling, then hold a hot iron over the paper. Don't press down too hard because to do so will push the oil further into the carpet. The idea is to heat the paper, then the powder, then the oil. Once the oil is heated it will become absorbed into the powder which can be vacuumed off.

For any residual mark, make a solution with 1 litre (2 pints) of warm water and a ¼ cup of household detergent. Wring out a cloth in the liquid and sponge the stained area from the outside edge of the stain towards the centre. Try not to get the carpet too wet; that is, don't let too much moisture get through to the backing of the carpet.

Keep a thick towel beside you and mop up excess water as you go. Leave the carpet for some weeks to be sure it is dry and that the stain will not reappear.

CARPET – POT PLANTS

Pot plants that sit on carpet should always sit in a saucer-like container so the water does not bleed onto the carpet. The water, going as it does through the soil, is filthy by the time it hits the carpet, and if this continues over a long period of time, the dampness will cause mould to grow and eventually rot the carpet. Dampen the carpet, using antiseptic disinfectant in the water to kill the mould spores and sprinkle oxygen bleach washing powder or nappy-soaking powder over the stain. Rub it in with the fingers. Leave it overnight. Vacuum off next day and repeat if necessary.

CARPET – RUST

For rust on pure wool carpet, try the kindest method first. Make a paste with salt and lemon juice. Cover the stains, making sure the paste is pushed into the fibres. Leave for 24 hours, vacuum off and repeat if the marks have faded. Bicarbonate of soda (baking soda) mixed to a paste with lemon juice, left to dry then vacuumed off, is the next treatment to try. Or use a commercial rust remover, following the instructions on the container.

CARPET – SCORCH

Light scorch marks on a carpet can be removed with plain, dry steel wool. Sometimes the addition of a little peroxide onto the steel wool helps to fade a scorch mark. For deep scorch marks, pick some threads from around the carpet at the edges, or from a spare piece, then use craft glue to stick the threads into the scorched area. Use scissors to cut the stuck-in threads to the size of the pile.

Very badly scorched areas may need to be cut out and replaced with a matching piece of carpet.

CARPET – SHAMPOOING

Before shampooing the carpet, test a trial patch with the shampoo of your choice. If possible, remove all the furniture from the room then vacuum the carpet. Apply shampoo, clean a small area at a time, and dry as you go with a thick towel, keeping the carpet as dry as possible. Hair shampoo works well if you don't have carpet shampoo. If a mechanical shampooer is being used, do all the room at one time. Leave until the room is completely dry before moving furniture back into it.

CARPET - SMELL

Mix together 500 grams (16 oz) of powdered borax with 500 grams (16 oz) of salt and sprinkle the mixture liberally over the carpet. Leave it for as long as possible so the smell will be absorbed into the powder mixture. Vacuum off and spray the carpet with a commerical odour neutraliser, available at supermarkets.

CARPET – SOOT

Cover the soot stain with lots of salt. Use your fingers to rub the salt into the fibres of the carpet. Leave for about an hour, then vacuum off. Repeat if necessary on badly soiled areas.

CARPET – SYNTHETIC

When the heat of an iron has melted the synthetic fibre in a carpet, the only thing likely to improve the look of the "melt-down" area is to rub gently with very fine sandpaper. The best result will be achieved by matching the carpet and having a carpet layer cut the melted section out and replace it.

CARPET – TEA OR COFFEE STAINS

Blot up as much liquid as soon as the spill occurs. Use a plastic sponge or a thick towel. Don't spread the stain by rubbing. Cover immediately with plenty of powdered borax. When the borax dries, vacuum off. Any residual mark can be lightly sponged with a little borax dissolved in warm water. Work from the outside edge to the inside of the stain, and don't get the carpet too wet.

CARPET – VASELINE

Put kerosene onto a cloth and dab, don't rub, the stain. When all the stickiness has been removed, lightly sponge with warm water and a little washing-up liquid.

CARPET – VOMIT

As quickly as possible, remove excess with a cloth and cold water. Then sponge with borax and warm water. Use 1 tablespoon borax to 600 millilitres (20 fl oz) of warm water. Don't get the carpet too wet. Follow up by sponging with wool wash which will remove any odour from the carpet.

CARPET – WINE STAINS

Soda water applied at once can be most effective. Keep mopping with kitchen paper. If left too long, use borax. Dampen the stain slightly and apply powdered borax over the stained area. The borax will act as blotting paper and absorb the stain and the moisture. Leave until dry, then vacuum off.

CARPET – WOOD STAIN

Manufacturers often fail to seal the bottom of the legs of wooden furniture, allowing some "bleeding" from the open cut of the wood. It is extremely difficult to remove from carpet. Try covering the stained area with a paste, using 1 tablespoon citric acid powder, 1 tablespoon powdered borax, 1 teaspoon eucalyptus oil and enough shellite (naphtha) to mix to the consistency of a thick cream. Push the creamy mixture into the fibre of the carpet and leave for 2 or 3 hours. Vacuum off. Repeat, if necessary.

CAT FUR

Most pet cats live indoors and they all shed fur. Cats always have a particular place where they curl up and sleep and it is that particular place which gathers the greatest amount of fur. The smartest thing to do is to put an old tea towel or sheet down for the cat to sleep on. Throw it away and replace it every so often to save yourself the effort of cleaning.

When fur does collect on the carpet, or on the velvet lounge, wring out a plastic cloth in hot or cold water, and wipe across the fur that has been shed. The plastic cloth will gather the fur.

CATS – TOM

Otherwise tomcats should be neutered if they are going to live indoors because spraying is inevitable. The problem is that it is an almost impossible stain to remove. On leather, urine from a tomcat removes the colour in the same way that bleach does. Wipe over the stained areas with a cloth wrung out in cold water with a dash of white vinegar on it. Then sponge with warm water and antiseptic disinfectant. When dry, disguise the stain with matching shoe colour dye.

CEDAR

Put brown vinegar on a damp cloth and wipe cedar furniture to remove the smeary look of polish. Buff with a clean, dry cloth. Matching shoe polish on a cotton bud will cover scratches.

CHAIRS

Fabric-covered chairs are usually sprayed with a water repellent which, as its name suggests, is a finish to help repel moist stains. Theoretically the stain is meant to sit on the top of the repellent and not go down into the fabric. It works well on light stains, in which case it is only necessary to wring out a cloth in 1 litre (2 pints) warm water with 1 teaspoon of detergent and sponge the stain.

CHAIRS – UPHOLSTERED

In a glass jar, mix together 4 tablespoons of powdered borax with 4 tablespoons of salt and 4 tablespoons of shellite (naphtha). Spread the mixture over the upholstered seat and back of the chair. Leave it overnight, then rub all over with a rough towel. Brush or vacuum any remaining powder from the upholstery. Any remaining "hard-to-shift" marks can be sprayed with stain remover, following the instructions on the container.

CIGARETTES

To remove the smell of stale cigarettes, leave a bucket of water in the room with a few slices of lemon in it. Another method is to burn candles in the room. For a wardrobe impregnated with the smell of cigarette smoke, put a few drops of commerical odour neutraliser on a ball of cotton wool and leave in the wardrobe.

To remove cigarette smoke stain from the ceiling of a car, sponge with bleach. Use 1 part bleach to 4 parts water. Cigarette burns on wooden furniture, providing they are not deeply burnt into the wood, can often be removed by rubbing with toothpaste. Always rub with the grain of the wood.

COCA-COLA

Coca-Cola spilt on carpet should be mopped up immediately with an absorbent cloth or sponge. Mop from the outside edge of the spill to the centre. Lightly sponge the residual stain with any commercial wool wash in lukewarm water. I have successfully removed dried Coca-Cola stains using this method, but if commercial cleaners or chemicals have been applied to the stain first it can cause a reaction which might set the stain.

COFFEE

Black or white coffee stains can usually be removed from woollen blankets or garments by dampening the stain with warm water then covering it with powdered borax. Leave for about

half an hour, brush most of the powder off, then sponge with warm water. Repeat two or three times until the stain is removed.

CONTINENTAL QUILT

It is possible to spread the feathers in a continental quilt by putting the quilt into the dryer with three or four clean tennis balls. The tennis balls help to spread the feathers. While the quilt is still warm from the dryer, take it outside and shake it vigorously. It is a good idea to lie the quilt flat in the sun before putting it away for the winter.

CORDIAL

Icy poles (popsicle/ice lolly), and soft drinks are made with cordial syrup that contains a vegetable dye for colour. Some cordials, particularly orange or red, are very difficult to shift. Once the stain is dry, pen remover will remove some cordial stains from carpet. Drizzle a little pen remover onto the stain, then cover with powdered borax. Leave to dry, vacuum off and sponge with 1 tablespoon of borax dissolved in a cup of water.

CORK FLOORS

Mop regularly with warm soapy water and add a little methylated spirits to the water. This helps the shine. For any marks that are difficult to remove, rub gently with a little toothpaste. If the surface has worn, it is not a good idea to wet it. Just rub over with turpentine on a clean cloth and lightly polish, or have the cork sanded and resurfaced.

CORK TILES

Cork tiles are always finished with a lacquer which, with time and continual use, wears off. Once the wear begins to show, it is advisable to re-lacquer. The usual method is to sand the floor, remove all traces of the sanding; then, paint the cork tiles with two or three layers of Estapol. There are professionals who do this work but it is possible to do it yourself. If you keep washing the floor once the surface is worn, the cork can absorb water, swell and lift.

COUCH – SMELLY

Mix together equal quantities of salt and powdered borax and sprinkle it all over the couch. Then spray the powder with commerical odour neutraliser. Leave it overnight if possible, then vacuum or brush it off. It would be a good idea to turn the couch upside down and repeat the treatment on the underside as well.

CRAYON

Melted crayon on fabric covered furniture is best treated by covering the stain with ice blocks in a plastic bag. When the crayon is hard, scrape as much as possible off with a plastic spatula. Next, cover the stain with talcum powder and put a couple of layers of kitchen paper on top of the

powder. Then hold a fairly hot iron just on the paper. Don't press down too hard because you could push the stain into the fabric.

When the grease from the crayon has come up into the talcum powder, brush the powder off and sponge the residual stain first with eucalyptus oil, then with spot and stain remover.

DAMP

In wardrobes, atmospheric changes can cause sweating and clothes will become mildewed, or develop yellow sweat marks, or rust spots. Don't put damp clothes in the wardrobe, or clothes that have just been steam ironed. Everything should be thoroughly aired before being put away. Leave wardrobe doors ajar from time to time to allow circulation of air. For persistent problems, put a container of damp remover or chalk in the bottom of the wardrobe.

For damp smell, open the windows and doors to let the air through. A heater turned on in the room, even with the doors and windows open, helps to dissipate the smell of damp.

Wipe window ledges and other surfaces with lemon juice or vanilla on a soft cloth. Spray with a commercial odour neutraliser.

DAMP WINDOWS

Dampness on windows is usually due to sweating, caused by atmospheric changes. This often results in mildew growing on the ledges and the curtains. Leave the curtains open as much as possible, particularly at night when the inside temperature is warm and the outside is very cold.

Air circulation is important so leave windows and doors open during the day whenever possible. A container of damp remover or chalk on the window ledge, or on the floor between the drapes and the window, will solve a persistent damp problem.

DIESEL SMOKE

For diesel smoke on furniture fabric, mix together 4 tablespoons of powdered borax, 4 tablespoons salt, and 4 tablespoons shellite (naphtha). Cover the smoke stains and leave for at least 24 hours, then use a clean, rough towel to rub over the stained area. Brush or vacuum the mixture off and repeat if necessary.

For difficult to remove spots, use carpet stain remover or carpet spot and stain remover, following the instructions on the can.

DINING CHAIRS – STAIN

The stains on dining chairs often contain fat or grease so it would be a good idea to smother the stained area with plenty of talcum powder, then put a tea towel over it and sit on it for a while. This will warm through to the stain and bring the grease up into the powder. It shouldn't take more than fifteen minutes. Then mix together 2 tablespoons of powdered borax, 2 tablespoons salt, and 2 tablespoons shellite (naphtha). Cover all of the seat of the chair, rub it in lightly with the palms of the hands, leave overnight then brush or vacuum off.

DOG HAIR

Use a foam plastic pad. Wring it out, until almost dry, in cold water, then wipe over the dog hairs from the furniture. First wipe in one direction, then the other.

ELECTRIC BLANKET

The blanket should be removed from the bed regularly, say once every month, then sprinkled all over, with equal parts of talcum powder, salt and powdered borax. Spray the powder mixture with commerical odour neutraliser then roll the blanket lightly so that both sides get the benefit of the powder mixture. Leave it for as long as possible before shaking the powder out. Vacuum or brush if necessary to remove the last traces of powder.

FELT PEN MARKS ON SYNTHETIC FABRIC

Use equal parts of talcum powder and powdered borax mixed to a paste with a little methylated spirits. Cover the stain and leave until the paste is dry, then brush off and wash in the normal way. Repeat two or three times. On vinyl or leather, wring out a cloth in hot water. Let it sit on the stain for 10 seconds, then try to remove the mark with pen remover. As some felt pens are waterproof, a different solvent may be required. Mineral turpentine, nail polish remover, or hair spray can be effective. Always test on an inconspicuous area first.

FURNITURE – BROCADE

To keep brocade-covered lounge suites clean, mix together 4 tablespoons of salt with 4 tablespoons of powdered borax, and 4 tablespoons of shellite (naphtha). It is a slightly damp powder. If you store it for later use, do so in glass, not plastic, with a tight-fitting lid. Sprinkle the powder over the brocade, gently spread it all over with the palms of the hands, then leave for an hour or so before brushing, or vacuuming, off.

On the arms of the furniture, where hands continually rest, spray with stain remover, following the instruction on the can.

FURNITURE – VARNISHED

On varnished furniture, scratches may be removed by placing a coarse cloth well soaked in linseed oil on the scratches. Leave for a short time, rub a little; remove excess and polish. Applying a little shoe polish of the same colour can mostly cover the deeper scratches.

FURNITURE – WOODEN

For white heat marks on wooden furniture, rub with Brasso or a commercial metal polish on a soft cloth. Another method is to rub gently with camphorated oil. Marks from glasses or vases can be treated in the same way.

Teak can be treated this way, but only use teak oil to polish. For some marks, toothpaste rubbed with the grain of the wood works very well.

GROUT

Many cleaning products contain bleach that can leach the colour from dark-coloured grout. A two-part epoxy grout, applied when the tiles are first laid, is stronger and more stable than the more commonly used grout. It is possibly more expensive but is totally waterproof and resistant to mould, soap build-up, and discolouration. Once the tiles are set and the grout has begun to discolour, Aqua Mix™ can be painted over the grout to any of twelve standard colours, or, mixed together to give other shades. Once cured, Aqua Mix™ will retain its original colour. It will also resist mould and be easy to clean without using too much elbow grease.

GROUTING

Soap residue on grouting should be scrubbed with a small, soft nailbrush. If the grouting is white, add bleach to the water. One-third bleach to two-thirds water will restore the whiteness of the grout and remove mildew. Sometimes, with constant cleaning, the grout wears down to the dark tile adhesive, causing the grout to look mouldy. Liquid correction fluid is good for patching small areas. If the grouting is coloured, use Epsom salts on a soft wet brush.

HEAT MARKS

White heat marks can usually be removed from wood by putting some Brasso or commercial metal polish onto a soft cloth and rubbing the mark with the grain of the wood. Toothpaste applied in the same way, works well for very light marks. When the white stain is removed, polish with a good furniture polish.

KNIVES

Knife handles of almost any type can be repaired by specialist restorers.

Knives will sharpen more readily if thoroughly warmed prior to sharpening. To clean knives of stainless steel, polish with a fine powder cleanser mixed with a little methylated spirits. Pearl-handled knives should be washed in warm soapy water; never in the dishwasher. Rub the handles with Vaseline, wipe off excess and polish with talcum powder. Ivory or bone handles should not be washed in hot water. Both will yellow with age, but hot water intensifies the yellow. Before trying to whiten ivory or bone knife handles, first clean them with powdered whiting mixed to a paste with lemon juice. Then stand them in a glass of ½ water and ½ bleach for 12 hours. Dry and polish with talcum powder. Be careful not to let the bleach solution cover the join where the handles meet the blades. It may weaken the adhesive.

LAVATORY

For the waterline in the toilet, I suggest you use heavy duty toilet powder. Keep it handy and sprinkle a little into the toilet every day. It is probably better to sprinkle the powder into the toilet at night when there is a longer time between flushes. Also, keep a toilet brush beside the lavatory for regular use.

LEATHER

The new, soft leather used in furniture is supposed to need no more care than to sponge now and then with warm, soapy water. The salespeople who expound this idea don't seem to know about small children with sticky chocolate in one hand, a ballpoint pen in the other. The leather certainly needs to be sponged over from time to time, but I like to treat it afterwards to a light rub with a commercial paste wax, thereby giving it a finish which is at least some protection against the onslaught of children, pets and others. Do not use oil, saddle soap, detergent, solvents or shoe polish on any of the new leathers.

Chairs and couches that have become grubby with an accumulation of different stains, such as hair cream, hair spray and newspapers, should first be treated with talcum powder. Sprinkle the talc over the stained areas, rub in with the palms of the hands, then rough rub with a firm towel. Next, wring out a towel in warm water with pure soap flakes dissolved in it and rub over all the furniture, paying particular attention to the soiled areas. Once the cleaning is complete, allow at least 24 hours for the leather to dry and become firm before finishing with a commercial paste wax. Buff up with a soft, dry cloth.

LEATHER MOULD

Sponge mould from leather furniture with antiseptic disinfectant on a soft cloth that has been wrung out in hot water. Any residual staining can be removed with a paste mixed with bicarbonate of soda (baking soda) and white vinegar. Nothing will prevent mould from growing again if the conditions are right. Wet, humid, dark and damp are the conditions under which mould will grow and survive. Dry, airy, light and caring are the conditions needed to combat mould.

Make sure the leather is wiped over regularly, the parts that are seen and the parts that are not. Be sure the leather is dry after wiping. Polish lightly with a commercial paste wax to restore surface.

LIGHT FITTINGS

An easy way to stop the carpet from getting dirty when cleaning light fittings is to hang an old, opened umbrella on the light fitting. The umbrella will catch the drips of dirty water, making cleaning less arduous.

LOUNGE SUITE CLEANER

For a fabric-covered lounge suite, a powder cleaner is best. In a glass jar, with a tight-fitting lid, mix together 250 grams (8 oz) of powdered borax with 250 grams (8 oz) of salt, then add ¼ cup of shellite (naphtha). Sprinkle the mixture evenly over the lounge suite, then rub all over with a clean, rough towel. Brush, or vacuum, to remove any residual powder. The more soiled areas, such as the arm rests, can be sprayed with carpet stain remover, following the instructions on the can.

LOUNGE SUITE – SMELL

The lounge suite probably needs to be treated from underneath to remove the smell. Turn it upside down and carefully remove the layer of fabric that is there to cover the springs. When the springs are exposed, mix together 4 tablespoons of powdered borax, 4 tablespoons of salt, and 4 tablespoons of shellite (naphtha). Double the quantity if you think it needs more.

Sprinkle the mixture all over the exposed area and leave it for 24 hours. Turn the couch right side up and bang it a little to remove the powder. The powder will not hurt the carpet and can be vacuumed off quite easily. Turn the couch upside down again, spray the inside with a commercial odour neutraliser, then replace the calico with tacks. The top side of the lounge can be treated with the same powder to freshen it up. It can also be sprayed with commercial odour neutraliser.

MAHOGANY

To care for mahogany, make sure it is always well dusted. Clean occasionally with a cloth dipped in linseed oil. Buff up with a clean soft cloth. White stains on a polished surface, caused by heat, can usually be removed by rubbing with Brasso or a metal polish on a soft cloth. Do not rub too hard. Polish after the stain has been removed.

MARBLE FIREPLACE

A light-coloured marble fireplace can be cleaned with a weak solution of household bleach and water. Use about 1 part bleach to 4 parts water or use warm water and ammonia. Remember though, marble is porous at the back, and eventually smoke is likely to penetrate through to the front of the fireplace. Once cleaned, polish the front of the fireplace with a commercial paste wax.

MARBLE – GREASE

Because marble is a porous stone, grease can be absorbed into it. Smother the stain with lots of talcum powder then cover the talcum powder with a clean tea towel, and without pressing down, gently move a hot iron all over the stained area. It takes time and patience but eventually the hot iron will heat first the towel, then the powder and lastly, the grease which will then be absorbed into the powder and can be brushed away. Once it is removed from the marble, use a clean soft cloth to rub all over with commercial paste wax. Buff it up with a clean, dry cloth.

MAT – CREASED

Buy a roll of carpet tape from your local carpet retailer. Turn the mat upside down and run the tape down the crease. Put a few strips across the crease and the problem is solved.

MATTRESS – BEDROOM

Any mattress should be changed round the other way every six months. People sit on the edge of beds and changing the mattress is like changing the tyres on the car for even wear.

MATTRESS – BLOOD STAINS

Make a solution using ½ litre of cold water and 2 tablespoons of salt. With a cloth dipped in the solution, sponge the stain. After the stain is removed, dry the mattress as quickly as possible. For this purpose a hair dryer works well. Dampen dried blood stain with hot water, then smother it with salt. Leave it for about fifteen minutes then use hot water to sponge the salt away. Work from the outside edge of the stain, dissolving the salt as you push it towards the centre of the stain. Try not to get the mattress too wet and keep a towel beside you to mop up as you go.

MATTRESS – GENERAL

When the covering of an innerspring mattress begins to split because of age, any type of repair using stitches or adhesive tape only puts a strain on a different part of the fabric and it will continue to split. If the inner springs are in good condition, the mattress can be re-covered professionally, or buy a firm fitting mattress cover from any good bedding specialist. Once the mattress is completely re-covered, the original covering becomes unimportant. It might be possible to get rid of a smell by smothering the mattress with powdered borax, then spraying the borax with commerical odour neutraliser. Leave it for a week if possible, then vacuum, or brush the powder off. Turn the mattress over and repeat the treatment.

MATTRESS – URINE STAINS

Old urine stains are very difficult to remove but I suggest you try my own "home brew cleaner". Into a 750 millilitre (26 fl oz) bottle, with a childproof screw-top, mix together ¼ cup each of methylated spirits and washing-up liquid. Add 1 tablespoon of ammonia, 1 teaspoon of eucalyptus oil and 1 dessertspoon of citric acid. Add sufficient water to fill the bottle. Use about ¼ cup of this mixture to 2 litres (70 fl oz) of warm water to sponge over the stains on the mattress. Don't get the mattress too wet. Mop as you clean, with a thick, dry towel. It may be necessary to sponge the mattress all over so it doesn't look patchy.

MITES

Fresh sprigs of mint under the carpet and in the cupboards will help to get rid of a plague of mites. For mites in the bedclothes, wash in wool wash and if possible put outside to air. Mites thrive on warmth so try to find room in the refrigerator for any articles that may be infested. Put one pillow at a time in a plastic bag. Leave for at least an hour in the refrigerator then replace with another.

MOTHS AND SILVERFISH

When moths and silverfish are eating your clothes, it is because they and their eggs are in the wardrobe and drawers. To get rid of them it is necessary to take all the clothes out and wash or dry clean every item. The drawers will then need to be scrubbed with hot water and a strong disinfectant. The scrubbing brush should be good enough to get into all the seams and joins of

the drawers. When cleaning is complete, make sure the drawers are thoroughly dry, then sprinkle them with Epsom salts. Now put a layer of paper down so the clothes do not come into contact with the salts.

The same treatment is needed for the wardrobe, but here it may be necessary to go round all the seams and joins with a hair dryer on "hot". This will cook any eggs so they won't be able to hatch. Also, bring to the boil, 2 cups of vinegar, 1 tablespoon each of cloves, grated ginger, lemon and orange rind, plus 1 teaspoon of dried chillies and 2 or 3 bay leaves. Simmer for 15 minutes, then remove from the heat and let it cool. Strain and discard the liquid. Put the strained spices into two or three open containers and put one on the top shelf of the wardrobe and the others on the floor. About once every six months, pour 1 or 2 tablespoons of water over the spices, cover with plastic and microwave on high for 60 seconds to revive the pungent aroma.

MOTHS – CUPBOARDS
Turpentine sprinkled in cupboards and drawers will often keep moths away. Another method is to sprinkle with Epsom salts or whole cloves. Highly scented soap helps to keep moths away from woollens. Sponging the drawers, and the inside of cupboards where clothes are stored with a cloth wrung out in warm water and cloudy ammonia is also good. Washing woollens and blankets in wool wash helps keep moths at bay.

PARQUETRY FLOORS
To clean parquetry floors, scatter with sawdust, damp tea leaves or damp bran, then sweep thoroughly. If the floor needs a little more attention, mop over with a cloth that has been wrung out in warm water with a little methylated spirits added to the water. Don't get parquetry floors too wet as water underneath will cause the parquetry to lift.

PICTURES
A tiny dab of Blu Tack on one of the bottom corners of all the pictures hanging in the house will save a lot of time and effort trying to keep them from going skew whiff!

POLISH
This is a real "old-timer" but it still works on polished wooden floors or furniture. Into a clean bottle, put 1 cup turpentine, 2 cups linseed oil and 1 cup water. Cork the bottle and shake well before applying with a soft, dry cloth. Use another soft, dry cloth and rub well for a good shine. Test before using because some of the new surfaces may not like the old-fashioned polish. Label the bottle.

POLISH BUILD-UP
Put 2 tablespoons of salt onto a saucer, then cover it with just enough vinegar to saturate the salt. Add about 1 cup of warm water then, wring out a cloth until almost dry, dip it in the solution and rub over the polish build-up on the table. Test on a small area first.

POLISH – WOODEN FURNITURE

Melt 2 cups of beeswax, remove from the heat, then stir in 2 cups of turpentine, 2 cups of olive oil (use linseed oil for dark woods). Now add 4 cups of dried lavender flowers and pour the mixture into jars to set.

QUARRY TILES

Improve the look of unglazed quarry tiles by mopping over with a mixture of half linseed oil and half turpentine. First, wash the tiles with hot soapy water and a little cloudy ammonia. Dry thoroughly before applying the linseed oil mixture. Glazed quarry tiles can be wiped over with kerosene on a soft, dry cloth. Sealed quarry tiles can be washed with hot water and a little methylated spirits.

QUILTS – CONTINENTAL

Most continental quilts can be washed in wool wash, either the commercial mixture or the home made variety, but check the fabric of the quilt before laundering it in the washing machine. Tumble dry with two or three clean tennis balls. The tennis balls spread the feathers, leaving the quilt soft and fluffy.

ROSEWOOD

Furniture made from rosewood should be rubbed every day with a clean soft cloth to retain its lustre. Only polish occasionally and use polish sparingly.

RUGS

Washable rugs can be washed at home but check that colours will not run. To wash at home, large rugs can be sponged, or even scrubbed, on the floor. Use the home made wooll wash and do on a warm day. Dry outside if possible, with the rug upside down. Flokati rugs are washable and some dry cleaners specialise in the cleaning and care of Flokati rugs.

Rugs or mats which curl at the corners can be made to lie flat by sewing or gluing flat curtain weights or magnets in the corners.

For a rug that develops a crease or fold, put a strip of carpet tape on the underside of the fold.

SAVE MONEY WHEN SHOPPING

- Always read the care instructions when buying garments. If the label reads "dry clean only", think about the cost of dry cleaning.
- Buy bath soap when it is on special, then scatter the cakes of soap among clothes or linen. This helps to keep moths and silverfish away. The added advantage is that soap left to harden for 12 months will last much longer when it is in use.
- For newly weds, who will have children, in the future don't buy white, shag-pile carpet, or an expensive soft-tone, leather lounge suite.

- Pets need a lot of care, particularly long-haired cats or dogs. Before getting a pet, think about the add-on cost of combs, brushes and veterinary care.

SMELLS

Smelly areas caused by cats, dogs, or even humans, and dead rats in the wall, can be eliminated by spraying with commercial odour neutraliser.

SMOKE ALARMS

Check the battery on the first day of every month.

TERRAZZO

Terrazzo floors are best cleaned with 1 tablespoon of detergent and 6 tablespoons of kerosene in half a bucket of hot water. Rinse with clean, cold water and dry with a soft towel. An application of commercial paste wax adds a polish to the terrazzo and helps to keep it clean. Terrazzo floors do not last forever. The surface becomes worn, particularly in the heavy walk areas, such as doorways. Because it is a bonded product, terrazzo becomes porous once the surface is worn. When it begins to wear, terrazzo can be sanded and resealed by a professional.

TILES

One way to clean tiles is to wipe them down with a solution of equal parts brown vinegar and kerosene. For white grouting use a weak solution of bleach and a nailbrush to scrub. For coloured grouting, use Epsom salts.

TILES – BLACK

To remove mildew from black tiles, use a soft brush to scrub them with very hot water and a dash of antiseptic disinfectant in the water. Let the tiles dry, to be sure all the mould is removed. To keep the tiles clean, and free from mould, into 2 litres (70 fl oz) of warm water, put ¼ cup of methylated spirits. Wring out a cloth in the solution and wipe all over the tiles. Buff up with a soft, dry cloth. This should be done once every week.

TILES – FLOOR

Dark-coloured floor tiles should be washed with hot water and methylated spirits. Use about ½ cup methylated spirits to a bucket of water. Squeeze the mop almost dry before going over the floor.

TILES – MOULD

Harsh scrubbing will remove the grout from between the tiles. When this occurs, the glue, which is often dark grey or black, is revealed. It then looks like a continuous mould problem. Renew the grout with Aqua Mix™; it is mould resistant and will make cleaning much easier.

TOILETS – CLEANING

I use a commercial toilet powder in the toilet but use much less than the recommended amount and I use it less often. In between times, I put about 2 tablespoons of washing soda into 1 litre (2 pints) of boiling water, pour it into the toilet and give a good scrub around with the toilet brush. A reader told me that she has successfully removed the calcium build-up caused by bore water with white vinegar. She applied it to the calcium build-up, left it for an hour; then scrubbed it off.

TOILETS – STAINED

For a rust stain down the back of the toilet, have a plumber check the water inlet and renew washers to stop the water leaking. It might be worth fitting a filter at the water inlet. To remove the stain, make a paste of equal parts powdered whiting and cream of tartar mixed with cold water. Add a few drops of peroxide. Pack the paste onto the stain and leave as long as possible. Repeat often.

UPHOLSTERY

Stains on upholstery should be removed according to the fabric specification. Do not use a water cleaner for suede or unwashable velvet. Only a powder cleaner is suitable for these fabrics. Never spot clean or clean upholstery, without first testing the cleaner on a part of the fabric that will not show if it marks.

VACUUM CLEANER

Make sure your vacuum cleaner is regularly emptied. Before vacuuming, pick up any hairpins or any other objects that are lying about because they can damage the motor. Regular servicing is a good idea if the vacuum is to last a lifetime. Put a few drops of vanilla essence, or any other pleasant smelling oil, onto a cotton ball and put it in the vacuum cleaner bag. The air will blow the scent when you are using the cleaner, making the rooms smell fresher.

VELVET

Crushed or rain-spotted velvet garments should be steamed. Hang them in the bathroom and leave all windows and doors shut when taking a shower or filling the bath. Another method is to hold a steam iron over the back of the velvet. Under no circumstances should you press down with the iron on to velvet, as it will flatten the pile.

Liquid Paper stains: Mineral turpentine will remove white correction fluid stains but a great deal of care is needed to remove the stain without spoiling the fabric pile. The treatment must be tested on an inconspicuous area first. Put a little mineral turpentine on to a pad of cotton wool and gently dab the stain, continually changing the cotton wool so the white correction fluid is not transferred back to the velvet. Modern velvet fabric is washable and it is necessary to sponge the mineral turpentine away once the stain is removed. Dry with a soft towel and brush the pile back the right way before it is fully dry.

Furniture covered with velvet can be freshened by rubbing with nylon net rolled into a ball. It lifts the pile and gets rid of dust. For cleaning, use a good powder cleaner.

Milk stains: Make a fairly thick paste with cream of tartar and cold water. Pack the paste over the stain, leave it to dry, then vacuum off. Any residue from the stain can be treated with a good powder carpet cleaner. Rub it in gently with the palm of your hand, leave overnight then brush off.

Bedspreads made of velvet, particularly those with rolled edges, become grubby around the hem where it touches the floor. Use any good quality carpet cleaning powder by lifting the hem onto the bed, then sprinkling the powder along the hemline. Rub it in a little so the powder is evenly spread. Leave for half an hour or so, then vacuum or brush off. If the hemline is left too long before cleaning and has become noticeably grubby, instead of vacuuming the powder off, use a thick, clean, dry towel and rub firmly before brushing the residual powder away. You could make up your own cleaner by mixing together 4 tablespoons powdered borax, 4 tablespoons salt and 4 tablespoons shellite (naphtha) or dry cleaning fluid.

WALNUT FURNITURE

If the furniture is genuine walnut, a scratch or stain can be removed by cutting a whole walnut and rubbing the mark vigorously with the nut. The juice will remove the stain. Watermarks on walnut furniture can usually be removed with Brasso or metal polish.

WARDROBE

Naphthalene is an all-pervasive smell that does not easily dissipate, so when it is used in the wardrobe, clothes cannot be worn unless they are first aired for a long time. Spice bags are every bit as effective as a deterrent for moths and silverfish, and the aroma is not offensive. Pomanders or spice balls are good to hang in the wardrobe, both for the fresh smell and to keep moths at bay.

To make spice bags, boil together for 15 minutes, 2 cups of water, 25 grams (¾ oz) of chopped root ginger, 1 tablespoon salt, ½ teaspoon cayenne pepper, 1 tablespoon of whole cloves, 25 grams (¾ oz) of peppercorns and the rind of any citrus fruit. Strain, allow the spices to cool, then put into loose-weave fabric bags, tie at the top with a pretty ribbon and hang in the wardrobe.

Wardrobes are usually chock-a-block full and I don't know anyone who has enough space for ideal storage. Perfection would be sufficient space between each hanger for clothes to hang without touching each other. We all know that does not happen. The other imperfect thing is that most wardrobes do not allow for the circulation of air. To help in the prevention of mustiness in the wardrobe, leave the doors open during the day when the bedroom is not in use, close them at night when the room is being used. Change the hangers around regularly so that no garment remains in the one spot for too long. Any clothing that has been worn should be washed or dry-cleaned before being put into the wardrobe for any length of time. On a day-to-day basis, be sure that all garments, whether they are dry-cleaned or washed, are thoroughly aired before being put away. A container of damp remover or chalk, on the floor of the wardrobe, will help to control dampness.

WARDROBES – DAMP

In each of the wardrobes, put a container of damp remover or chalk, available from hardware stores. You will be surprised at how much dampness is converted to water in the container, which naturally needs attention from time to time – the water has to be emptied and more powder added to the container. Keep airing the wardrobe by keeping doors open whenever possible.

WATERBED

The mattress of most waterbeds is made of vinyl and the underlay must be aired regularly as perspiration build-up can encourage the growth of mould. The water inside the mattress needs to contain a fungicide. Some manufacturers recommend adding a measured amount of fungicide every three to four months. When buying a water bed make sure you get one that is on casters. This makes it easier to move about. With any new purchase, read the instructions carefully and follow them.

STORAGE

BABY CLOTHES

The most important thing about storing baby clothes, shawls and other items, is to make sure that everything is clean and perfectly dry. Do not use plastic bags, or any other form of plastic wrapping, because it is likely to cause condensation that will result in yellowing or rust marks. The container in which they are stored should be of cardboard not plastic. Spread the bottom of the container with Epsom salts, then two layers of tissue paper, making sure the articles do not come into direct contact with the salts. The baby-wear can be wrapped separately in tissue paper, or put in layers with tissue paper between each layer. Lavender bags, or wrapped scented soap, can be scattered throughout the container. From time to time, check the stored articles, working on the principle that a pinch of prevention is worth more than a kilo of cure. Many stationery suppliers stock textile storage boxes made from acid-free corrugated cardboard.

BOOKS

Books which are to be stored can be packed in cardboard boxes, but they will need air space to help combat the atmospheric changes. Elevate the first boxes from the floor by putting down either a few bricks, or wooden or plastic blocks, with a couple of flat pieces of wood resting across the bricks to form a slatted shelf to hold the boxes. About three planks of wood across the top of the first boxes will allow some breathing space between the first and second layer of boxes. Continue adding the boxes of books in this manner. Leave a breathing space of at least the thickness of a brick at the top of the stacked boxes, and a similar space at the back, between the boxes and the wall. Talcum powder, sprinkled on the covers, will help to stop the covers from sticking to each other. Sprinkle a mixture of Epsom salts and naphthalene flakes over and around the boxes, but not touching the books.

CLOTHES

Clothes on hangers should not be stored in plastic. Woven nylon bags with a zip are suitable for short-term storage. Lightweight cotton or calico is best because, unlike synthetics, it is less likely to build up and retain humidity. A humid atmosphere is a great breeding place for

moths, silverfish and other chewy creatures, as well as mould and rust. Naphthalene is an insect deterrent, but cuddling into the shoulder of a suit smelling of naphthalene or mothballs might also be a deterrent to the opposite sex. Spice bags are great and the smell is pleasant. Epsom salts is also good but the salts should not be in direct contact with the clothes.

HANDBAGS

Handbags can be stuffed with items such as underwear, tea towels, etc. to retain their shape. Wrap handbags separately in pillowslips.

LEATHER

The most important thing to remember when storing leather clothing is that it must be perfectly clean and dry. Pay attention to the lining too. Rather than hang leather for summer storing, it is better to put tissue paper inside the garments, wrap in more tissue paper, and loosely fold in a clean, dry sheet. Don't forget to put tissue paper in the sleeves so the folds at the elbow do not set in the leather. Store on the top shelf of the wardrobe.

LINEN

Roll rather than fold the article. Take linen out every now and again and hang on the line to air. If they must be folded, fold off-centre in a different place each time. If this is not done, the creases can set and become impossible to remove later on.

The best storage area for linen is a very dry area, with shelves or drawers lined with acid free paper. Sprinkle Epsom salts under the paper to deter moths and silverfish. Don't let the salts touch the linen.

PHOTOGRAPHS

One of the commercial powder insecticides can be used when storing photographs but don't let the powder come into direct contact with the photographs. The most important thing is a dry storage area. If the photographs are to be stored on shelves in a cupboard, use the high shelves. Don't use plastic and don't stack too many on top of each other. The weight pressing down on flat photographs can spoil the emulsion on the surface.

Upright storage is better that flat storage. If at all possible, the best method of storage could be in a filing cabinet with suspension files. Talcum powder between photographs, tissue paper, or both, are good packing mediums.

SHOES

Shoes can be stuffed with newspaper. Put a few drops of commerical odour neutraliser on the paper and wrap separately. Worn sheets or towels are good for wrapping, covering or separating items. Always store in a dry, well-ventilated area. Boxes should be on pallets or some other means to stop them from sitting flat on the floor. Some air circulation under boxes is always desirable.

A brick under each corner of a wooden box provides enough air circulation. Cardboard boxes may need more support, such as a flat plank of wood on bricks. The amount of support will depend upon the weight.

WOOLLENS

Wash woollens before storing. Silverfish are attracted to unwashed garments. A few cakes of highly scented soap, wrapped in a waxed paper, in among woollens also assists in keeping moths and silverfish away. It is a good idea to take the garments out to air about every two months. Powdered sulphur or Epsom salts deter silverfish, but don't let it come in direct contact with garments.

HOUSEHOLD

ACRIFLAVINE

Acriflavine is a highly coloured antiseptic, similar to iodine but without the sting. If spilled, particularly on carpet, it should be treated immediately. Check the label on the bottle to see if it is water-, or alcohol-based. For water-based Acriflavine, dampen the stain and cover with white denture powder. Leave for fifteen minutes, then sponge or wash with warm water and an oxygen bleach powder such as nappy-soaking powder or oxygen bleach washing powder. For Acriflavine with an alcohol base, methylated spirits will generally remove the stain.

ALABASTER – SOILED

Rub soiled, light-coloured alabaster with a cloth dipped in turpentine, or, if badly stained, try toothpaste, or powdered whiting mixed to a paste with bleach. Pack the paste on the stain and leave for an hour before washing off. Polish afterwards with beeswax or a silicone polish. I use commercial paste wax or a good car polish.

ALLERGIES

Look online for an allergy association in your area. They can be very helpful with information on where to obtain recipes and special foods or products.

For an allergy to eggs, it is necessary to use a substitute as the binding agent in recipes. For rissoles, use rice instead of eggs. Meat loaf can be made with half ground mince and half sausage meat. In some cakes or boiled puddings, grated carrot can be used.

Dust allergies are common. To help with dust-free sleeping, put such things as pillows, blankets, covers and other items that are not washed frequently into the tumble drier for 15 minutes on cold setting. Dust can be kept down by sprinkling an uncarpeted floor with damp used tea-leaves, damp bran or sawdust. Always dust furniture with a damp cloth.

ALUMINIUM

To clean and brighten aluminium, use a soapy steel-wool pad. Try to rub in the same direction.

ANGORA AND MOHAIR

Angora, mohair, or any fluffy woollen jumper or cardigan sheds fibre. Half an hour in a plastic bag in the refrigerator before wearing often helps to stop the shedding, but only for a short time. Another method is to lightly spray the garment with hair spray or a good commercial water repellent. Try a little on the inside first to make sure the spray does not flatten, or spoil, the fluffy look of the garment. Sometimes lightly sponging with white vinegar helps. Another idea is to wash the article in warm water with 1 teaspoon of shampoo. Rinse in cold water, roll in a towel to spin dry, turn inside out and lie flat to dry. When dry, brush fluffy woollens with a soft brush.

ANNIVERSARY

	Modern	Traditional
First	Clocks	Cotton
Second	China	Paper
Third	Crystal, Glass	Leather
Fourth	Appliances	Fruit, Flowers
Fifth	Silverware	Wooden
Tenth	Diamond	Tin, Aluminium
Twelfth	Pearl	SilkLinen
Fifteenth	Watches	Crystal
Twentieth	Platinum	China
Twenty-fifth	Diamond	Silver
Thirtieth	Jade	Pearl
Fortieth	Ruby	Ruby
Fiftieth	Golden	Golden
Sixtieth	Diamond	Diamond

ANTS – ARGENTINE

Argentine ants can be distinguished from other varieties as they don't have the pungent smell when squashed. It is a good idea to check with your local council or government as some of them provide an extermination service for Argentine ants.

ANTS – IN THE HOUSE

Black pepper sprinkled under rugs and carpets deter both ants and silverfish. Another way to deter ants is to sprinkle their tracks with powdered borax, alum, or talcum powder. They hate walking over powder. Another ant deterrent is paste made with 2 cups sugar, 1 cup water, and 2 tablespoons of borax. Boil for 3 minutes, put a little on tin or plastic lids and place in the path of the ants. They are attracted to the sweet sticky contents and get stuck in it. The containers are easily disposed of when the ants have gone.

Another method is to use diatomaceous earth, a powder, used for cleaning the filter in swimming pools. It is sold under a number of different brand names. Sprinkle it about where the

ants are congregating. I have tried it out on the ants around my place and it seems to work well without being harmful to birds and other creatures. As with talcum powder, don't breathe it in.

ARALDITE

Araldite is a very strong glue, not meant to be removed with nail polish remover. You might be able to remove it with a paint thinning solvent, available from paint shops or hardware stores. Don't forget to test it on an inconspicuous part of the fabric first.

BABY SHOES

I have one of my baby shoes dipped in bronze and use it as a pencil holder. It is a constant source of wonder to me that my foot once fitted into such a small shoe. See if there is one in your local area.

BAG – BEADED

Try lightly sponging a stained beaded evening bag with warm water and a little wool wash. Have a clean, dry towel handy to dab it dry so there is no tell-tale water mark left behind. Because of the beading, it is not advisable to use a volatile cleaner. Another method is to rub equal quantities of talcum powder and bicarbonate of soda (baking soda) all over the beads. Leave for an hour of two then brush off.

BALL POINT PEN

The inks in ballpoint pens vary enormously. Most ballpoint pen marks can be removed from almost any material, including leather and vinyl, if you act quickly. Add a few drops of pen remover to a tissue or cotton wool and dab the stain away. Long-term marks or blobs may need to be treated two or three times. For ballpoint pen marks that have indented vinyl, first wring out a cloth in hot water and cover the mark to heat the vinyl before quickly applying the pen remover. Sponge with warm, soapy water when the marks have disappeared. Methylated spirits will remove some ballpoint pen marks. Test on an inconspicuous part of the material or leather before using any treatment to remove the stain.

BALLPOINT – RED

Red ballpoint pen marks can often be removed with methylated spirits. Put a pad of clean, waste cloth under the stain, then put methylated spirits onto a clean cloth and dab the stain. Keep changing the cloth to an unused area so the pen mark does not re-infect the garment. If that doesn't work, use pen remover. Follow the instructions on the bottle.

BATIK

Batik is a handmade Asian fabric, often strikingly colourful and unlikely to undergo the permanent colour processes that commercially manufactured fabric does. There is some

commercially manufactured batik coming on to the market now but it is more expensive. The old-fashioned method of rinsing in salt or vinegar to stop colour running is not effective on many of the hand made batiks.

Very colourful batik is not washed often in its country of origin. It is usually worn sari style over a plain blouse so it is not in direct contact with the skin. When it is washed, cold water is used, no soap or detergent, and it is immediately hung outside to dry.

BEE STINGS

Some people seem to attract bees more readily than others, and a sting is always painful. For immediate relief from painful bee stings gently remove the sting and dab honey over the affected area. If you are one of those people to whom bees are attracted, it is a wise precaution to always keep a jar of honey ready. Do make sure it is a bee and not a wasp that has caused the sting. For wasp stings, see Wasps.

BEESWAX

Put plenty of layers of paper towel over the stain, then hold a hot iron over it. Don't press down heavily on the iron, just keep holding it so the heat goes through to draw the beeswax up into the paper. Keep changing the paper until the wax is removed. Then use kerosene on a soft cloth and dab off any residue wax. Finally, sponge with warm water and wool wash.

BEETROOT

With kitchen paper or an absorbent cloth, blot up as much as possible. If the stain is on carpet cover it with powdered borax. The borax will absorb the stain so use plenty. Leave for a few hours then vacuum off.

If beetroot has stained table linen or clothes, soak in milk for a few hours, or put the stained portion of the article in a shallow dish of cold water with a slice of bread on the stain. The bread will absorb the colour. Do this before washing the article.

BIRD DROPPINGS

For dried bird droppings on clothing or outdoor furniture, scrape off as much as possible then sponge with warm water and nappy-soaking powder.

BIRO

For biro marks on clothing, drizzle pen remover on to the stained area. The marks will change to a pinky colour. At this stage, sponge, or wash the fabric with warm water and a little wool wash. On leather, wring out a cloth in hot water and hold it over the stain for two or three seconds. Put a few drops of Penoff onto a cotton bud and dab the biro mark. When the mark begins to fade or change colour, sponge with warm water and a little wool wash. Once the mark is removed, polish the leather. If the ballpoint pen contains indelible ink, this treatment will not work.

BIRTH STONES

Certain precious stones have always been sacred to specific months of the year. Ancient civilisations also attributed symbolic qualities to precious stones.

Stone and Meaning

January	Garnet, signifying faithfulness.
February	Amethyst, peace-making.
March	Bloodstone, courage and wisdom. Aquamarine was later attributed to this month.
April	Sapphire, repentance, and diamond, innocence. In more recent times, only the diamond is placed with April and the sapphire attributed to September.
May	Emerald, true love, and cornelian, contentment. Cornelian is a clear red quartz.
June	Originally agate, for health and longevity, but latterly pearl or moonstone.
July	Ruby, true friendship, and onyx, reciprocal love.
August	Sardonyx, conjugal happiness. This is a type of quartz, banded with reddish brown and other colours.
September	Originally chrisolite, freedom from evil. The sapphire is now generally the accepted stone for this month.
October	Opal, signifies hope.
November	Topaz, for friendship.
December	Turquoise, for happiness and love.

BLACKBOARD

When chalk leaves scratches on a blackboard it is usually because the chalk contains a small piece of grit or some other foreign substance. Cut a piece from the chalk, or rub sandpaper over it until the grit is removed and the chalk is smooth once more. If the blackboard becomes too scratched it will need repainting with special blackboard paint.

BLEACH

Avoid the use of chlorine bleach wherever possible. If bleach is splashed onto fabric it will remove the colour. It is sometimes possible to renew small spots of colour by matching with a waterproof felt pen. Dab on a little of the colour and a cover-up job can be effected.

Or mix a small amount of matching dye and apply it with a cotton bud. It is a good idea to colour the back of the stain first, let it dry to see the colour before recolouring the front of the garment. Never use bleach on poly/cotton fabrics.

Always check fabric care labels on clothing.

BLINDS – CONDENSATION

Put one or two containers of damp remover, (from hardware stores) between the blind and the window in each room to keep the amount of condensation to a minimum.

BLOOD

Blood stains can be removed with a saline solution made with 1 tablespoon of salt to 500 millilitres (16 fl oz) of cold water. Soak or sponge the stain as quickly as possible. Where the blood has dried, pack the stain with a paste made with salt mixed with a little cold water. Allow to dry and brush off. For blood on a mattress, spread with a thick paste of raw starch and water. Leave to dry, then brush off.

BLOSSOM

To use spring blossom in vases, it is best to cut branches when the buds are just showing colour. Crush the base of the stem before putting into water. When the petals open, spray with hair spray to stop them dropping too soon. A little cloudy ammonia in the water helps blossom branches to last longer.

BLOWFLIES

In the early spring and summer, blowflies collect in porches, garages, balconies and around doorways. Grow basil in pots to put in these areas it helps to keep the flies away.

BLU TACK

The best way to remove Blu Tack from walls and hard surfaces is with Blu Tack. Roll a little fresh Blu Tack between the palms of the hands and, when it is soft and pliable, roll it over the old Blu Tack. It may need to be done a couple of times for complete removal. Any residual stain can be sponged with eucalyptus oil or kerosene. On carpet, cover the Blu Tack with a plastic bagful of ice cubes to harden it, then use a plastic spatula to remove the bulk. Sponge any residual stain with eucalyptus oil or kerosene.

BOOKS – GREASE MARKS

Try smothering the grease marks on the pages of the book with talcum powder. It will be necessary to put the talcum powder on both sides of the page, before putting a weight on the book. Hopefully the pressure will push the grease into the powder. Leave it for about two days before brushing the powder away.

Repeat the treatment if necessary.

BOOKS – MOULDY

To get rid of mould from hardcover or leather-bound books, wring out a cloth in very hot water, add a dash of antiseptic disinfectant to the cloth and wipe the mould away. Be sure to pay attention to the top and bottom of the spine of the book as mould spores can gather in those

areas. Make sure the books are completely dry before putting them back on the shelves. A light dusting with talcum powder helps to ensure the book covers are dry.

BOOKS – MUSTY

A mixture of half talcum powder and half powdered sulphur is often helpful in getting rid of the musty smell from books which have been badly stored over a period of time Sprinkle the powder between the pages of the books, leave for two or three days, then gently remove the powder. A very soft brush, such as a sable make-up brush, is ideal to use.

BOOKS – WET

Hold the book over a hot, steaming saucepan to separate the pages that have stuck together. Once the pages have been steamed and carefully separated, smother the pages with talcum powder. The powder stops them from sticking together again. Leave them until thoroughly dry before shaking the powder out from between the pages. The pages can then be ironed flat, using a hot iron and plain white paper to cover each page before applying the iron.

BORAX

Borax is a white, crystalline sodium borate, occurring naturally, or prepared artificially, and used as a cleansing agent, particularly in the manufacture of glass and pottery. For home use, it is commercially produced and sold in 500 gram (16 oz) plastic containers at hardware stores or supermarkets. Boracic acid is a different product and is only available on prescription.

BORER

Kerosene or cloudy ammonia sprayed into borer holes will generally kill them. Don't refill the holes with woodfiller until you are absolutely certain that all the borers have been killed. Have your cupboards or furniture checked by a professional if you suspect borers.

BORE WATER

If bore water is all that is available for the washing, the best thing to do is make sure that all the taps are fitted with very good filters.

BOWLS – CLOTHING

White jumpers, cardigans or dresses that are worn when playing bowls will become yellow with time.

Garments of pure cotton can be bleached. Use about 1 part bleach to 6 parts cold water to soak the garment after washing. Rinse well and turn inside out to dry. Knitted cotton should be laid flat on a towel to dry.

Synthetic fibres usually whiten with addition of bicarbonate of soda (baking soda). To a bucket of warm water, add 2 tablespoons bicarbonate of soda (baking soda) and soak the garment overnight before washing in the normal way.

Pure wool stays white longer if it is always washed with pure soap rather than detergent. Always turn white garments inside out to dry and do not hang them in direct sunlight. Bowling hats made of fine, white straw, develop sunburn and will yellow with continued use. White shoe cleaner, evenly applied, extends the life of a hat avoiding having to discard it.

BRASS

For difficult to remove spots on brass, try lemon juice mixed with a very fine powder cleaner. Wash well with soapy water afterwards. Make sure the article is thoroughly dry, then polish with a good brass cleaner. Worcestershire sauce is very good for cleaning brass.

Lacquered brass sometimes develops spotting and the lacquer starts to lift. Strip the lacquer completely. It is best to use the same brand of stripper as the lacquer. If you don't know the brand, seek advice at a good paint store.

Old-fashioned carriage lights were made of solid brass but with modern copies, the look is achieved with a coating of brass over another metal then finished with a top coat of clear sealant. Usually the clear sealant is the first to suffer penetration from atmospheric particles. If treated quickly, it is only necessary to remove and replace the sealant. Any good hardware store can advise on the best and cheapest product suitable for the purpose. When left for too long, the particles penetrate through to the brass and the lights will then need to be re-dipped.

BRICKS

Crumbly bricks around a fireplace will naturally attract dust and soot, making cleaning an extremely time-consuming task. No matter what flooring is in front of the fireplace, a sheet or plastic cover will need to be put down before cleaning begins. Get professional advice on the possibility of sealing the bricks around the fireplace. A firm brushing, followed by vacuuming, will help to clean the bricks.

Bricks contain salts that leach out, leaving white powdery marks over the brickwork. The marks can be brushed off with a firm brush, or scrubbed away with equal parts of white vinegar and warm water. It is important, however, to check for dampness.

There are various ways to remove paint from bricks but get some expert advice. Hydrochloric acid can be scrubbed on and sprayed off with water. Professionals can do sand blasting. With either method it is easy to strike problems with the mortar which, if old, could disintegrate.

Also, the bricks may become porous, particularly on the weather side of the building. This would create a damp problem inside the house. A newer method is to spray on chemicals under pressure, re-grout if necessary; then glaze with a weather protective coating.

BRONZE CUTLERY

A lot of cutlery, goblets, etc. are made in Thailand from bronze. They look wonderful at the time of purchase, but unfortunately the sheen doesn't seem to last very long. Wash the cutlery in hot water with pure soap flakes and clean any remaining stains with Worcestershire sauce on a soft cloth. Lightly rub over with cooking oil before putting away. Or make a paste with lemon juice

and toothpaste to rub bronze to a soft sheen or use Polier, which is excellent for cleaning Thai cutlery and gives it a protective coating.

BROOMS

Clean brooms about once every month by washing in hot soapy water with disinfectant. If possible leave in the sun to dry. Always stand brooms with their heads upward to stop the bristles bending out of shape. Or put a hook in the end of the broomstick and hang it in the broom cupboard.

BRUSSELS LACE

Some Brussels lace was made with pure silk, some with pure cotton, and some with a mixture of both. All Brussels lace is delicate and used to be made of very fine net with motifs sewn on by hand, but nowadays it is made by machine. To wash the older ones, dissolve 1 tablespoon pure soap flakes in 2 cups hot water. Leave it to cool, then add 1 tablespoon ammonia, 1 teaspoon eucalyptus oil and 1 dessertspoon citric acid. Put the lace into a large screw-top jar, cover it with water that has been boiled and allowed to cool, add about half the mixture, then screw the top firmly on and shake for 30 seconds. Leave for 10 minutes, then shake again. If the lace is too big for this method, put it in a clean, white pillowcase and use half a bucket of water to dunk it in. Rinse in water that has been boiled and allowed to cool. Put the lace flat between two thick towels and pat dry. Iron with a warm iron between sheets of tissue paper so the point of the iron will not catch and tear the lace.

BURNS

On furniture, burn marks from cigarettes and other hot things placed on a table can often be removed by rubbing with a little toothpaste or Brasso or metal polish. Always rub with the grain of the wood. If you rub some of the colour from the wood, rub over with a little matching shoe polish to bring the colour back.

CAMELLIA

A flat dish, where the flower stems can be in water, is certainly the best way to display camellias. Stop the petals of the flowers from turning brown by sprinkling them with salt.

CAMPHOR WOOD

When a camphor wood chest loses its pungent aroma, rub the inside of the lid with fine sandpaper and the smell of the camphor wood will be like new again. Empty the chest before sandpapering and vacuum it out afterwards to get rid of the fine shavings.

CANDLES

Scraps of old candles can be melted in a saucepan, over a very low heat, watching it all the time. As soon as melting is almost complete, remove the saucepan from the heat and take out any old wicks. Craft shops sell moulds and wicks. Wicks are also available from hardware stores. You can

use cream cartons or jelly moulds to make your own more interesting shapes. Don't forget to get a wick of a suitable size for the thickness of the candle. Commercial moulds have a hole through which the wick can be threaded.

To make sure the wick is centred on your own interesting moulds, set the end of the wick in the centre of the mould with a little wax. When the wax is set, bring the wick to the top of the mould and tie it to a piece of string secured across the top centre of the mould. Then pour in the melted wax.

CANDLE CREASE – SUEDE SHOES

Put the shoe into a plastic bag and leave it in the freezer for about two hours, then take them out and use a plastic spatula to lift as much as possible of the frozen candle grease from the

Suede: Don't use a knife to do this because you could cut the suede and ruin the shoe completely. Use methylated spirits to remove any residual stain. With suede, it is often a good idea to rub a stain gently with very fine sandpaper.

CANDLE SPIKE

Any candle, no matter what the size, is likely to break and crumble as it is pushed onto a spike holder. Make a hole in the bottom of the candle with a hot nail to prevent the problem.

CANDLE STAIN

Residual staining after candle wax has been removed from fabric, can usually be removed by sponging with eucalyptus oil. On heavy fabrics, it may be necessary to use kerosene, but test on an inconspicuous area first.

CANE

Old cane chairs can be scrubbed with liquid sugar soap and water, then left to dry thoroughly. The cane can then be given a very thin primer coat and finished with a gloss paint. For the natural look, two coats of clear lacquer should be sufficient to prolong the life of a much loved chair. Whether applying primer, paint or lacquer, it should be only a thin coating so as not to clog the weave of the cane. Mildew can be removed from cane baskets or chairs by scrubbing with a strong solution of salt and water. Use about ½ cup of salt to 1 litre (2 pints) of cold water.

CANVAS

Canvas blinds, chairs and sails get badly stained if put away soiled. Salt water is the best cleanser, so if possible take them to the beach with a scrubbing brush.

Otherwise, scrub them with salt and water. Trail sails behind your boat, dry them in the sun and sprinkle with talcum powder to deter mould spores from generating when the sails are in storage.

CAPERS

Gather the green seeds of nasturtiums and soak them for three days in salt and water. Use

about 1 cup of salt to 1 litre (2 pints) of water. After three days, drain the salted water from the nasturtiums and bring to the boil sufficient vinegar to cover the seeds. Add spices to the vinegar, such as, a dash of nutmeg, a little horseradish and a few shallots. Simmer for 10 minutes. Sterilise bottles, add the nasturtium seeds and cover them with the strained vinegar. Cover with plastic and screw the lids on.

CARAVAN TANK

To clean the tank in a caravan, drain it, and if there is a filter on the tap, remove it for cleaning or replacing. Leave the filter off and fill the tank with clean water. Add the juice of 6 to 8 lemons and leave for at least 24 hours. Drain the tank and repeat the process. Fill the tank once more with clean water then drain it, to get rid of the acidic taste of the lemon juice. This treatment is sufficient to clean most tanks, but if bore water has been used in the tank, further treatment with a commercial cleaner may be necessary.

CAR – SPILT MILK

It is worth taking the carpet out and scrubbing it on both sides with wool wash. While the carpet is out, wash the floor of the car with hot water and a dash of antiseptic disinfectant. When the floor is dry, spray with a commerical odour neutraliser. When the carpet is completely dry, spray both sides of it. Lightly sprinkle talcum powder over the floor before putting the dry carpet back.

CARNATIONS

These flowers will last longer in a vase if you give them lemonade to drink. Flat lemonade will do. Or add 1 teaspoon of sugar to the water.

CARPET – SOOT

Cover the soot stain with lots of salt. Leave for about an hour then vacuum, off. Repeat, if necessary.

CARPET – WOOD STAIN

It is a great mistake to put furniture, particularly wooden furniture, onto a carpet immediately after cleaning. If the choice is putting the furniture onto damp carpet, or leaving it out in the rain, naturally it goes inside. But it is then important to put plastic or foil under the feet of the furniture because it is an area which is very seldom sealed, and damp carpet acts like a straw, sucking the sap and oil from the wood, and of course, staining the carpet.

Fade the stain with the application of 2 tablespoons borax mixed with 2 tablespoons salt and 2 tablespoons shellite (naphtha). Cover the stain with the powder; gently spread it into the carpet with your fingers, then leave for at least 24 hours. Repeat the treatment once a week until the stain fades away.

CAR – SAND

Water is the best thing possible for cleaning sand, salt or mud from under the car. Salt and sand

should be washed away as quickly as possible. Put a circular garden sprinkler under the car and turn the tap on hard. It makes the task very easy.

CAR SICKNESS

The regular motion of a car can cause sickness. Keep a packet of barley sugar in the car and children or adults can suck the candy to settle nausea. Stop regularly and walk around the car at least three times – it changes the motion.

Some passengers perspire – try sitting on newspaper; that helps! Sucking junket tablets also works but because of the taste, children usually spit them out.

CAR STATIC

Spray the seat covers with an anti-static spray, available from supermarkets and some pharmacists. Keep a bottle in the car and spray your clothing lightly when you get in the car. The regularity of spraying will depend on the weather and the quantity of synthetic clothing you wear.

When you wash the seat covers put fabric softener in the rinse water and be sure to use fabric softener when washing any synthetic clothing, even your underwear.

CD CASES

To remove the stickiness after removing price tags from plastic CD cases, put a little eucalyptus oil onto a tissue and gently rub the glue residue off. Once the sticky residue is removed, lightly spray the plastic case with car polish, then buff it up with a soft, clean cloth.

CELSIUS TO FAHRENHEIT

To convert Celsius to Fahrenheit, multiply the Celsius figure by nine, divide the result by five, then add 32.

CEMENT

To remove cement from clothing, soak the garments in cold water with 1 tablespoon of salt and 1 cup of vinegar.

CHARCOAL

The best thing for removing charcoal stains from clothing is salt. Dampen the stains, cover them with salt, leave for about an hour and then soak the clothes in cold water for an hour and wash as usual.

CHEWING GUM

Put the garment in the freezer for about an hour. When you remove it, crumble the stained area with your fingers. Stretch the knit or weave as you crumble, to remove the gum from behind the stitches. The residual stain can be removed by sponging with eucalyptus oil.

CHINA – CRACKS

The bleach method can be successful in cleaning the hairline cracks in china but the water needs to be very hot. The hot water opens the cracks and lets the bleach do its job. An old-fashioned method of solving this problem was to simmer china plates in milk for about 30 minutes. The milk would seal small cracks and scratches.

CHINA – REPAIRS

There are clear china glues on the market. Hardware stores stock different brands, most of which are very good, but it might be better to have repairs done professionally.

CHRISTMAS LIGHTS

The Christmas tree lights won't become tangled if they are wrapped around cardboard tubes. Push the plug into the tube, then roll the lights loosely around the outside of the tube and secure with a rubber band. Now roll cling wrap over the lights and continue with another layer of fairy lights. When complete, put the roll into a large plastic, supermarket bag and hang it in the wardrobe or garage until next year.

CHRISTMAS MINCE

This recipe for Christmas mince can be made now and kept in the fridge until the week before Christmas when you want to make the mince pies: 250 grams (8 oz) each of raisins, sultanas, currants, and apples, 125 grams (4 oz) chopped peel, the rind and juice of 1 lemon, 1 cup brown sugar, 1 tablespoon golden syrup, 1 teaspoon each of nutmeg, allspice and cinnamon, ½ teaspoon salt, 30 grams (1 oz) butter, 3 tablespoons rum or brandy.

Method: Peel and grate the apples and put them into a basin with dry ingredients. Add the lemon and syrup. Melt the butter with the spirits and thoroughly mix with all the ingredients. Store in screw-top jars in a cool dark place, or in the refrigerator.

CHRISTMAS PUDDING CLOTH

To successfully remove the cloth from the Christmas pudding, prepare the cloth before mixing the pudding. First plunge it into boiling water to sterilise. Wring it out and spread on a flat surface then liberally sprinkle with flour. This method causes the flour to adhere to the cloth so that it can be removed without taking the surface off the pudding. Another method is to add half a lemon to the water when boiling a Christmas pudding. This helps prevent the cloth sticking to the pudding. Very good for bought puddings.

CHRISTMAS TREE

Fresh Christmas trees should have the bottom cut off before putting them into water. Like cut flowers, they need to drink to stay alive. A diagonal cut is best for them to be able to absorb more water. Also, drill a hole up through the bottom of the tree and push cotton wool, or plastic

sponge, up the drill hole. The cotton wool becomes a wick to suck more water up into the tree.

Another good tip for Christmas trees is to hang small bells on the lower branches. The tinkle will let you know when little fingers or pussy paws become active.

CLINGING GARMENTS

Synthetic fibres cling and have a tendency to ride up. The best thing is to spray the garments with Statique (from supermarkets or pharmacists) before they are to be worn, preferably before ironing. Also, garments which cling should be hand washed, rinsed with a fabric softener, and never dried in a tumble drier.

CLOTHING – YELLOWED

Lie the garment flat in the bath, with the yellowed side uppermost, and enough water to just cover it. Now sprinkle denture powder all over the yellowed area and "puddle" it around for an even spread. Leave for about two hours, then wash the garment in warm water and nappy-soaking powder. Turn it inside out and dry away from direct sunlight.

CLOUDY AMMONIA

Cloudy ammonia is used for many different cleaning jobs and is sometimes used in the wash to soften fabrics. Keep the bottle out of the reach of young children.

COCKROACHES

A good deterrent for cockroaches is to sprinkle their paths liberally with highly scented talcum powder or powdered sulphur. A commercial insect powder also helps. Cockroaches are most at home in dark, damp areas so make sure that cupboards, skirting boards, etc. are thoroughly dry at all times.

CONCRETE – GREASE

Use 1 part detergent to 6 parts kerosene on the stain, leave 5 minutes and hose. Or cover the grease with kitty litter, leave for half a day, then sweep the kitty litter away. Best done on a sunny day.

CONDY'S CRYSTALS

A stain from Condy's crystals should be treated with calamine lotion. Cover the stain with calamine lotion, let it dry; brush off. Condy's crystals spilt on the bath or handbasin can also be treated with calamine lotion. Sometimes baby oil removes Condy's crystal stains from an enamel bath. Lemon, cut and sliced, and then rubbed over the stains is also worth a try.

CONTACT

Methylated spirits will remove the adhesive residue of adhesive shelf paper. When adhesive is

removed after being down for a long time, it may be necessary to scrub the sticky residue off with steel wool and methylated spirits. Acetone can also be used but methylated spirits is better because it is less volatile and the smell dissipates more rapidly.

COPPER

Some modern copper products are coated. Soap and water are all that is needed to clean them. For uncoated copper, use Worcestershire sauce on a soft cloth. Polish with a dry cloth. Another method, also very good, is salt and lemon juice mixed to a paste, or use a commercial copper polish paste, which cleans and coats the surface.

CORNED MEAT

This is the same as pickled, pumped and salted.

CRAFT GLUE

Try removing craft glue (this won't work with water-based glue) with acetone but test first on a small, inconspicuous area of the garment to see what effect the acetone has on the fabric. Also, make sure you wash the acetone out of the fabric as soon as the stain is removed.

CRAFT GLUE – DRIED

Pour Sceney's lacquer thinner into the bottle. Use about as much lacquer thinner as there is glue in the bottle. Put the top securely on and leave overnight. Then remove the top and stir the contents until they are mixed together. If the glue is still too thick, repeat the process, using less lacquer thinner. Continue to do this until the glue is the correct consistency.

CRAYON

If the walls are papered with washable wallpaper, use toothpaste. Just rub it on gently until the crayon is removed then wipe off. If the paper is not washable, try a little shellite (naphtha), or acetone, on a soft cloth.

For painted walls, cover the marks with three layers of paper towel, then hold a hot iron onto the paper to draw the grease from the crayon into the paper. Rub any residual mark with talcum powder.

CRICKET GLOVES

Most cricket gloves can be cleaned by scrubbing with a solution of 3 parts water, 2 parts methylated spirits, and 1 part cloudy ammonia. Don't soak them in the solution, just put the gloves on in turn and scrub with a nailbrush.

CRICKET WHITES

You will have no trouble with cricket whites if you use one of the commercial wool wash

detergents. For bad stains, put a little wool wash straight onto the garment and rub. In other words, use the wool wash as a stain remover before putting the clothes into the wash. It gets rid of grass stains as well as those stubborn, red ball stains.

CROCHET

Gum arabic water is good for stiffening crochet work. Gum arabic powder is available from artists' supplies shops. To 1 litre of boiling water add 125 grams (4 oz) gum arabic powder. Stir until the gum melts, then strain through a piece of muslin, bottle, cork and store for use later. For an average proportion, use 1 tablespoon gum arabic water to 1 cupful of water. This can vary according to the stiffness desired.

Another method is to use sugar starch. In a saucepan moisten ½ cup cornflour (cornstarch) with enough water to make a thin paste. Add 1 cup water and stir over heat until it turns clear. Add an ice cube and ¾ cup sugar. Strain. Squeeze mixture through the item to be stiffened then hang to dry. For decorative pieces, such as wedding bells, hang on the line by a thread and shape occasionally while they are drying.

To deepen the colour of cream or ecru cotton crochet, soak in a bowl of very well strained black tea. The strength of the tea determines the depth of colour. Start light and do two or three times for darker. Stir now and then so that streaking does not occur.

CRYSTALLISED FLOWERS

One way to crystallise flowers is to dip them in a thin gum arabic solution and then sprinkle them with Epsom salts. This is particularly good with holly leaves for Christmas decorations. The holly leaves look as though they are covered with frost. Flowers treated in this manner must not be eaten.

CUPBOARDS

Old cupboards often develop a musty smell. When this happens it is best to empty the cupboards and give them a thorough wash, preferably with a 1 in 4 solution of bleach. Make sure the cupboards are thoroughly dry before putting anything back into them. A few drops of commerical odour neutraliser on a small pad of cotton wool will help to keep cupboards smelling fresh. A few bay leaves in kitchen cupboards helps to keep insects away. Or, after making spiced vinegar, put the strained off spices into an open container and leave on one of the shelves.

CURRY STAIN

The two most worriesome ingredients of a curry stain are oil and turmeric. The oil should be treated first. Use lots of talcum powder and warmth to draw the oil from the stain and into the powder. Next, apply glycerine to soften the yellow stain of the turmeric, and smother it with powdered borax mixed to a paste with hydrogen peroxide. Leave for about 10 minutes, then wash as usual.

CURTAINS

Before washing curtains always check the material they are made from. Many materials are dry-clean only, in which case, don't try to wash them: have them dry cleaned. Light synthetics (nylon or terylene) can be washed, but do so in lukewarm water, drip dry and rehang before they are quite dry. Ironing will then be unnecessary.

CURTAINS – MOULDY

Soak the curtains overnight in warm water with a dash of antiseptic disinfectant and ½ cup of cream of tartar, then wash in the normal manner. Thin synthetic curtains should be washed and rinsed in the same temperature of water, then drip dried. It would be a good idea to put a container of damp remover on the windowsill during the winter months when the condensation is at its worst. Hardware stores sell these products.

CURTAINS – RUBBER BACKED

Wring out a cloth in very hot water, add a dash of antiseptic disinfectant to the cloth and wipe over the mildewed area of the rubber-backed curtains. This will kill the mould and remove most of the mildew stain. Any residual stains can be wiped with a cloth wrung out in a weak bleach solution. Use about 1 part bleach to 6 parts water. When the stains are removed, use clean, cold water to remove the bleach solution from the rubber backing. Rubber-backed curtains can be washed with warm water and wool wash but take care not to let the rubber meet when hanging them to dry because the rubber can become stuck together. Also, don't hang them in strong sunlight or heat to dry.

CURTAINS – TERYLENE

Soak them overnight in a bucket of cold water with ¼ cup of cream of tartar and 1 teaspoon of citric acid. Next day, wash the curtains in warm water and pure soap flakes. Dissolve the flakes in hot water before adding to the wash water. Rinse in water of the same temperature as the wash and drip dry away from direct sunlight.

DECANTER – OLD

Old glass decanters sometimes show their age with a dingy appearance. Try putting a teaspoon of dishwashing machine powder into the decanter, then fill with hot water. Shake a little to dissolve the powder. Leave overnight. Next day, put hot water into the sink, empty the decanter into it and wash inside and out. Rinse until clear. Rinse again with 1 teaspoon of methylated spirits in the rinse water.

DECANTERS

To clean a decanter, put in 2 tablespoons of fine sand, mix with a little vinegar and warm, soapy water, then shake well. Uncooked rice with a few tea leaves and water is also a successful cleaning method. Shake well.

To remove the stain of red wine from a glass or crystal decanter, put 1 tablespoon of baking powder and 1 cup of lukewarm water into the decanter. Shake well. Empty, then add warm water with a few drops of detergent and a little cloudy ammonia. Rinse well before using.

DECANTER STOPPER

To loosen and remove a stopper that is firmly stuck in a decanter, pour a little glycerine around the stopper, then stand the decanter up to its neck in warm water. Next, wrap a cloth wrung out in cold water around the top of the decanter. Gentle movement should now remove the stopper but don't try to force it. Repeat the treatment rather than use force.

DENIM

Denim material is hard-wearing and also very tough to iron. Try putting it in the refrigerator for a few hours. This helps to remove the creases. Another method is to soak overnight with a small packet of Epsom Salts. Add a couple of teaspoons of vinegar to hold the colour. The best way to soften denim is to soak it in cold water with a cup of powdered Borax and a cup of vinegar for at least 24 hours. Then wash in fairly hot water with ½ cup of Borax and ½ cup of pure soap flakes dissolved in hot water and ½ cup of salt. Add fabric softener and vinegar to the rinse water and tumble dry with three clean tennis balls in the drier.

DENTURES

Use a commercial denture cleaner. Follow the instructions carefully and rinse teeth well after cleaning. Your pharmacist will be able to get it in for you.

DOLLS

It is sometimes difficult to know whether a doll is washable or not. If you are not sure, play safe and use a powder carpet cleaner or a mixture of half talcum powder and half borax. Cover the soiled areas with plenty of the powder and put the doll in a plastic bag or pillowcase for a few hours. Hold the top of the bag together and give poor old dolly a good beating before taking it out. Then rub over the doll with a rough towel before brushing the powder out.

- **Cabbage Patch** and similar dolls should be undressed before cleaning.
- **Clothes** should be washed and ironed.
- **Shoes** are usually plastic and can be washed. Wipe completely dry after washing.
- **Bodies** should be cleaned regularly. Wring out a cloth until almost dry, in warm water and wool wash. It is best to use a rough towel or face washer. Sponge all over the body, paying particular attention to the fingers. Don't get the doll too wet. Sponge away water marks with a little white vinegar on a damp cloth. Sponge the face lightly with a cloth wrung out in warm water and wool wash. Use a towel to dry completely.
- **Ballpoint** pen marks can be removed with pen remover.
- **Hair** on most dolls manufactured today is almost certainly synthetic. It can be washed in

the same way as human hair. Hold the doll upside down over a basin of warm water and shampoo the hair. Use a small amount of fabric softener after the wash. Rinse well, then towel, or blow dry. Take care not to get the rest of the doll wet.

- **Rag dolls** can be washed, depending on the material with which they are stuffed. If the stuffing is a mystery, play safe and either lightly sponge with wool wash, or spray with carpet stain remover, wait until it changes to a white powder, then brush or beat to remove the stain remover.

- **For felt-pen marks**, wring out a cloth in very hot water and apply it, like a poultice, to the soft, plastic face or body of the doll. Leave it for long enough to heat the plastic, then rub the mark with pen remover on a soft cloth. When the mark begins to change colour, sponge it with warm water and a little wool wash. Felt-pen marks might fade with the application of pen remover or methylated spirits. Some pens contain indelible ink that is impossible to remove without damaging the doll.

DOUBLE-SIDED TAPE

To remove double-sided tape, scrape off as much as possible, then dab the remainder with eucalyptus oil and rub with a rough towel. Some adhesives may need nail polish remover.

DRESS ODOUR

When you wash the garment, put a little antiseptic disinfectant in both the wash and the rinse water. Don't use too much. About a teaspoonful should be sufficient.

DRIED FLOWERS

The fastest and easiest way to dry flowers is in a microwave oven with silica gel. Chemists and craft stores sell silica gel. The best type is in the form of blue crystals because they turn pink as moisture is absorbed into them so it is easy to determine when they are worn out. The bonus is that they can be put into a warm oven and restored to absorbency as the colour changes to blue again. Cover the bottom of a microwave-safe container with silica gel crystals or powder. The powder is best for delicate blooms. Now layer the flowers, face down, gently on the gel, and just as gently, cover the blooms with more silica. Don't pile it on or the blooms could be damaged. Now put the container, uncovered, into the microwave, with ½ cup of water next to it. Microwave on high for 1 to 3 minutes, depending on the delicacy of the blooms. Leave the flowers in the gel until they are cool enough to handle, then remove them and shake the silica off.

DRIZA-BONE COATS

Driza-Bone coats always have a care instruction label sewn into a seam of the garment and the manufacturers instructions are: "Do not wash with detergent or hot water. Do not dry clean, iron, or use starch. Only if the garment is extremely dirty, hand wash in lukewarm water with pure soap,, then re-proof the garment using Driza-Bone Garment Dressing." I don't think it would be outside the manufacturers instructions to first rub the mould spots with white, two-day-old, bread

to remove the surface mould, then wring out a cloth, until almost dry, in warm water. Add a dash of antiseptic disinfectant to the cloth and sponge any residual mould discolouration.

DUST MITE

For an infestation of dust mites, particularly in the bedroom, have the room treated by a professional. Once treated, it is important that continual care is taken to prevent further infestation. Use a straw broom regularly, and vigorously, to sweep all the edges of the carpet. Then, go around the edges with a hair dryer, on hot, to cook any eggs and prevent them from hatching. Move the bed regularly and vacuum under it. Turn the mattress every six months. Put the bedding in the sun whenever possible. Feather pillows can be put into the tumble dryer with two or three tennis balls. Dust mites hate heat and disturbance, so give them as much of this treatment as possible.

DYE

Before dyeing any garment that has become blotchy because bleach has removed patches of colour, it is essential to remove all colour for the garment to dye it evenly. Get some commercial colour remover and follow the directions on the packet. Don't re-dye until the garment has dried to a fairly even colour all over.

On garments that have picked up dye from other garments in the wash, spray the stained area with a hardworking commercial stain remover, leave for about two hours then wash in the normal way. Or, use a commercial colour run remover, following the instructions on the packet.

On laminex, toothpaste mixed with methylated spirits will usually remove a dye stain. White cotton garments can be soaked in cold water and bleach, but don't use bleach on synthetics or wool.

Another method is to soak the garment in warm water, cover the dye mark with bicarbonate of soda (baking soda) and leave until the stain disappears. Repeat two or three times if necessary. For stubborn marks, a strong solution of tartaric acid may work. Test all fabrics before using any remedy for removing dye marks.

EGGS – BOILED

Prick the blunt end of the egg with a darning needle before boiling. It helps to prevent cracking.

To soft boil eggs, immerse the eggs in warm water, bring to the boil and boil for three and a half to four minutes, depending on the size of the eggs.

To hard boil, eggs should be at least five days old or they will not peel evenly. Put the eggs into cold water, bring to the boil, and boil for ten minutes. When boiling is complete, plunge the eggs into cold water. Peel under cold, running water.

Farm fresh eggs should be kept out of the refrigerator for at least four days before boiling them or they will be difficult to peel.

EGGS – CRACKED

If eggs crack while boiling, pour salt quickly over the crack.

EGGS – KEEPING

The yolks of eggs can be kept for three or four days if placed in a cup with enough cold water to cover the yolks. Keep in the refrigerator. Tip a little of the cold water off before using for cakes, scrambled eggs or omelettes. Egg whites freeze well, but mark the quantity on the container in case you forget. To preserve eggs, put plenty of Vaseline on the palms of the hands and liberally cover each egg. Store in a crock, or similar container, in a cool place.

EGGS – PICKLED

Mix together in a large saucepan:

   8 cups **vinegar**

   25 grams (¾ oz) **root ginger, chopped**

   1 tablespoon **salt**

   ½ teaspoon **cayenne pepper**

   1 tablespoon **whole cloves**

   25 grams (¾ oz) **peppercorns**

   1 **bay leaf**

   1¼ cups **sugar**

Bring to the boil and simmer for about 10 minutes. Remove from the heat; allow to cool. Strain and pour over peeled, hard-boiled eggs in a jar with a screw-top lid. Best left for two or three weeks before eating. Eggs will change colour but can be kept indefinitely.

EGGS – POACHED

Lightly grease pan, add cold water then eggs. Bring to the boil and simmer until the white sets and the yolks are cooked. Gently lift from the pan with an egg slice.

EGGS – SCRAMBLED

To make scrambled eggs go further, beat the eggs with a knob of butter and sufficient milk, then add a tablespoon of evaporated milk for every two eggs.

EGG – STAINS

Dampen the stain with warm water then cover it with a paste made with powdered borax and glycerine. Leave it for about half an hour then sponge with warm water. Use warm water and a little wool wash to remove the glycerine.

EGGS TO TEST

Don't depend on your nose to know if an egg is fresh: try an easier way. Put the egg in a container of water. If it sinks to the bottom, it is fresh. If it floats to the top, don't throw it out. Crack it open. You will know immediately if it is fresh enough to be used for cakes, omelettes, or scrambled eggs.

EGG WHITES

A tiny pinch of cream of tartar added to egg whites, before beating makes them froth quickly and they will be stiffer when beaten. Egg whites will not beat if very fresh, or if taken straight from the refrigerator. Room temperature is best. Don't beat egg whites in plastic bowls. Grease residue, even after washing, can adhere to a plastic surface and prevent egg whites from stiffening.

EMBROIDERY

The transfer marks for embroidery can usually be removed by putting methylated spirits on the marks, then turning the pattern on to a clean cloth and ironing the back of the work. The pattern is transferred to the cloth.

Some of the modern transfers are of different ink from the older ones and with these I have had some success with pen remover. Drizzle the pen remover over the marks and, when they change colour, sponge with warm water and washing-up liquid.

EUCALYPTUS OIL

For stains of unknown origin, or stains that have dried, a dab of eucalyptus oil is often a good idea. Eucalyptus oil is also good for removing some glue stains.

FABRIC – CREASING

Some fabrics seem to crease or crush the minute you sit down in them. To help control the problem, turn the garment inside out and spray with any good spray starch. Iron on the wrong side. Wear a cotton slip under dresses that crease easily. Adding 2 tablespoons of salt to the rinsing water will keep some fabrics a little crisper and help to control excessive creasing.

FABRIC – VELVET

Silk velvet should only be dry cleaned. Velvet containing synthetic fibres will wash well, but it is necessary to follow the care instructions, which should be on a label on an inside seam of the garment. For chairs, use a powder carpet cleaner.

FELT HAT

For hats made of felt, like Akubras, there are a number of cleaning methods. The inside headband usually attracts a mixture of sweat, dirt and body oil, and so needs the most attention. First smother the band with talcum powder and leave it in a warm place overnight. Rub the talcum powder off with a clean, rough towel. Now wring out a cloth in warm water, add a dash of neat, commercial wool wash to the cloth and sponge the band. Don't get it too wet. Let it dry thoroughly. Now mix together 4 tablespoons powdered borax, 4 tablespoons salt, and 4 tablespoons shellite (naphtha).

Spread the mixture all over the hat, rubbing it in with the palms of the hands. The mixture needs to be spread evenly and left overnight. Rub it off with a clean, rough towel.

For any difficult to remove spots, spray them with carpet stain remover, following the instruction on the can. Once clean, it is probably a good idea to spray the whole hat with a water-repellent. Felt hats can be steamed back into shape.

FLEAS

A plague of fleas can be one of the worst experiences anyone can have. The cheapest and easiest way to get rid of them is to buy a bulk amount of salt. About 5 kilograms (11 lbs) will not go amiss. The back door, the front door, and any other entry to the house will have a step in front of it. Smother each step with lots of salt. It should look like a snowfall. Inside the house, sprinkle salt around the edges of the carpet, under the beds, and anywhere else that fleas have gathered. You will be surprised at how quickly you will rid the place of fleas.

A word of warning though. When the fleas have gone, don't sweep the salt from the steps into the garden. Sweep it onto a shovel or dustpan and dispose of it with the rubbish. Many of the plants and shrubs in the garden will object to a dose of salt.

FLIES

Nothing will keep really determined flies away, but here are a few deterrents. Sprinkle a little vinegar on a damp cloth and wipe over mirrors and windows after cleaning to keep flies from sitting and spotting. Ferns are a good deterrent to flies. Keep one in a pot in the kitchen, beside doorways. A few drops of lavender oil on a wet sponge can be left about where flies like to gather. Freshen every 4 days.

FLOORS

For vinyl floors, use a commercial vinyl floor cleaner to rejuvenate the floor. Follow the instructions on the bottle. The heavy walk areas may need a little more attention than the rest of the floor. For vinyl floors that are difficult to clean, put about 1 tablespoon of caustic soda into ½ bucket of hot water and use a squeegee to wash the floor.

FLOUR TEST

It is easy to test which flour is selfraising and which is not, by putting a teaspoon of each flour in different containers, then adding a little water. The one that fizzes, or bubbles, is the self-raising flour. In future, to save yourself the trouble of making the test, label the containers.

FLOWERS

Flowers cut from the garden should go straight into a bucket of water where they can be left until you are ready to arrange them in a vase. Flowers purchased from a florist, or store, should have the end of each stem cut off before being put into water.

Once cut, the stems immediately begin to heal, by sap bleeding over the wound (the same as when you cut your finger). The sap sets and the flowers cannot suck up the water so necessary for their survival.

FLUFF

Some clothing, particularly if made from synthetic fibre, attracts fluff. If possible, wash the clothing and put a good brand name fabric softener in the rinse water. Another method is to spray evenly over the outside of the garment with a commercial anti-static spray.

FRUIT SALTS

For homemade fruit salts mix:

60 grams (2 oz) **tartaric acid**
60 grams (2 oz) **bicarbonate of soda**
60 grams (2 oz) **cream of tartar**
155 grams (5 oz) **caster sugar**
30 grams (1 oz) **Epsom salts**

Mix well; bottle and store in a dry place. Use 1 teaspoon to a glass of water.

FRUIT STAINS

Fruit stains on carpet can usually be removed by dampening the stain with warm water then smothering it with powdered borax. Leave for three or four minutes, then sponge with warm water. Repeat two or three times if necessary.

Another method is to drizzle pen remover onto the stain, leave for a minute or two, then sponge with warm water and any good detergent.

On clothing,s dampen the stain, cover it with denture powder, leave for 20 minutes then wash as usual. Fruit stains can usually be removed from a tablecloth by wetting the stained area, then covering it with lots of powdered borax. Let it sit for about 20 minutes then run water from the hot tap through the powder. As the powder dissolves, it will be possible to see if the stain is disappearing. It may be necessary to repeat the treatment. When the stain has almost gone, put the cloth into ½ bucket of warm water with 1 tablespoon of either oxygen bleach washing powder or Bio-Ad powder. Leave for a couple of hours, then wash in the usual way. Sometimes, drizzling Penoff onto a fruit stain works well.

FUR

Never store furs in a plastic bag. Make up a bag from an old sheet with a few herbs such as rosemary, verbena, a cinnamon stick and a few cloves, in it to discourage moths.

GARLIC PASTE

Put 4 to 6 cloves through a garlic crush, or food processor; moisten with a little olive oil and mix to a paste. Put the mixture into jars, cover with clarified butter and store in the refrigerator.

GENTIAN VIOLET

On clothing or carpet, cover the stain with calamine lotion. Leave until it dries then brush or

vacuum off. Or, dab gently with methylated spirits on a cotton wool ball. For a severe stain, particularly on carpet, mix methylated spirits and powdered borax to a creamy paste. Cover the stain, allow to dry, vacuum off and repeat if necessary.

GLASS

Clean mirrors or windows with equal parts water, kerosene, methylated spirits and cloudy ammonia. Polish with a soft dry cloth after cleaning.

Cloudy glasses: Drinking glasses sometimes go cloudy, particularly if a dishwater is used. If this occurs, wash them by hand in hot soapy water with a little cloudy ammonia in the water. Another method is a little salt and vinegar rubbed around the glass with the dishwashing sponge, then rinse well in hot clear water. Store drinking glasses upside down when not in use so that dust does not accumulate in them.

On wood-burning combustion heater doors. When the glass is cold, scrunch up newspaper which has been dipped in a solution of water and methylated spirits to clean both sides of the glass.

GLASS FROSTING

Dissolve Epsom salts in hot water – it needs to be a fairly strong solution but the strength depends on personal needs. Trial and error is the best way to decide quantities. Brush the hot liquid onto the glass. As it cools, the liquid crystallises to provide the frosting.

GLORIA'S CARPET CLEANER

This is my own mixture that I use for all sorts of things, including removing stains from fabric upholstery. Into a 750 millilitre (26 fl oz) bottle with a screw-top, put ¼ cup of methylated spirits, ¼ cup of washing-up liquid, 1 tablespoon of ammonia and 1 dessertspoon of citric acid. Now fill the bottle with cold water, screw the top on and shake before use.

For stains on the carpet, wring out a cloth in warm water, add a dash of the cleaner to the cloth and gently remove the stain. To clean walkway areas, put about ¼ cup of the cleaner into 2 litres (70 fl oz) of water. Wring out a towel in the liquid and sponge the soiled area.

GLOVES – KID

To keep pale-coloured kid gloves from becoming soiled, put them on, then rub your hands through warm flour. Be sure the gloves are quite dry so that flour does not stick to them like a paste. For gloves that are only slightly soiled, use a pale-coloured India rubber. An old-fashioned method for cleaning pale-coloured kid gloves, is to dip a baby's nappy in milk, then rub it over a cake of pure soap. Then, with the glove on the hand, clean with downward strokes, by wiping from the fingers to the wrist. Put them on a thick towel to dry, continually changing their position and pulling the kid to shape correctly as they dry.

GLUE

For superglue there is a solvent available from hardware stores. It should be applied according to the directions on the container.

Many of the new plastic-based glues cannot be removed from fabric without ruining the garment and the only hope is to remove as much as possible before the glue sets. Dab with eucalyptus oil or tea tree oil. If your fingers are stuck together with glue, just pour some eucalyptus oil over them, rub firmly together and the glue will come away easily. Some residual glue marks, particularly those that are tacky to touch, can be removed with either shellite (naphtha) or acetone.

Glues vary in content, depending on the use, and on the manufacturer. It is best to use a solvent for the particular brand of glue. Take care to test the solvent on an inconspicuous area of the fabric, or surface, from which the glue is to be removed.

GOURDS

When properly preserved, gourds make a most attractive table decoration. Pick them from the vines when ripe, leaving a short stem attached. Allow to dry in the sun, but if that is not possible, dry in the oven, at a very low temperature with the door left slightly open. Or dry in the microwave on defrost. When completely dry, spray with a clear lacquer. Gourds are ripe when the stem behind the fruit begins to dry.

GRASS STAINS

Most grass stains can be removed by wringing out a cloth in warm water and adding a dash of wool wash to the cloth, then sponging the stain before washing in the normal way. Remove grass stains as soon as possible. If the material is cotton, use 2 parts methylated spirits to 1 part cloudy ammonia and 3 parts hot water. Soak the stain in the mixture before washing.

GRAVESTONES

For rust marks on granite headstones, commercial rust removers can be used. To ensure the granite remains an even colour, apply the rust remover evenly all over. Wash down thoroughly with clean water on a dull day so the headstone does not dry and leave streaks. Some stonemasons supply a product especially formulated for cleaning granite and it might be worth while getting some quotes for quantity and price. For one or two fairly small marks, try dipping a cloth in a little cold water, then add a little citric acid to the cloth and rub over the mark. Keep the granite of tombstones looking smart by polishing with commercial paste wax. Apply the polish with a clean, soft cloth and use another such cloth to buff up.

GREASE – CAR SEAT

One of the hazards of take-away foods is transporting them. It is so easy for grease, particularly from cooked chickens, to leak onto the car seat. For velour seats, smother a grease stain with lots

of talcum powder and cover the powder with a towel or sheet to keep the powder in place. Now there are two options. Carry passengers sitting on the stain. The sheet will protect their clothing from the powder and the heat from their bodies will draw the grease up into the powder.

The second option is to use a hot iron. Hold the iron over the towel until the grease comes up into the powder. Be careful not to touch the velour with the iron. Any residual stain can be sponged away, working from the outside edge to the centre, with warm soapy water and wool wash.

HAIR BRUSHES

To clean hairbrushes, use warm soapy water with a little cloudy ammonia. Or use shampoo and warm water. If the hairbrush has a wooden back, smear the back of the hairbrush with Vaseline before washing. When it is clean, rinse and wipe the Vaseline off the back. Shake the water out of the bristles and run under a cold tap. Shake and leave to dry.

HAIR COLOUR STAIN

Hair colouring, no matter what the brand, is almost impossible to remove. The first thing to try, is undiluted shampoo. Rub gently and, if it begins to fade the stain, keep repeating the treatment. Rinse the shampoo from the stain after each application. A hairdresser told me she uses Penoff to remove hair colour stains from vinyl couches.

HAIR SPRAY

Hairspray holds the petals of flowers, extending their life; particularly good for spring blossom. To remove hairspray from mirrors, rub with methylated spirits on a soft cloth.

HANDBAGS

Oil or grease stains on leather handbags need to be covered with lots of talcum powder; because the powder is likely to slip off, put the handbag into a pillowslip. Then put the bag onto a sunny window ledge so the warmth will heat through the pillowslip and the powder, pulling the oil or grease up from the leather and into the powder.

Perspiration and body oils from your hands cause white leather to yellow. It is a process of deterioration that cannot be reversed. It can, however, be covered quite successfully with a good leather paint. It will be necessary to clean the leather first. Use a rough towel or a soft brush, and warm water with hair shampoo to clean the leather. When the leather is thoroughly dry, wipe it over with methylated spirits on a soft cloth. Let it dry again before applying the colour. White will probably need two coats to give the desired density.

Reptile or snakeskin handbags can be cleaned by wringing out a rough towel in hot, soapy water and rubbing firmly over the surface of the skin. Once clean, the skin should be rubbed with lanoline lotion, then buffed with a clean, soft cloth.

For beaded handbags use powdered borax. Rub the borax into the handbag and leave for at

least an hour and then shake the powder out. A soft, baby's hairbrush can be used to get rid of any residual powder.

Canvas bags can be washed or scrubbed with warm soapy water. To avoid mildew forming, make sure the bag is dry before storing. For fabric handbags use a powder carpet cleaner. Clean leather handbags with a soft cloth dipped in warm water to which has been added a little cloudy ammonia. When thoroughly dry polish with leather cream, or use a silicone cream car polish. Don't use coloured polish on handbags as it is liable to come off on clothing. Always test first.

Lining should be brushed thoroughly then rubbed with a rag dipped in dry cleaning fluid or shellite (naphtha). Don't make it too damp or interlining, as well as the skin, may be damaged.

Patent leather can look like new if polished with Vaseline and then thoroughly rubbed with a soft, dry cloth.

Vinyl can be washed in warm soapy water to which has been added a little cloudy ammonia. Polish with a cream-type furniture polish or car polish.

HAND CREAM

For sensitive or freckled skin, and to help fade age spots, this hand lotion may help. Steam 10 large cupfuls of elderberry flowers with 2 tablespoons of water for about 5 minutes. Add 250 grams (8 oz) of Vaseline and simmer for about half an hour. Remove from the heat and strain through muslin into jars.

HATS

The first thing to do is to smother the stained area of a leather hat with talcum powder and leave it in a warm place for about 12 hours. The warmth will draw the oil into the powder. Residual staining can be sponged with warm water and a little wool wash. If the hat is suede leather, use a suede brush to buff up the nap. Once the hat is clean, regular use of eucalyptus spray on the inside hatband should stop the build-up of oil and sweat. Spray the band of the hat, then give it a brisk rub with a clean towel.

If a satin brimmed hat has been soiled from being handled, the marks will be body oils, perspiration, and possibly a little make-up. First cover the satin with dry cream of tartar and rub it in with the fingers before brushing off with a dry towel. After this treatment, any soiled areas remaining can be lightly rubbed with a towel wrung out in warm water and wool wash. The cloth should be wrung out until almost dry so the stiffness of the brim will not be affected.

If the satin is discoloured by glue coming from the base underneath the satin, it will need to be replaced. It may only be necessary to cover the existing satin binding with another piece of satin. Cut the fabric on the cross to do this.

White straw hats inevitably yellow as time goes by, even if they are not exposed to the sun. There is no satisfactory way to remove the yellow but painting with white shoe colour can rejuvenate the hat. Care must be taken not to paint any coloured trimming, even if it means removing the trimming and replacing it after the hat has been treated.

HEATER

Moisture and resin, rising from the burning wood, causes creosote to form on the glass door of a wood-burning heater, particularly if the fire is left burning overnight. The heater does not get enough combustible air and, as a result, does not burn efficiently. The best way to remove the creosote is to wipe over the door with a damp cloth to lubricate the surface. Then use a razor blade or scraper to remove the build-up. This can be done when the glass is hot or cold. Or use slightly damp newspaper, which is a good cleaner, and can be discarded into the heater and burnt. To retard the build-up, make sure the wood is thoroughly dry.

HEMLINE

To remove a hemline mark, rub with white vinegar, then wring out a cloth in water and a little cloudy ammonia and iron over the cloth, along the line of the hem on both sides.

HYDRANGEAS – DRYING

Pick hydrangeas when they change to autumn colours and put them, headfirst, into a tub of water for an hour or two. Remove them from the water and shake well. Then scrape and bruise the stems and put into hot water. After two days take them out of the water and stand the stems in $1/3$ glycerine to $2/3$ water for at least five days. Top up each day with water as it evaporates. Don't add any more glycerine. After five to eight days, the hydrangeas are suitable to use in a dried arrangement.

ICE CREAM

On chairs or sofas, sponge with a cloth wrung out in very hot water. When dry, sponge with dry-cleaning fluid. If very obstinate, sponge again with lukewarm water and any good detergent. Wipe clean with a soft dry cloth. On clothing, sponge with fairly hot water and any good detergent or pure soap.

INDOOR PLANTS

Indoor plants add softness to a room but they need care. Don't polish the leaves with oil: it could burn them. For happier plants, use milk with about 1 teaspoon to 1 cup of water. During the winter, ferns like a drink daily because of the reduced humidity caused by heating. Try to keep ferns away from the direct source of heat. An easy way to increase the humidity around indoor plants is to keep them sprayed with water. Never stand indoor plants on carpet. Put a plate or saucer under the plant to prevent water and earth from staining the carpet.

INK

Test before using any method to remove ink stains.

Ballpoint pen marks can be removed from most surfaces with pen remover (from newsagents and supermarkets). On fabric, where possible, put cottonwool or kitchen paper under the mark, then dab the stain with pen remover on cottonwool. Change the cottonwool frequently to

avoid transferring the mark back to the fabric. Once the marks fade, sponge with warm water and any good detergent.

On leather, use pen remover sparingly and be sure to test on an inconspicuous area before use.

On wood, put pen remover onto a cottonwool pad and rub with the grain. Polish afterwards.

Marks from felt-tipped pens are almost impossible to remove. Remember the ink they contain is designed by manufacturers to be permanent. If pen remover will not remove the mark, try making a paste with equal parts of talcum powder and powdered borax mixed with methylated spirits. Cover the stain and leave for about an hour, then wash with wool wash. If it doesn't remove the mark entirely, it may lighten sufficiently to make it less noticeable.

Printers' and some indelible inks. Dissolve 1 dessertspoon of oxalic acid (from pharmacists) in about a breakfast cup of warm water. Put the stained part on a folded towel or cloth and dab with clean pieces of cottonwool dipped in the solution. Do not rub. When the stain has faded, rinse thoroughly with bicarbonate of soda (baking soda) added to the rinsing water.

INSECTS

Old-fashioned citronella, available from pharmacists, is very good to deter many insects. It can either be dabbed on face and hands, or a few drops dabbed onto a tissue or piece of cottonwool will help to keep the insects away.

INSECT BITES

Raw onion juice rubbed onto an insect bite will help to relieve the painful itch. Or, rub the affected area with methylated spirits, or, dab the bite with eucalyptus oil.

IODINE

Applying bottled mustard over the stain can treat iodine stains. Remove the mustard and sponge any residual stain with methylated spirits on a dry cloth.

IVORY – TO WHITEN

The traditional method for bleaching ivory was to rub it with finely ground pumice stone and water. Then while it was still wet, it was exposed, under glass, to the sun. This method prevented it from drying or cracking.

Another method was to dip it, for no more than 5 minutes at a time, in 1 part chlorine bleach to 6 parts water. Ivory is no longer traded so the value of beautifully carved pieces will increase as time goes by. Delicately carved pieces would be impossible to bleach by the traditional method without breaking some of the very fine lattice-like design. The chlorine bleach dip is possible, but risky. Best done by a professional restorer.

JAM STAINS

Jam stains can be removed from almost any fabric or surface by sponging with a solution made

with 500 millilitres (16 fl oz) of warm water to 30 grams (1 oz) of borax.

JEWELLERY

Most jewellery can be washed in hot soapy water. Use pure soap, not detergent. For filigree and marcasite, leave pieces to soak for half an hour to loosen dirt that can build up in the pattern. An old, very soft toothbrush can be used for stubborn dirt. Once clean, rinse the jewellery in warm water with a little methylated spirits in it. Toothpaste is also good for cleaning jewellery but be sure to wash all the paste off. The lustre of jewellery is enhanced with continual wear.

JAG

Some jugs always drip onto the table or table cloth after use. A little butter or glycerine smeared under the lip will stop a jug from dripping. An easier method is to put a saucer under the jug and then train the family to use it.

KEYS

Bore a hole off-centre before putting the front door key on your key ring. The key will stand out at an angle and is easily found in the dark.

KNITTING

Before knitting, dust talcum powder over your hands to stop them from becoming sticky and slowing you down. Put the ball of wool into a plastic container with a hole in the lid for the wool to feed through. Tape around the hole so the wool doesn't catch. This will keep the wool clean and untangled. Use dark needles for light coloured wool and light needles for dark wool. It makes it much easier to count stitches. Be sure to buy wool that is suitable for your needs. Always buy a little extra for repairs.

LABELS

For unwanted labels on furniture, soak a cloth in eucalyptus oil, put over the label, leave for about three minutes only, and it should come away. Test on an inconspicuous area first.

The sticky substance under labels on glass can often be removed by rubbing with Brasso or metal polish. Printed labels on material can sometimes be removed by sponging lightly with methylated spirits. Then place downwards on paper towel, cover the back of the garment with a clean dry cloth and press with a steam iron.

To remove labels from bottles or jars, leave them in a sink filled with hot water for a while. Or, put in the dishwasher, but don't forget to remove the label from the draining cover. Marks left by sticky labels can often be removed from refrigerators by dabbing with a little eucalyptus oil on a cottonwool pad. Other things worth trying are toothpaste, nail enamel solvent, or acetone. To remove stickers from shiny surfaces, put wet newspaper over the sticker, and leave for 15 to 25 minutes, by which time it can usually be removed without much trouble. Another method is to

cover the sticker with wet cellophane or plastic. Leave for about half an hour before removing the plastic and peeling the sticker off. Some stickers can be removed by smothering them with oil. Another method is to cover them with warm butter or margarine. Brasso also works well. The sticky residue left behind after the label is removed can be rubbed with toothpaste, eucalyptus oil or acetone.

LACE

Don't iron directly onto lace as the point of the iron will often catch the lace and tear it. Always cover with a cloth before ironing. To keep lace looking crisp and fresh it can be washed in gum arabic water. From a shop which sells artist supplies, buy 125 grams (4 oz) of fine white gum arabic powder. Put it in a bowl and add 1 litre (2 pints) of boiling water. Stir with a wooden spoon until the gum melts, then strain through a piece of muslin into a bottle; cork, and keep for use as needed.

An average proportion to use is 1 tablespoon gum water to 1 cupful of water, but this can vary according to the stiffness desired. This solution was always considered to be a superior starch for fine lace and crochet.

LAMINATED SURFACES

After years of use and cleaning, particularly with abrasive cleaners, laminated surfaces lose their lustre and colour. While there are still years of life left in the laminate, it can look a little tired. Wash the surface with hot water and any good detergent. Let it dry then wipe it over with methylated spirits to be sure it is grease free. Now smooth a colour over the surface. A matching shoe colorant would probably be suitable. Use a lighter colour than required and build it up with two or three coats. When the colour is evenly spread all over, and dry, polish it with commercial paste wax and buff up with a soft, dry cloth. Polish it regularly with the wax to maintain the surface and the colour.

LAMINEX – WOOD GRAIN

Wood-grain laminex cupboards should only need to be washed with hot water and any good detergent. Don't go overboard with the use of detergent or the laminex will dry streaky. If there is a need for an additional shine, polish with commercial paste wax and buff up with a soft, dry cloth.

LAMPSHADES

Water-based cleaners should not be used on fabric covered lampshades because the wire frames are likely to rust through to the fabric. One of the safest ways to clean a lamp shade is to rub with dry shampoo. Or mix together 2 tablespoons powdered borax, 1 tablespoon salt and 2 teaspoons shellite (naphtha) and use the palms of your hands to rub the mixture all over the lampshade. Leave for half an hour then brush off with a soft brush. Or, spray the lampshade with carpet stain remover, following the instructions on the can.

Clean parchment lampshades with a handful of starch dissolved in a cup and a half of warm water. Rub the mixture into the shade with a sponge. Be sure not to get the sponge or the lampshade too wet. When the lampshade is clean, go over it with a damp sponge to remove the starch. If the lampshade is very dirty, use more starch in the mixture.

It would be better to use a powder cleaner for a velvet lampshade. Make up a mixture, using 4 tablespoons of powdered borax, 4 tablespoons of salt, and 4 tablespoons of shellite (naphtha). It is a slightly damp powder. Rub it into the nap of the velvet, then rub briskly with a clean, rough towel. Repeat, if necessary.

LAVENDER – DRYING

Pick the long stems before the flowers fall, tie in bunches and hang, upside down, in a dark place. When fully dried, skim the flowers free of the stalk and to each 225 grams (8 oz) of flowers add 15 grams (½ oz) each of dried thyme and mint, 7 grams (¼ oz) of caraway seeds and 1 ground clove. Mix altogether with 15 grams (½ oz) salt and put into bags. The bags are good for perfuming drawers and wardrobes. Highly scented things help to keep moths away.

LICE

Children sometimes bring home lice in their hair or clothing. The eggs, called nits, can be dropped onto clothing and carpet around the house. Fresh air, sunshine and disinfectants are the remedies for lice. If they are in clothing, the clothes should be disinfected as much as possible, put out into the air, preferably sunshine, turned inside out so that the air and sun can get into all the seams. A hot iron rubbed over clothes will kill the nits. Or put the clothes into the tumble drier for about 20 minutes.

Kerosene is the old-fashioned treatment for head lice, but many schools supply free shampoo for the treatment of head lice. For the treatment of nits it is a good idea to wash the hair with vinegar and water, then comb with a very fine comb. Pharmacists carry special combs for nits and will advise on commercial treatments for lice.

LINSEED OIL

There are two types of linseed oil: raw and boiled. Never try to boil linseed oil yourself. It needs to be done commercially.

Wooden floors are sometimes polished with linseed oil that can build up, particularly around the edges. To remove build-up, rub with a piece of old towelling dipped in a mixture of half turpentine and half brown vinegar, then wash with hot soapy water.

LIPSTICK

First try cold water to remove a lipstick stain from fabric. If that doesn't work, put glycerine on the stain, leave for a few hours then wash in hot, soapy water. For a lipstick of very intense colour, drizzle a few drops of pen remover on the stain, dab with dry cloth and sponge any residual mark with warm water and wool wash.

LIQUEUR – BRANDY

1$^{1}/_{3}$ cups **water**

1½ cups **sugar**

1 heaped **dessertspoon cocoa**

3 drops **glycerine**

½ teaspoon **vanilla essence**

1¾ cups **brandy**

Put water, sugar and cocoa into a saucepan and bring to the boil. Simmer for 20 minutes. Remove from the heat and add glycerine and vanilla essence. When cold add the brandy. Bottle and cork.

LIQUEUR – CHERRY BRANDY

Here is the recipe I use for cherry brandy:

1½ cups **hot water**

1 cup **sugar**

1 teaspoon **cochineal or red colouring**

1 teaspoon **almond essence**

1 cup **brandy**

Dissolve sugar, cochineal and almond essence. When cold, add brandy and bottle. It is better left for at least four weeks before drinking.

LIQUEUR – COFFEE

1 cup **sugar**

1 cup **hot water**

4 heaped teaspoon **coffee powder**

1 cup **rum or brandy**

Dissolve sugar and coffee in hot water, add a little vanilla essence. Allow to cool, add rum or brandy. Keep for two weeks before using.

LIQUEUR – CRÈME DE MENTHE

1½ cups **hot water**

1 cup **brandy**

2 teaspoons **glycerine**

1 cup **sugar**

1 teaspoon **peppermint essence**

Green food colouring

Mix well together and bottle.

LIQUEUR – IRISH COFFEE

1½ cups **water**

1¹/3 cups **sugar**

1 tablespoon **instant coffee**

3 drops **glycerine**

1 teaspoon **vanilla**

1 cup **brandy**

Bring water, sugar and coffee to the boil and simmer for 30 minutes. Remove from the heat and stir in glycerine, vanilla and brandy. Bottle when cold.

LIQUEUR – IRISH CREAM

3 **eggs**

400 grams (14 oz) **condensed milk**

1 cup **whisky**

300 millilitres (10 oz) **cream**

1½ tablespoons **chocolate topping**

1 teaspoon **vanilla essence**

Blend for 1 minute and bottle.

LIQUEUR – ORANGE

Finely peel 6 oranges (no pith) then chop the peel. Squeeze the juice and put with the peel, into a jar with 60 grams (2 oz) of crushed coriander seeds and 1 cinnamon stick. Melt 470 grams (1 lb) sugar until it becomes syrup and add to the jar with 1 litres (2 pints) of gin. Seal and leave for three months then strain through blotting paper. Bottle and leave for another three months.

LIQUID PAPER

Mineral turpentine will remove Liquid Paper stains. On hard surfaces, test first to make sure the surface will not be damaged.

On clothing, test on an inside seam to ensure that colour will not run. Put some mineral turpentine onto a clean cloth and dab the white correction fluid stain away. Then sponge with warm water and detergent to get rid of the stain remover.

LIZARD SKIN

Wring out a clean, soft cloth in warm water. Add a few drops of hydrogen peroxide to the cloth and wipe all over the skin. Once the skin is clean, go over it with a fine cream to keep it soft. A good face cream is suitable.

LUREX

Gold and silver lurex and embroidery threads can be dry cleaned, but they sometimes become dull. To brighten them, sprinkle with a little cream of tartar and gently rub with a soft brush.

MARBLE

To clean and freshen marble, rub with a cloth dipped in turpentine. If it is badly stained, use a paste made 1 one part bleach to 1 part cold water. Bees wax polish gives a good surface to marble. An alternative to bees wax is commercial paste wax.

For soft marble that seems to mark easily, treat the mark with a very fine powder cleanser mixed to a paste with methylated spirits. Rub in with the fingers, or a soft cloth, and when the mark has disappeared, polish with bees wax furniture polish or commercial paste wax. You may need to repeat this three or four times.

If the mark is a coloured stain from claret, etc., add some bleach to the paste, or try toothpaste. Smoke-stained marble can be rubbed over with a mixture of bleach and water. Use 4 parts water to 1 part bleach. Finish by polishing with bees wax.

New synthetic marble needs no more care than soap and water. It is much lighter in weight than real marble and practically indestructible.

MARBLE VANITY TOPS

Marble vanity tops can be polished to a fine sheen with commercial paste wax. The best way to apply it is to wring out a cloth in hot water. The cloth should be wrung out until it is almost dry. Then apply some wax to the cloth and thoroughly cover the marble tops. Buff up with a soft, dry cloth and repeat the procedure once a week until the surface shines like new.

MARCASITE

Bracelets and brooches made of marcasite become dull very quickly, especially if not being used. The best way to bring them to a bright shine is to rub firmly with soft tissue paper.

MARKING PENS

Marking pens, used to identify clothing, contain indelible ink that is designed to remain intact when garments are washed or dry cleaned. This means that anything used to remove the identification will probably ruin the garment. If you need to change the identification, I suggest you write the new identification on tape, then sew the tape over the old name.

MASKING TAPE

A good masking tape should peel off easily when the job is finished. A little methylated spirits will remove the residue. For more difficult tape, when the stickiness won't seem to budge, or has been left for too long, use shellite (naphtha), Brasso or lacquer thinner.

MASONIC APRON

Sprinkle carpet-cleaning powder all over the apron. Rub it in with the palms of your hand. If the apron is particularly grubby this may not clean the surrounding ribbon. For extra treatment, cover the ribbon with any good bleach powder, wring out a cloth until almost dry and rub the powder into the ribbon with the cloth. A nailbrush worked in the same direction as the grosgrain, is also a good idea. Make sure you don't get any moisture onto the skin when cleaning the ribbon. If the skin has yellowed, paint it carefully with white shoe cleaner. Rubbing with dry cream of tartar can clean gold braid or thread on Masonic aprons.

MERCUROCHROME

Cover the mercurochrome stain on the carpet with calamine lotion, allow it to dry, then brush off. On fabric, sponge the mercurochrome stain with equal quantities of methylated spirits and water, then work glycerine into the stain, wash in soapy water and rinse.

MICE

If you can find where mice are coming in, and they have learned to ignore a trap, pack around their entrance with steel wool. Another method is to sprinkle around cupboards and under the sink with oil of peppermint, or oil of cloves, or cayenne pepper. Lots of highly scented talcum powder sometimes helps. In desperation, use a rat poison powder but be careful that children and animals cannot get anywhere near it. A tasty temptation is to load the mouse-trap with raw bacon and see if they can resist it.

MILDEW

You must kill the fungus in order to remove mildew. Hot sun will kill it. For white, natural-fibre materials, use weak bleach, 1 part bleach to 4 parts water. On dark material, sponge with antiseptic disinfectant. A paste of salt and lemon juice is good for delicate fabrics.

For stubborn stains on clothes, make a paste of powdered starch and water and pack over the stain. Leave until it is perfectly dry, re-damp and allow it to dry again, preferably in the fresh air. Repeat until the mildew marks have completely disappeared.

On coloured fabric, salt and lemon juice mixed together or cream of tartar and lemon juice mixed to a paste are less likely to fade colour while removing mould marks. Because it is a gentle method of removing stains, it will not be as miraculously effective as some of the commercial cleaners, so stains may need to be treated two or three times. Sponging with 1 tablespoon of antiseptic disinfectant in a litre of warm water will kill the mould spores. Residual staining can be rubbed with pure soap, then rubbed between the hands or gently scrubbed with a soft brush before washing the article in the normal manner.

On wallpaper, hold a folded towel over the spot with one hand, while you hold a heated iron over the towel with the other hand. Don't have the iron too hot as you will not want to mark the wallpaper. The towel will absorb any moisture from the mildewed area and at the same time,

kill the mould. Any excess mildew can be brushed off. If any marks remain, rub over with bread that is two days old.

MILK – SPILT

Milk spilt in the car should be mopped up with cold, not hot, water. Hot water cooks the milk into the fibres of the fabric, making it harder to remove. If possible, remove the car seats and clean the underside as well as the surface. Use lukewarm water and wool wash. Mop up as much of the moisture as possible with a thick, dry towel, then sprinkle lots of powdered borax over the top and underside of the car seat. This will serve to absorb both smell and moisture. Leave for as long as possible, then brush or vacuum off and spray both sides with commercial odour remover.

MIRRORS

To clean mirrors, wring out a cloth in warm water, put methylated spirits on the cloth and rub over the glass to remove the dirt. Then polish with a soft, dry cloth. If the frames are gilt take care not to touch the frames with the methylated spirits. Gilt frames can be cleaned by rubbing with a cut lemon then sponging with a solution of ½ litre (1 pint) water and 1 tablespoon bicarbonate of soda (baking soda). Rub gently with a soft cloth and polish with chamois leather. A slice of two-day-old bread also cleans gilt frames.

MIRROR SCRATCHES

Light scratches on mirrors can sometimes be removed by rubbing with jewellers rouge. Put the rouge paste on to a soft cloth and rub the scratches. Clean the rouge off with methylated spirits on a soft cloth.

MOSQUITOES

For mosquitoes, use citronella. A few drops on a tissue or a piece of cottonwool, dropped here and there, will retain the pungency and repel the pests. Citronella can be dabbed directly onto the skin to keep mosquitoes from biting. Another hint, particularly for campers, is creosote, available from hardware and paint stores. Dip a piece of rag into creosote, put it where the mosquitoes are congregating. Commercial repellents are excellent but some people are allergic to them.

To make your own citronella candles, soak the string to be used for the wicks, in citronella, for about twenty-four hours. As the citronella-soaked wick burns, the aroma will turn the mosquitoes away.

MOTHER-OF-PEARL

Do not use hot soapy water on mother-of-pearl. Rub with a soft cloth dipped in olive oil. Polish with silk. Another method is to rub with Vaseline, then polish.

MOTHS

Spice bags are good for deterring moths, either in the pantry, or when storing clothes. To make spice bags, bring to the boil, 2 cups of vinegar, 1 tablespoon each of cloves, grated ginger, lemon rind and orange rind, 1 teaspoon of dried chilli and 2 bay leaves. Simmer for 15 minutes, then strain and cool. Discard the liquid and put spice into gauze, or similar fabric bags. Secure the tops of the bags and use as required. These spice bags are also good to hang on coathangers in the wardrobe.

MOULD

High humidity provides perfect conditions for mould spores to grow. To discourage the growth of mould, alter the conditions to allow a flow of air. Open windows and doors, plus ceiling fans, will help. Wardrobe doors in the tropics should be louvred and, if not, leave doors open as much as possible. Don't put clothes into wardrobes until they have been aired. Anything that has been steam ironed should not even be folded until it is aired. All wardrobes and closets should have at least one container of damp remover in them. The containers need regular attention so read the instructions carefully.

Always add antiseptic disinfectant or household disinfectant to the water when washing clothes or linen. To rid the walls of mould, scrub them with hot water and antiseptic disinfectant. Leave to dry, then use a hair dryer on hot for a final dry.

Mould on the ceiling is best treated with one of the commercial removers. Read the instructions on the container and follow them carefully. Wear rubber gloves and protect eyes and clothes. Remove, or cover, anything that might be splashed. Make sure the window or the door is left open to dissipate the fumes.

Most white windcheaters are made with a mixture of cotton and synthetic fibre and it is unwise to use chlorine bleach. When the garment is patterned with fabric paint, it is difficult to find anything that is strong enough to remove the mould without ruining the design. It is worth making a creamy paste with powdered starch and lemon juice, then applying it to the mildewed area, taking care to avoid the painted design. Rub it in with the fingers so that the paste gets in behind the knit of the fabric. Leave it until the paste dries, brush it off, and repeat if necessary.

White cotton garments can be soaked for two or three hours in a bleach solution. Use about 1 part bleach to 6 parts water. Or, cover the stain with a paste made with lemon juice and salt. Leave it overnight, then wash the garment in the normal way. It may be necessary to repeat the treatment two or three times.

To remove mould from washable fabric, always begin with the safest method. First sponge with antiseptic disinfectant to kill the mould spores. Next, mix salt and lemon juice to a paste, cover the mould stains, leave for at least two hours, brush off and repeat two or three times. Because it is the most gentle method, this treatment will not always work so it will be necessary to move to the next treatment which is to soak the garment overnight in cold water and about two tablespoons of oxygen bleach such as nappy-soaking powder or oxygen bleach washing

powder. After soaking, wash in hot water and any good detergent. Do not use chlorine bleach unless you are sure the fabric is white, pure cotton or linen. Discolouring or blackish marks on the back of a rubber bath mat is an indication of the presence of mould. Put the bath mat into the bath and scrub it with a stiff brush and a weak solution of chlorine bleach. Use about 1 part bleach to 6 parts water. It is a good idea to do this regularly, about once a month, to keep the mould spores at bay. Hang the bath mat to dry after each use.

Mould can be removed by soaking white cotton towels in a bleach solution. Use about 1 part bleach to 6 parts water. Coloured, or synthetic-fibre towels, should be soaked overnight in hot water and about a tablespoon of antiseptic disinfectant to kill the mould. Wash with nappy-soaking powder to get rid of the mould marks.

Mildew on suits and jackets that have been kept in a closed wardrobe can usually be removed by wringing out a cloth in hot water, adding a dash of neat antiseptic disinfectant to the cloth, then sponging the spots. When the spots have been removed, steam iron the garments to ensure all the mould spores are killed. Hang the clothes in an airy place to dry thoroughly before putting them back in a wardrobe.

Mould can be removed from furniture by sponging with a solution made from 1 teaspoon of cloudy ammonia to ¼ litre (½ pint) of hot water. Wipe dry very quickly. Or, wring out a cloth in very hot water, add a dash of neat antiseptic disinfectant and wipe with the grain of the wood. Dry quickly with a thick towel.

In bathrooms use 1 part bleach to 4 parts water or one of the commercial mould removers. Condensation can cause mould to grow on curtain linings. Wring out a cloth in very hot water, add a dash of antiseptic disinfectant to the cloth and rub the stains. Any residual marks can, be removed by sponging with a cloth wrung out in a solution of 1 part bleach to 6 parts water.

Mildew on a mattress can be removed by covering the stains with a mixture made with 1 tablespoon powdered borax and 1 dessertspoon bleach. Leave for an hour, then use a soft brush to ensure the powder gets into the weave of the fabric. Vacuum off, sponge with a towel wrung out in hot water and repeat the treatment if necessary. If the mattress is only lightly mildewed, lemon juice can be used instead of bleach.

Scrub a tent with a strong solution of salt and water. One bucket of cold water and 250 grams (8 oz) salt. It wouldn't hurt to add more salt if the mildew is extensive. It is always a good idea to test on a small inconspicuous area before beginning any treatment.

NAIL POLISH

The best way to remove nail polish from fabric is with nail enamel solvent. Unfortunately, the brand name polishes seem to have dropped a solvent from their range of products. The other alternative is to use acetone or lacquer thinner. Put a cottonwool ball under the stain, carefully add a little solvent to the stain, cover immediately with another cottonwool ball and pat the colour from the garment to the cottonwool balls.

Keep changing the cottonwool until the colour disappears, then dab with eucalyptus oil and

wash the garment in the usual way. Test on an inside seam first to see how the treatment reacts with the fabric.

NAILS

Equal parts of sugar, lemon juice and oil can clean stained fingernails.

NAPTHALENE

It is recommended you do not use naphthalene when packing children's bedding or clothing. If you suspect that bedding and clothing has been stored in naphthalene, air the items out of doors for three days prior to use.

NEWSPAPER CUTTINGS

As newspaper deteriorates quickly, it is important to preserve it carefully. The best way to preserve newspaper cuttings is to paste the cuttings to acid-free paper with wallpaper glue. Use a glue with the least amount of insecticide. Just dab a little here and there on the cuttings. Never use sticky tape or plastic. Paper is affected by changes in humidity, so store in a well-aired, dry place.

NICKEL

Rub daily with a dry cloth moistened with methylated spirits. Polish with a soft dry cloth afterwards.

NICOTINE

For nicotine-stained fingers, put 1 teaspoon of sugar into the palm of your hand, add a squeeze of lemon juice and rub over the stains.

ODOURS

For cars or wardrobes, a few drops of commerical odour neutraliser on a small piece of cottonwool will keep most odours at bay.

When cooking cauliflower or cabbage put a couple of slices of bread in the pot, or a couple of slices of lemon. This will save the strong smell going through the house. Cooking in a little milk also reduces the smell.

The odour from cigarette butts will disappear with a few slices of lemon in a bucket of water placed in the room. Use the same treatment to get rid of the smell of fresh paint. Burning a candle also works.

Milk spilt in the car or on carpet should be sponged with wool wash and when dry sprinkled with a few drops of commerical odour neutraliser. Another method is to make a paste with cream of tartar, cover the stained area, leave it to dry, then brush off.

To remove the smell of onions from your hands, rub baking powder over palms and fingers, then rinse.

Plastic containers should be washed thoroughly in plenty of hot water to which a little bleach has been added. Rinse, dry and put in the deep freeze for an hour or so.

In the refrigerator use a small saucer of dry mustard or a small container of bicarbonate of soda (baking soda). Leave it in the refrigerator and replace every two months.

The smell of fish can be removed from a cooking utensil by sprinkling it with dry mustard. Leave it for a while, then wash in the normal way.

Baby vomit smell should be treated quickly with a paste made from bicarbonate of soda (baking soda) and water. Cover the stain, leave for an hour, then sponge or wash.

For a smell that stays in the microwave oven, put the peel from juiced oranges into the oven and microwave on high for two minutes.

New towels and cotton fabrics, particularly from third world countries, sometimes have an unpleasant smell, probably from the type of finish used before the fibre is woven. One quarter cup of methylated spirits added to the wash is usually sufficient to solve the problem. Test for colourfastness.

For cat urine on floorboards, scrub with hot water and any good disinfectant, paying particular attention to the joins in the floorboards. Once the floor is dry, spray with a commercial odour neutraliser. It may be necessary to spray every two or three days until the smell of cat urine dissipates.

To deodorise the kitchen after cooking, fill one or two small dishes with bicarbonate of soda (baking soda) and put them near the stove. The bicarbonate of soda (baking soda) should be replaced about once a month, depending on how much cooking has been done, and also on how much the kitchen is able to be aired.

On clothes, it is worth trying odour neutraliser. Spray the clothing inside and out, then leave in the air for at least an hour. if the smell persists, wash the clothes in warm water with some antiseptic disinfectant in the water. When it is dry, spray with odour neutraliser,

ODOUR – GLORIA'S ROOM FRESHENER

For ridding a room of unwanted odours, such as cigarette smoke or animals, or just the stale smell of a house that has been closed for a period of time.

Mix together 20 drops each of lavender oil, eucalyptus oil, tea tree oil, clove oil and citronella. Add 200 millilitres (7 fl oz) of mineral water and 100 millilitres (3 fl oz) of methylated spirits. Put the mixture into a bottle with a spray pump. Label the bottle and shake before using.

It is quite safe to spray the carpet, but be careful not to spray the mixture on oil paintings, watercolours that are not under glass, or on polished wood surfaces.

OIL

For oil spills on vinyl, smother the stain with talcum powder and leave for 24 hours. Remove the powder and sponge with eucalyptus oil. Repeat, if necessary.

On clothing or carpet, pack the oil stain with plenty of talcum powder. Cover the talcum powder with paper towel. Now hold a hot iron over the paper, but under no circumstances push

down on the iron. Just hold it lightly on the paper to let the heat absorb the oil into the powder. Repeat, if necessary.

On wallpaper rub gently with bread which is two days old. If that doesn't work, hold three layers of kitchen paper over the stain and press with a fairly hot iron. On concrete, oil can be removed by mixing 6 parts kerosene with 1 part detergent. Leave for 5 minutes and hose off. Or cover the stain with powdered cement, leave for 24 hours, then brush off. Another method is to use ½ phenyl, ½ hot water, and scrub with a stiff broom.

On shoes, pack the stain with a powder of 2 tablespoons powdered borax, 1 tablespoon salt and 2 teaspoons shellite (naphtha) or dry cleaning fluid. Put the shoe into a plastic bag to contain the powder and leave on a sunny window ledge for at least 12 hours. Repeat if necessary, then polish with a good matching-colour shoe polish. Smother the oil stains on sheets with talcum powder, roll them up and put in a warm place for a few days. Shake the powder off. Some powder will remain on the oil stains. Rub lightly then put into the washing machine with your favourite detergent and add about 2 tablespoons of household disinfectant to the wash.

By the way, it will not hurt to shake the powder from the sheets onto the carpet. It helps to clean the carpet.

ORANGE CORDIAL STAINS

Orange cordial is one of the most difficult stains to remove. There is no magic solution, and not all orange cordial stains respond to the same treatment. I have had some success by drizzling a few drops of pen remover onto the stain, then immediately covering it with powdered borax. Leave for about two hours, brush or vacuum off, then sponge any residual stain with a cloth wrung out in warm water with a dash of methylated spirits in it.

Another method I have had success with, is to dampen the stain, cover it with denture powder, leave for 2 or 3 hours, vacuum off, then sponge with a cloth wrung out in warm water and nappy-soaking powder.

PAINT – ACRYLIC

Water-based or acrylic paints can be removed from clothing with cold water, but only when the stain is still fresh. Once dry, water-based paint stains are almost impossible to remove. It is worth trying acetone, used in the same manner as turpentine on oil paint, but test first to see how the acetone affects the fabric. If that doesn't work, I suggest embroidery, applique, or some other form of cover to hide the stain.

PAINTING

Before painting anything, make sure you have at hand the correct remedy for the splatters that will certainly occur.

For acrylic or water-based paint, you will need a clean rag and water. On clothing this type of paint gets into the fibres and can be removed only while the paint is still wet.

For oil-based or enamel paint, put turpentine onto a clean cloth, then dab the stain, changing the area of the cloth from time to time, so that paint is not transferred back to the garment.

Knitted fabrics need to be stretched with the fingers for stain removal in order to get to the back of each stitch.

To reduce clean-ups when painting, put a large runner of plastic, or an old sheet, over the area where the drips are likely to happen. Put old socks, or plastic bags, over your shoes. Use rubber bands to secure a rag over the handset of the phone before painting begins. And because you might have to answer the door, put a plastic bag over the door handle. Before replacing the lid on a paint tin, rest a piece of plastic on top of the paint. It keeps the air out and stops a skin from forming.

Stop loose bristles from shedding onto fresh paint by combing or brushing the paintbrush before work begins.

Paint wrought iron with a sponge instead of a brush, it is easier and gives a better finish. Paint fly screens horizontally and the paint is less likely to drip and fill the mesh. Use a piece of old carpet instead of a brush to paint screens. Put a coat of vinegar on concrete before painting. It helps to prevent peeling.

To re-paint cane, strip off any old paint, using a commercial stripper. Wash off with warm, soapy water and leave for at least a week before repainting.

An onion, sliced and on a plate, will help to remove the smell of paint from a room. Another method is to slice 3 or 4 lemons into a bucket of hot water and leave in the room.

PAINTINGS

Oil paintings should be dusted only with a soft brush. Do it regularly to prevent dust build-up. Never rub an oil painting with a cloth. The best way to store paintings is to hang them on a wall. If they must be packed away, make sure the storage area is dry and airy so that mould will not grow. Don't stack paintings. Air should be allowed to circulate between them.

PARSLEY

Parsley stains can be removed by sponging with warm water and borax. Parsley can be washed, dried, chopped and frozen for continual use straight from the freezer. After planting parsley seed pour boiling water over it and it will germinate within three weeks.

PEARLS

Talcum powder is good for returning the original lustre of pearls, but for make-up stains it may be necessary to resort to stronger treatment. Dissolve a little shampoo in hot water, then wring out a cloth in the water and wipe the pearls, taking care not to get the stringing agent wet. A little water will not hurt catgut, cotton or whatever else has been used for stringing, but leave the pearls lying flat until no moisture remains. The other alternative is to take them to a jeweller for cleaning.

PERFUME

Perfume stains on white painted wood should be rubbed with eucalyptus oil on a soft cloth. Then, if the stain persists, put a cotton bud into neat bleach and gently apply it to the stain. Wipe the bleach away quickly with a wet cloth.

If perfume is spilt on clothing, act quickly. Rub in a little glycerine, leave for a couple of hours, then wash in warm soapy water and rinse well. If the garment is non-washable sponge gently with warm water and borax.

Don't spray perfume when standing close to a polished timber dressing table. It is easy for the fine spray to cover the timber surface. The spirit in the perfume will destroy the polished surface of the wood.

PETROLEUM JELLY

If on clothing, or carpet, sponge the stain with a clean cloth dipped in a little kerosene.

PETS

If pets shed hair or fur on couches, chairs or carpets, dampen a plastic sponge with water and a little vinegar and wipe over it. It will pick up the hair or fur very quickly. For pets with a heavy animal smell, sprinkle a little citronella or commerical odour neutraliser around where they sit, or sprinkle either on a cloth and leave in the same area. Brewers yeast rubbed on dogs' coats helps to prevent fleas.

To keep pets off the garden use a bird and animal repellent.

PEWTER

To keep the lovely soft glow of pewter, polish it regularly with powdered whiting mixed with a little oil. Wash pewter in warm water and washing-up liquid. Be sure to rinse in hot water, and dry naturaly. Polish with a soft cloth.

Another method is to use very hot water and soap-impregnated steel wool pads. Rub all over the surface of the pewter until it is evenly shiny, then wash and rinse in hot water. Dry with a soft cloth. Wash and dry the pewter once more, then seal and polish with commercial paste wax. This method keeps pewter looking brilliant for years before it needs doing again but it is not recommended for pewter purists or museum collections.

PHOTOGRAPHS

Before putting photographs under glass, in a frame, be sure the glass is completely dry. Even with care, humid conditions can cause the surface coating of a photograph to stick to the glass. Some of the photo processing shops might be prepared to attempt the removal but I doubt they would guarantee the result.

If you're prepared to take the risk, remove the glass from the frame with the photograph attached, then immerse it, photo uppermost, in just enough tepid water to cover the glass. In about ten minutes the photograph should float off the glass. Remove the photo and put it, face up, on a

flat, paper-covered surface to dry. It would be better to use a photographic emulsion for a precious colour photo, but often taking the risk with the water treatment gets the result.

PIANO KEYS

From David Bernard, a reader who worked for a piano refurbishment company 30 years ago, I discovered the professional method of restoring piano keys. The keys are removed and lightly sanded. Ivory keys are then put out in the sun with a constant application of hydrogen peroxide. After several days, the keys will return to the original colour. They are then lightly buffed to give a smooth finish.

Ivory keys can be recognised by the fact that they are in two pieces and the seam can be found where the large section of the key joins the long narrow section. Piano keys that are made from a composition, or from celluloid, are always in one piece and can only be treated by sanding and buffing.

For simply doing the best you can without calling in a professional restorer, wipe the keys regularly with methylated spirits on a warm, soft, cloth. For ivory keys, after wiping, leave the piano lid open as often as possible. Leaving the lid open can help prevent yellowing, but it will be necessary to dust more often.

PILLING

Fluff or lint balls that gather on some fabrics can be removed with a small gadget made specifically for the purpose. It looks like a miniature electric razor. There are small hand-held ones that cost no more than a few dollars, going up to battery operated, then to the more sophisticated electric variety. They are usually sold in sewing machine specialty shops.

Another method is to wring out a plastic kitchen cloth until it is almost dry, then brush the pilling away. Stretch the fabric and brush in one direction. Another important point: be sure that any excess colour is removed from the plastic before using it.

The latest idea for this problem comes from a reader who tells me that she has saved her sanity using the humble, disposable shaver to remove pilling. She also uses it to remove the bits of tissue that sometimes get into the washing machine by mistake.

PLAY DOUGH

To make play dough, the children will need a sieve, a saucepan, a wooden spoon, and a chopping board. Play-dough mixture can be made with 1 cup flour, 1 cup salt, 2 tablespoons cream of tartar, 1 cup water, 1 tablespoon vegetable oil and a few drops of food colouring. Sift flour, salt and cream of tartar into a saucepan and gradually stir in the water and oil until it is smooth. Add food colouring, a few drops at a time, until it is a nice bright colour. Cook over medium heat until the mixture comes away from the sides of the pan and forms a ball. This should not take more than two or three minutes. Remove from the heat and leave until lukewarm. Knead on the board until it is soft and pliable. Use an old chopping board because some of the colour may

be transferred from the dough. Mould into any shape and allow to set. If left overnight the shape will become quite hard and can be painted.

To keep some of the play dough for another day, wrap it tightly in plastic because it dries quickly when exposed to air.

POLLEN

First use sticky tape to lift off as much as possible and to prevent spreading the stain. Residual stains of tiger, Christmas and other lilies, can be removed by pressing a little tomato juice and pulp onto the stain. Wash the tomato juice off immediately so it doesn't have time to dry. Another method is to make a paste with glycerine and denture powder. Pack over the stain, leave for half an hour then wash off. Pen remover is often successful in removing pollen stains, particularly from clothing.

POMANDERS

Pomanders are usually made with oranges or lemons combined with aromatics. The chosen fruit should be thin skinned without blemishes. Start at the stalk end and, in circles, press about one cup of cloves into the fruit until it is covered. Then, on a sheet of tissue paper, mix together 1 dessertspoon of orris root powder (available from pharmacists) and 2 dessertspoons of cinnamon. Roll the fruit in the powder, twist the paper around it, and store in a cupboard for a few weeks.

In damp weather it is a good idea to leave the fruit for only two weeks, then put in a very low oven to assist the drying process. The cloves siphon the juice from the fruit that eventually shrinks and hardens. Shake off excess spice powders, tie a ribbon around it and hang in the wardrobe. The pomander will impart a gentle aroma for about three years. It is a natural alternative to keep moths out of the wardrobe.

POTPOURRI

Pick the flowers or herbs to be used in potpourri on a fine day, after the dew has gone. Spread them out to dry, on mesh in the shade, or in the oven turned to low and with the oven door left slightly ajar, or in the microwave on defrost.

Any scented flowers can be used but usually, thyme, basil and other herbs are added. To 6 handfuls of dried flowers and herbs, add 2 teaspoons each of powdered cloves, cinnamon and orris root powder.

PRAMS

In this day and age most prams, pushers and strollers are covered with vinyl, the quality of which varies with the price. No matter what the price or quality, the same amount of care should be given to the item the baby travels in, as to the baby itself. At least once a month, wash the vinyl both inside and out, with very hot, soapy water. Make sure it is thoroughly dry, then spray the vinyl with a good upholstery polish. Fold-up baby carriages must be dry before being folded.

If the pram is to be left folded for more than three weeks, smother it with talcum powder and store in a dry place.

For mildew, mix the juice of one lemon with three tablespoons of salt and rub into the mildewed area with the palms of your hands, or use a nailbrush. Leave the mixture on for half an hour before washing off. Another way is to sponge, or scrub, with hot water and antiseptic disinfectant. Or scrub with a solution of 1 part bleach to 4 parts water. Pram tyres should be rubbed occasionally with glycerine. This not only cleans, but also helps preserve them.

QUASSIA CHIPS
Quassia chips come from the bark of a tree and after steeping in boiling water, the liquid is used to destroy the insects that breed in and around wood. After straining off the liquid, the chips can then be put in the ceiling to deter possums, or scattered in the garden to deter cats and dogs. The liquid can be sprayed around doorways to deter animals. Some pharmacists, nurserymen and hardware stores stock quassia chips.

RATS
Rats should be attended to by pest exterminators or contact your local council. Prevention is better than cure so don't allow rubbish to accumulate and don't leave food scraps about. Rats can be very vicious if cornered so don't try to attack them yourself.

RATTLING DOORS AND WINDOWS
Stick a strip of foam rubber around the area that rattles. This will stop the noise and keep draughts at bay.

RECORDS
It is not necessarily desirable, but it is possible, to wash vinyl records. It needs to be done very carefully, in lukewarm water, with no more than about two drops of detergent. Keep the labels out of the water and use a circular motion to wash with the grooves. It is best to use a damp piece of velvet, remembering to always wipe with the grooves or, buy a special record brush. Do not wash compact disks.

RED CLAY SOIL
Red clay soil is not easy to remove, particularly from carpet or upholstery. Use a firm brush to get as much of the dried soil from the fabric and then vacuum. Next, mix together in a 750 millilitre (26 fl oz) soft drink bottle with a screw-top, ¼ cup washing-up liquid, ¼ cup of methylated spirits, 1 tablespoon of ammonia, 1 teaspoon of eucalyptus, 1 dessertspoon of citric acid. Fill the bottle with cold water and shake well.

Put ¼ cup of the mixture into 1 litre (2 pints) of warm water. Sponge over the stained areas with the mixture. Use a clean absorbent towel to mop up the moisture as you work.

RED WINE

If spilt on the carpet, use kitchen paper to mop up any excess, and always dab, don't wipe. Then smother the stain completely with powdered borax. Leave until the next day when the wine will have absorbed into the borax powder. Brush or vacuum off.

On clothing use soda water, and always work from the outside to the middle so as not to spread the stain.

RINGS

To remove a tight ring from your finger, pass the end of a piece of fine string under the ring. Now wind it evenly around the finger upwards as far as the middle joint. Then take the lower end of the string under the ring and slowly wind it upwards. The ring will gradually move along the string and come off. Another method is to wet the finger, rub it with soap, then press the ring over the knuckle, turning it on the finger as you do so.

ROSES

Roses will last longer if the bunch of roses, when first cut, is put into a bucket of water almost up to their heads. Then reach down into the water and snip the ends of each rose stem, slitting it a little as well. Leave them standing in the water for at least an hour before arranging in vases. Use a potato peeler to strip the ends of the stems of roses. Saves getting thorns in your
fingers.

To stop petals falling, put five coins in the bottom of the vase. The roses will eventually die, but the petals will stay put.

To revive drooping roses re-cut the bottom of the stem and stand in boiling water for two or three minutes, then put them back into cold water.

ROSE WATER

To 18 cups of distilled water add 2 tablespoons of rose essence. Leave for 3 weeks. This can be used for either cooking or in the bath.

RUBIES

To clean ruby rings or necklaces, even if they are set with diamonds, sapphires, gold or silver, mix together 1 cup warm water, ¼ cup ammonia, and 1 tablespoon of dishwashing detergent. Put the jewellery in, leave for 10 minutes, then scrub with a soft toothbrush. Rinse under the hot tap, then dip in, and straight out, of methylated spirits. This cleaning method is not suitable for pearls, opals, turquoise, coral or any porous gemstone.

RUST

Used strictly according to the instructions, a commercial rust remover will remove rust marks from clothing. Test on an inconspicuous area first to be sure it is compatible with the fabric.

Bleach will remove rust in some instances, but do not use bleach on coloured materials, synthetics or wool.

For rust in washable material, boil 1 teaspoon of cream of tartar in 2 litres (70 fl oz) of water and soak the stain. Bad stains will need lemon juice mixed with bicarbonate of soda (baking soda) to remove them. A paste made with salt and lemon juice is safe for most fabrics. Leave it on the stain until the paste is dry. Brush off and repeat, if necessary.

On woollens, try a paste made of glycerine and yolk of egg. Leave for ½ hour, then wash off in lukewarm water and wool wash.

On silk, wash in warm water and wool wash and rinse. Then rub in plenty of dry bicarbonate of soda (baking soda) and leave for 12 hours. Wash again in warm water and silk care wash.

Rust on concrete can be removed with spirits of salts, but make sure you wear strong rubber gloves.

Rust build-up inside a kettle can be prevented by putting 1 or 2 marbles into the kettle.

To prevent garden tools from becoming rusty, smother with Vaseline when they are not in use. For rust-free steel wool kitchen pads, put them in a plastic bag in the freezer after use.

SALAD

Stains from salad are mainly due to oil or grease in the dressing. Put paper towel under the stain, then cover the stain with talcum powder, another paper towel over the powder and hold the hot iron over it. Or, just cover with talcum powder, roll up and leave in the laundry overnight. Eucalyptus oil will remove any residual stain before washing as usual.

SCORCH

Light scorch marks can often be removed by rubbing gently with dry steel wool.

For white cotton fabric, soak the whole garment, or sponge the mark with a solution of 1 part bleach to 4 parts water.

On a silky synthetics where there is some concern about the colour, make a paste of glycerine and borax, pack it over the scorch mark and leave it to dry before brushing off. Some scorch marks can be removed with a 50-50 solution of hydrogen peroxide and water. Don't leave it soaking: do it quickly, then wash the garment thoroughly. With this method, it is always necessary to test the fabric on a seam that will not show.

On denim pack the scorched area with a paste made with equal parts of cream of tartar, Borax and water. Allow to dry then brush off.

Try treating the scorch mark on carpet with white toothpaste. Use a toothpaste containing cream of tartar. Leave it to dry, brush off and repeat if necessary. Sponge any residual mark with warm water and nappy-soaking powder or oxygen bleach washing powder. Sometimes a light rub with very fine sandpaper can be effective but test first to see that the fibre does not fur. Cover the scorch mark on a wool garment with cream of tartar toothpaste. Leave the toothpaste to dry, brush it off, and if the mark has begun to fade, repeat the treatment.

SCREWS

To loosen nails and screws that have become rusted into wood, drop a small quantity of paraffin oil over them. Allow this to soak in, and after a short time the screws may be taken out. Inserting a screwdriver into the head and tapping it firmly with a hammer will often succeed in starting a stiff screw.

SCUFF MARKS

Scuff marks from rubber-soled shoes, or trolley wheels, can usually be removed from vinyl floors by putting kerosene on a cloth to rub the marks with. Because of the different compositions used in rubber-soled shoes, and trolley wheels, methylated spirits might work better than kerosene. Steel wool or scourers should not be used because they will, most likely, scratch or remove the surface of the vinyl. Once the scuff marks have been removed, wash the floor with vinyl floor cleaner.

SEAGRASS MATTING

For seagrass matting that has developed an unpleasant odour, cut up some unskinned onions, put on plates around the room, close doors and windows, and leave for 48 hours. Then remove the onions and air the room. Now spray with commerical odour neutraliser. If possible, lift the matting and clean underneath it. To clean seagrass matting, put 2 cups of salt into a bucket of water, stir to dissolve some of the salt, then scrub the matting. Dry thoroughly or mould could eventually grow under it.

SEA SHELLS

When they are removed from the water and become dry, shells do tend to lose their lustre. If they are kept in a jar with salt water, the colour is retained. Coating the shells with Vaseline retains the lustre and the colour, but the best method is to spread the shells on a sheet of newspaper and spray or paint with clear lacquer.

SEAWATER

For seawater stains on fabrics, sponge with warm water to dissolve the salt. If the stain persists, spot clean with methylated spirits, then launder or dry clean.

For seawater stains on shoes, try 2 teaspoons of methylated spirits to 1 dessertspoon milk. Rub on, leave to dry, then repolish.

SEPTIC TANK

Septic tanks use a natural dissemination of waste with bacteria, so care must be taken with the use of toilet cleaners. Never use bleach, or any product containing bleach because it will destroy the bacteria and the function of the septic tank. Choose a cleaner that is specially recommended for use with septic tanks.

Commercial cleaners, other than those recommended for your particular septic system, should

not be used. Sludge, in the form of undecomposed solid matter, sinks to the bottom of the tank, while oil waste forms a scum on the surface of the water. Between the sludge and the scum, is the effluent that runs through an outlet pipe and is eventually absorbed into the ground. Every four years or so, septic tanks should be pumped out to prevent the sludge and scum from clogging the outlet pipe and drainage area.

Bad odours are a sure indication that the system is overloaded and should be pumped out. Check the operation recommendations for your system, and for more detailed advice, speak to the people who installed the system.

SHAMPOO

To make chamomile shampoo, mix in a basin, 1 tablespoon of borax, 1 tablespoon of pure soap, and 30 grams (1 oz) of powdered chamomile flowers. Mix in and beat to a thick lather with ¼ litre (8 fl oz) of hot water. Let it cool before using.

SHAWLS – BABY

Forty or more years ago loving care was put into making the most intricate handmade shawls for babies. Invariably white to begin with, time yellows the material, and because time also weakens the weave or knit, it is advisable to treat an old shawl with as much tender loving care as that with which it was made. These old shawls were always meant to be washed by hand in lukewarm water.

Use the old-fashioned wool wash that is made by mixing together, 4 cups pure soap flakes, 1 cup methylated spirits and 50 millilitres (2 fl oz) eucalyptus. Store the mixture in a jar with a tight-fitting lid and use about 2 tablespoons to a bucket of water to wash a shawl. Rinse in lukewarm water and lay the shawl flat to dry. Dry away from direct sunlight.

SHEEPSKIN

To whiten a sheepskin, put the skin on a flat surface and scour well with warm water and soap. Rinse with clean water and hang to drain. Then hang up to bleach in a large packing case, or some other container which can be made airtight. Put 250 grams (8 oz) of sulphur in a tin, set it alight, and place it under the skin, being careful not to have it close enough to burn the wool. Close all openings, and leave until the next day. Then hang out to dry and beat with a broomstick to fluff up the wool. Most sheep or lambswool skins that have been made into rugs or garments are washable but, as some are not, it will be necessary to test a small area first. To do this, dissolve a few pure soap flakes in warm water; wring out a cloth in the water and sponge a small inconspicuous area of the skin. Leave it to dry. If the skin dries hard, it is not washable and will need to be cleaned with powder carpet cleaner. If the skin is washable, use wool wash to wash it in lukewarm water. It is not necessary to rinse, but if the item to be washed is very dirty, wash it twice.

Vacuum sheepskin car seat covers, then sponge them with the wool wash mixture. Do them

at a time when the car is not going to be used for two or three days so they have plenty of time to dry. If the car is in continual use, remove the covers for cleaning.

SHELVES

To remove old adhesive shelf paper, cover the adhesive paper with paper, then run a warm iron over it. It will peel off easily. Try lining shelves with floor tiles. They are easy to clean and last forever.

SHINY FABRIC

The surface of trousers and suits can become shiny in parts. Sponge the shiny area with brown vinegar, or strong cold tea. Finally, hold the steam iron over the sponged area, but do not press down. Hang it in the air to dry.

SHOE POLISH

Shoe polish can usually be removed by putting a little methylated spirits, or kerosene, onto a soft cloth, then dabbing the stain. Keep changing the position of the cloth so the stain is not transferred back to the fabric. Any residual stain can be removed by sponging with warm water and a little wool wash.

SHOES

Don't put wet shoes next to a fire or radiator. Direct heat dries out the leather. Pack the shoes with newspaper that absorbs the moisture, while at the same time keeping the shoes in shape.

For dirty shoes or boots, rub over with a clean cloth and cloudy ammonia, then polish. Never store boots or shoes in plastic. They sweat and can become mouldy. To restore leather shoes or boots, make sure they are clean. Rub with a dry brush to get rid of mud and dry grit from the seams. Don't forget underneath the heel. Then go over the shoes, both the upper and the sole with methylated spirits. Thoroughly dry, then go over the shoes again with liquid paraffin, (obtainable from pharmacists or hardware stores). Leave for 24 hours, rub with a soft cloth; polish.

White patent leather shoes can be sponged with methylated spirits and then sponged with detergent to get rid of any dirty marks. Polish with Vaseline. For cracks on white patent leather, touch up with a dab of white correction fluid.

Fabric shoes made from denim, or similar material, can be washed or scrubbed with wool wash or detergent.

Scuff marks on shoes can be sponged off with kerosene on a soft cloth. Or rub off with an art-gum eraser (from stationery stores).

Satin shoes. Use a good powder carpet cleaner. Just rub the powder into the shoes with the palms of the hands, brush off with a soft cloth.

Suede shoes. Use a very fine sandpaper or a pencil eraser for scuff marks. To steam clean suede shoes, first clean off dirt with a brush or dry sponge, then hold the shoes over a pan of boiling

water. When the steam raises the nap, stroke the suede in one direction with a soft brush. Dry the shoes before wearing.

For shoes that have become smelly, pharmacists sell specially formulated foot powder that can be sprinkled liberally into the shoes and left overnight. Shake the powder out lightly before the next wear. Or mix 2 tablespoons powdered borax with 1 tablespoon bicarbonate of soda. Divide the powder mixture onto two pieces of tissue paper. Sprinkle a few drops of commerical odour neutraliser onto each. Lightly roll the tissue and push into the toe of each shoe. This will absorb the odour and can be used two or three times before discarding.

SHOES – CARE

To keep shoes fresh and free from odours, sift together 2 cups of bicarbonate of soda, 4 tablespoons of talcum powder and 4 tablespoons of powdered borax. Now add, stirring continually; 20 drops lavender oil, 30 drops lemon oil, 10 drops cinnamon oil and 10 drops pine oil. Stir twice daily for three days, then store in a glass jar with a sprinkler lid. Sprinkle into shoes about three times weekly.

SHOES – MOULDY

Remove the laces from sports shoes and open them as much as possible, and put in the sun. Leave them in the sun as long as possible to allow the heat to kill the mould spores. Now mix together, 4 tablespoons of powdered borax, 4 tablespoons of salt and about 6 drops of commerical odour neutraliser. Put half the mixture into each shoe and leave for 24 hours. It may be necessary to repeat the treatment two or three times.

SILK FLOWERS

Without continual care, dust, which inevitably settles upon the delicate silk, becomes ingrained and very difficult to remove. The silk flowers should be turned upside down and shaken to loosen the dust. Then, with the heads of the flowers still pointing to the floor, use a soft brush to gently dislodge dust particles. Shake again and repeat if the petals still look dusty. The flowers can be steamed lightly by holding them upside down over a bath of hot water. Leave them upside down until completely dry. They can be very lightly sprayed with a fine hair spray when they are dry. I cannot emphasise too much that silk flowers are very delicate and need gentle handling.

SILK – GREASE

Smother the grease stain with talcum powder, leave the garment in a warm spot for about twenty-four hours, then brush the powder away. Often it is sufficient for the grease to be absorbed into the powder and no further treatment is necessary. The next step, if the stain is still obvious, is to soak the silk garment in half a bucket of lukewarm water with about 1 tablespoon of household disinfectant, for half an hour, then wash as usual. Use a special silk wash to wash silk garments.

SILK – RUST

The safest way to remove rust marks is to make a paste with lemon juice and cream of tartar, cover the rust spots, leave to dry, then brush off. Repeat two or three times as necessary. Marks that have been there for a long time may need more treatment but it is better to persevere than to use a harsher treatment on silk.

SILK – YELLOWED

To keep silk white, add 1 teaspoon of cream of tartar to 1 litre (2 pints) of warm water and soak the garment for 10 minutes before washing. A few drops of methylated spirits helps to give silk a sheen. Before ironing silk garments, put them in a plastic bag in the freezer for half an hour.

SILVER

Putting pieces into an aluminium saucepan with about 1 tablespoon pure soap flakes, and enough boiling water to completely cover them, can clean silver forks, spoons and other small items. Let them sit in the saucepan for 20 minutes, then rinse in very hot water and polish with a soft, dry cloth. If you don't have a saucepan deep enough to cover the silver, change the water after the first 20 minutes and reverse the silver to clean the other ends. Not every household has aluminium saucepans. Don't substitute with stainless steel or enamel line a basin with two layers of aluminium foil and follow the same treatment. There are a number of good commercial silver cleaning products on supermarket shelves. Don't put knife handles in, as glue might deteriorate.

Rub black spots on silver with a mixture of powdered whiting and kerosene. For stubborn spots, cover them with the mixture and leave to dry before washing in boiling water.

For egg-stained silver, rub with salt, then clean or wash as usual.

SILVER CLOTH

To make a silver cloth, or a mitt, for polishing, bring to the boil 2 litres (70 fl oz) of water, 2 tablespoons of whiting and half a cup of cloudy ammonia. Put in two clean, soft dusters, (or three or four towelling mitts, see below). Keep the solution boiling, stirring the dusters, or mitts, in it for 10 minutes. Take the saucepan to the line and peg the dusters, or mitts, to drip dry. Do not wring. Store the impregnated articles in plastic bags to be used many times before washing and impregnating again. Cotton gloves can also be impregnated with the solution to make silver cleaning easy.

To make the mitt, put your hand flat onto two layers of towelling and, beginning at the wrist, draw a line around the hand following beside the little finger, round the top of the fingers, down beside the forefinger, then around the thumb, and down to the wrist. Cut the mitt out, leaving a margin for the seam, and wide enough at the wrist to get your hand in when sewing is complete.

For gifts, or to sell on stalls, fold the mitt and put it into a clear plastic box, label it and attach a festive bow.

SILVERFISH

Silverfish can be eradicated completely but it takes time and a lot of patience. General eradication can be done to kill live silverfish, by spraying with any commercial low-irritant spray. The problem is that as fast as they can be sprayed, more hatch, so it becomes a double job - spray the live ones, then cook their eggs to prevent them from hatching. The eggs are usually laid in corners and along edges, such as where the carpet meets the wall, in cupboards where the shelves meet the wall, and in all the seams of drawers.

Cupboards and drawers should be washed with very hot water and dried along the edges with a hair drier turned on hot. It is not wise to spray near food so put Epsom salts in food cupboards. For the carpet edges, use a hair drier or a steam iron. Put a towel between the carpet and the iron to prevent damage to the carpet. No matter how thoroughly the job is done, the eggs are so small that some always escape and will hatch, hopefully in gradually lessening numbers. It takes months of repetitive treatment to rid the house completely of silverfish.

Books need special attention because the eggs can be inside and down the spine of books. Old books are particularly susceptible because paper was not always treated, at the manufacturing stage, to resist the ravaging of insects. Use a powder insecticide, or sulphur powder, and continually take the books out and fan the pages. It really is hard work.

Sprinkle cloves in the linen cupboard to deter silverfish. Or, finely peel any citrus fruit, dry the peel in the oven and put in linen cupboards, but don't let cloves or peel come into direct contact with the linen.

SILVER – TO STORE

Sprinkle the silver with talcum powder before putting it away. Another method is to put about ten sugar cubes in the container in which silver is stored. Acid free, white or blue tissue paper is very good to wrap around silver for storing. Do not use rubber bands that can do irreparable damage to silver. Another no-no is newspaper. Printers' ink can oxidise and remove the silver plating on teasets and other items.

SLATE

To keep slate looking fresh, use equal parts of linseed oil and turpentine applied with a soft, dry cloth. This will prevent smudges for quite some time. This is not suitable if the slate is sealed with a poly sealant. For a sealed slate floor, simply wash regularly with half a bucket of hot water and a quarter cup of methylated spirits. Buff up with a clean, dry cloth.

SMELLS – LIDS

Wash plastic lids in a weak bleach solution. Use 1 part bleach to 6 parts of water. Rinse in very hot water then put the lids in the freezer for an hour or so. Another method is to mix 2 tablespoons of cream of tartar, 1 tablespoon of bicarbonate of soda, 1 tablespoon of dry mustard and put the lids into a plastic bag with the mixture. It doesn't really matter how long they stay in it.

SMELLS – SHOES AND BAGS

Wring out a cloth in hot water, add a dash of antiseptic disinfectant to the cloth and wipe the handbags and shoes all over, both inside and out. Then sprinkle the inside of the shoes and the handbags with plenty of talcum powder. Leave them in a warm spot for at least 24 hours, then shake the powder out. I always shake out talcum powder on to the carpet. It's easy to vacuum off and helps to clean the carpet, thereby doing two jobs for the price of one.

Before putting shoes or handbags away, pack them with newspaper, and if they still smell a little musty, sprinkle the newspaper with a few drops of commerical odour neutraliser.

SMOKE STAINS

For smoke stains on brick, scrub with 1 part bleach to 4 parts water. On paint, apply the same mixture of bleach or try a little powder cleanser on a cloth.

On washable fabric, dampen the stain, cover with nappy-soaking powder, leave for an hour, then wash normally. Repeat, if necessary. On non-washable fabric, cover with salt, leave for a few hours, then brush off and sponge with detergent.

For cotton blend synthetic use ½ cup cream of tartar to ½ bucket of water.

SOAP AS PRESENTS

It is a good idea to make soap early in the year for Christmas presents because the longer it is left before use, the longer it will last. Here are two different soaps, one for use in the bathroom, and the other for gardeners or for men who have a workshop at home.

Bath soap

Bring to the boil 4 cups of water.

Add and dissolve 1.75 kilograms (60 fl oz) dripping.

Remove from the heat and pour into a plastic bucket.

Then mix in 3¼ cups olive oil and a few drops of essential oil.

Leave to cool for a while.

Then add 710 grams (25 oz) caustic soda.

Pour into moulds and leave to set. Don't use aluminium containers for soap making.

Garden soap

Before you start, pour 1 cup of boiling water over 1 cup of lavender flowers, to make ¾ cup of lavender water.

To make the soap, use a non-aluminium bowl that can be fitted into a saucepan to be used as a double boiler.

Into the bowl put 250 grams (9 fl oz) pure soap flakes.

Stir in ¾ cup lavender water.

Put the bowl into the saucepan, which should be about full of boiling water. Let it simmer gently, stirring occasionally, until the soap melts – in about 2 hours.

Now stir in and mix well ¼ cup olive oil, 400 grams (14 oz) fine sand and 2 tablespoons dried lavender flowers.

Cut a hole in the base of a 500 gram (16 fl oz) plastic margarine container and thread a rope through it. Hold the rope upright and pour the thick soap into the container.

Leave for at least a week before removing the container.

SOAP – CASTILE

Bring to the boil 4 cups water.

Add, and dissolve 1.75 kilograms (80 fl oz) dripping.

Remove from the heat, pour into a plastic bucket, and then mix in 3¼ cups olive oil..

Leave to cool then add 710 grams (25 fl oz) caustic soda.

Pour into moulds and leave to set.

Important: Do not use aluminium containers for soap-making.

General hints:
- Stir frequently while soap is cooling to prevent water and soap from separating.
- Use salt-free, clarified dripping.
- If the soap mixture shows signs of boiling over, dash in a little cold water.
- Put in a warm (not a cold) place to set.

SOAP – SCRAPS

Honey soap is easy to make from leftover soap scraps and leaves hands feeling soft and smooth. Cut the soap into small pieces and, to each cup of soap scraps, add ¼ cup of rolled oats and 1 tablespoon of honey. Use a double boiler, or put into a stainless steel, or glass saucepan, with a little water and simmer until the mixture becomes transparent. Add 2 tablespoons of glycerine to the simmering mixture and stir in. Turn the mixture into moulds and leave to set. Don't use aluminium containers for making or moulding soap.

SOAP - HONEY

Cut thinly 125 grams (4 oz) of yellow soap into a double saucepan, occasionally stirring until it is melted. Keep it over the double boiler and add 1 tablespoon palm oil and 1 tablespoon honey. Then add a few drops of cinnamon oil. Let it all boil together another 6 or 8 minutes, then pour out and let it stand. Cut up and it is ready for immediate use.

SOAP – LAUNDRY

To make a soap suitable for the laundry, such as rubbing on collars and cuffs, cut up soap scraps, cover with water and simmer in a stainless steel or glass saucepan, until the soap becomes liquid. Let it cool, then to each cup of soap jelly, add 2 cups of powdered whiting, 2 tablespoons of mineral turpentine and 1 teaspoon of eucalyptus oil. Stir thoroughly. Put into moulds to set. Do

not use aluminium containers to make or mould soap. This soap is particularly good for greasy clothes, or removing greasy spots from the carpet.

SOAP – LIQUID

Liquid soap is almost impossible to make from pure soap because it tends to solidify. To refill pump containers it is best to use shampoo. If the shampoo is too thick, it can be thinned by adding water. Bath gel is also useful for filling liquid soap containers but it must be thinned with water before the containers are filled. Some people make liquid soap from scraps by putting the scraps into a large container with water into the microwave. I haven't tried it.

SOAP MOULDS

I don't use professional soap moulds. Far more interesting and innovative is to use plastic jelly moulds, old plastic soap containers, or even plastic lids. Add a personal touch with a dried flower or petal from your garden, in the bottom of each mould. It sets into the soap and makes a pretty gift.

SOAP – SAND

To make sand soap, cut up a large bar of household soap (about the size of three cakes of laundry soap) and put in a saucepan with about 1200 millilitres (42 fl oz) of water. Heat slowly, stirring continually until the soap dissolves. Then stir in 1200 millilitres (42 fl oz) each of clean sand and wood ashes. Remove from the heat and stir until the mixture begins to thicken. Then put it into moulds to set. Do not use aluminium containers for soap-making.

SOAP – BALLS

Another way to use leftover soap scraps is to chop them up quite small and push them into the toe of a discarded nylon stocking. Put the stocking with the soap in it into a bowl of hot water. Let it stand for about five minutes, then mould it into a ball with your hands and tie a knot in the stocking as close to the soap as possible. Put the soap ball into a plastic bag and then into the freezer to set. If the soap is well pushed together the nylon can be cut off before use. If not, leave the soap in the nylon for use.

SOAP – STAIN REMOVER

Mix together in a basin, 4 cups pure soap flakes, 1 cup methylated spirits, 50 millilitres (2 fl oz) eucalyptus and 1 cup boiling water. Stand the basin in very hot water, over heat if necessary, until the mixture is clear. Turn into moulds and leave to set. It can be covered and put into the fridge for setting. After removing from moulds, wrap in waxed paper and leave for about three weeks before using to sponge make-up from collars, or to remove small stains from clothing or carpet. With time, there is a lot of shrinkage to the soap but it does not affect the cleaning qualities. Do not use aluminium containers for mixing or moulds.

SPA BATH

Spa baths should be disinfected after each use to prevent fungus forming in the pipes. Before emptying the water, put 2 capfuls of bleach into the bath, mix it about with your hands, then run the pump for about 1 minute before draining and wiping the surface clean. The pipe and system should be cleaned no more frequently than once a month. This should be done by filling the bath with bathing temperature water, then add ½ cup of dishwasher powder and mix thoroughly. Run the pump for about 6 minutes, drain, refill with warm water, run the pump for 2 minutes, then drain. If your particular spa bath has cleaning instructions that differ from this, follow the instructions of the manufacturer.

SPIDER STAIN

The removal of a stain from a squashed spider, or other insect, can depend on the type of insect, and what it has been eating. The best thing to try is to sponge with warm water and a little wool wash. Another method is to dampen the stain, smother it with denture powder, leave for an hour, then wash with nappy-soaking powder.

SPIDER WEBS

Usually seasonal, spiders' trailing webs are great dust collectors. However, they do love a diet of silverfish and other insects, so they have their uses. Creosote, on a cloth wiped over suitable surfaces will often discourage spiders. If creosote cannot be used, try antiseptic disinfectant.

SPOONS – SOUVENIR

Silver souvenir spoons can be coated with a metal sealant.

STAMPS

To remove stamps from an envelope put the envelope in the freezer for a few hours, the stamp can then be lifted off with smooth-end philatelic tweezers. If on plain paper, soak in lukewarm water for 10-15 minutes after which time they should lift away quite easily. Lie face down on blotting paper, kitchen paper or a clean towel. If on coloured paper, use cold water. (A pinch of salt for each cup of water will discourage any colour runs. Do not use too much as this may "blister" the coloured inks). Otherwise buy a specific stamp remover solution.

STATIC

Anti-static spray controls static electricity in synthetic garments. It is available in supermarkets and some pharmacists. If you don't want to go to the expense of using a formulated product, use a fabric softener in the final rinse when washing garments that cling. This method is usually effective but works better when a top quality fabric softener is used.

STICKING DRAWERS

To make wooden drawers run smoothly, rub the sticking areas with bees wax. A good silicone polish will often do the job just as well.

STORAGE CONTAINERS

The best storage containers are good, old-fashioned, tea chests but they are becoming harder to obtain. Removalists have supplies of cartons. Some of the cartons are designed to hang clothes and these are excellent. Pad coathangers with old stockings to prevent hard-to-remove creases across the shoulders of garments. In the bottom of the containers put Epsom salts, or highly scented soap, covered with acid-free tissue paper. Don't cover clothes with plastic. It can cause rust or mould due to sweating.

STRAW MATTING

Clean by scrubbing with salted water. Use about 2 cups salt to a bucket of water. Wipe the matting dry as you go. The salt will prevent the matting turning yellow. Straw or plaited matting will last longer and keep cleaner if given a coat of clear lacquer when new.

SUEDE – CLOTHING

Suede jackets, skirts and trousers can be cleaned by spraying with a suitable suede cleaner. Shoe shops and some shoe repairers carry such sprays. Follow the instructions on the can. Finally, brush with a firm-bristled brush to lift the nap. Always test on an inside seam first, to be sure the colour or suede surface is not effected by the cleaner.

Another method is to mix together 4 tablespoons borax powder, 4 tablespoons salt and 4 tablespoons shellite (naphtha). Sprinkle the powder over the garment, leave for 20 minutes, then rub with a towel before brushing off.

For grease marks around the neckline, cover with talcum powder. Leave for at least an hour, brush off and repeat if necessary.

Some suede garments are washable but check the label for washing instructions.

SUIT – CARE

To care for business suits it is best to own at least two suits that should be worn on alternate days. Don't wear the same suit two days in a row or it will become stretched at the elbows, knees, across the bottom and the elbows and the top of the legs will become creased. Pure wool fabric, and even wool and synthetic mix fabrics, have the resilience to settle back into shape, particularly if they are first hung in the steam of the bathroom and then in the air. For men, a trouser press is a good investment. The saving in dry cleaning would soon pay for a trouser press. Use clip hangers for both trousers and skirts. Don't hang them across the bar of coat hangers. Brush suits regularly and don't leave them hanging in plastic bags.

SUIT SHINY

A dark coloured suit that has become shiny in parts can often be restored by wringing out a cloth in hot water, adding a dash of brown vinegar to the cloth, then sponging the shiny parts. If the nap has worn off restoration is not possible. Women's suits can be restored by the application of bias binding or ribbon around the collar, lapels, etc.

TABLES

For heat marks on wooden tables, camphorated oil can be rubbed with the grain. If that is not successful, rub with Brasso or metal polish, then polish.

Hot milk spilt on a wooden table can be rubbed with a flannel wrung out in hot water and vinegar. For the next week rub daily with camphorated oil on a cloth wrung out in hot water. If the mark remains, polish with Brasso or metal polish, then with a good furniture polish.

Glass tops: A tablespoon of fabric softener in 2 litres of water and 2 cups methylated spirits is a terrific lint-free cleaner for glass tabletops. Apply with a soft cloth and polish immediately with a chamois or a soft, dry cloth.

Chrome legs: Rub with a piece of smooth, damp aluminium foil. The foil turns black but the chrome will shine. Left over soda water is also good for cleaning chrome.

Also see Wood furniture (page 183).

TAPESTRY

To clean a tapestry wall hanging, make up a mixture of 2 tablespoons powdered borax, 2 tablespoons salt, 2 tablespoons dry-cleaning fluid or shellite (naphtha). Sprinkle all over the tapestry and rub with the palms of your hands. Leave for about an hour, then either shake the powder out or beat the tapestry from the back to remove all the powder.

TEAK – STAINS

A dark stain on a teak table may be able to be removed by covering the mark with a paste of powdered whiting mixed with ammonia. Apply it like a poultice, covering only the dark stain, then cover with a piece of cling wrap. Leave for two hours then check to see if the stain is fading. Repeat, if necessary.

TEAPOT

For an aluminium teapot, use a paste made with salt and vinegar. Pack the paste into the spout and leave it overnight. Next day, wash it out with very hot water. Repeat, if necessary. Or boil apple peel and cores in the pot for 10 minutes. Let it stand another 10 minutes then wash and rinse.

The inside of a china teapot can be cleaned by filling it right to the top with cold water, then adding a tablespoon of white denture powder. Let it stand overnight, then empty it and use a cloth or brush to ensure that cleaning is complete. Rinse well with hot water. The spout can be packed with salt and a cotton bud used to rub the tea stains off. Do not use bleach or detergents

on decorative china teapots, particularly those that are decorated with gold.

For silver or pottery teapots which are stained inside, put in 3 or 4 denture cleaning tablets or 2 teaspoons denture powder, half fill the pot with cold water and leave overnight. Next day, empty the teapot and rinse first in hot water, then in cold water.

Enamel teapots can be cleaned on the inside with salt. To clean the spout, pack with salt mixed with lemon juice and leave overnight. Next morning, remove the salt and scald with very hot water.

TEDDY BEARS

Grubby teddy bears should be put into a pillow slip, then smothered with a mixture made with 4 tablespoons powdered borax, 4 tablespoons salt and 4 tablespoons shellite (naphtha) or dry cleaning fluid. For more than one teddy, the mixture will need to be doubled. Leave the bears in the pillowslip for about 48 hours, making sure the powder mixture has been well rubbed over it. When the bear is taken from the pillowslip, use a clean, soft towel to rub all over. Shake, or brush out any remaining powder.

TERRACOTTA

Grease and oil can sometimes be removed from a small terracotta container by smothering the stain with talcum powder. Put the article in the oven on the lowest setting. It might need to be wrapped in foil to prevent powder from settling in the oven. The warmth should draw the oil or grease into the powder that can then be brushed off.

Terracotta pots contain salts that bleed through. Empty the terracotta pots; clean them thoroughly with hot water, detergent, and about 2 tablespoons of cloudy ammonia. Leave them in the sun for a couple of days to be sure they are completely dry, then seal the inside surface with insect repellant. Be sure the inspect repellant is dry before re-using. The outside surface can be cleaned with equal parts of white vinegar and warm water. Don't seal the outside because the lime bleeding will sit under the seal.

TEXTA OR FELT-TIPPED PEN STAINS

For a dried felt-tip pen stain on clothing, first soften it with a little glycerine. Don't forget to put a cloth, or paper towel, under the stain to avoid pushing the felt pen colour through and creating another problem area. Now drizzle some pen remover on to the stained area. The colour should change to a pinkish look. At this stage, sponge with warm water with a little detergent. If the felt pen contains indelible ink, lacquer thinner, acetone, or shellite (naphtha) may be worth trying but test to see that the fabric will not be affected.

TEA TREE OIL

Tea tree oil can be used as a solvent for gum residue or as a cleaner, in the same way that eucalyptus oil is used.

TORTOISE SHELL

To polish tortoise shell put a little olive oil onto a soft cloth and rub over the surface of the shell. If the tortoise shell has lost its surface and developed a matt finish, use Vaseline on a soft cloth, two or three times before applying the olive oil.

TOYS

Stuffed animals and dolls used for toys, collection, or decoration usually have instructions for care sewn into a seam. Where no care instructions exist, play safe and do not immerse the article in water. Spray with a carpet stain remover, following the instructions on the can, but instead of vacuuming off, rub with a rough, dry towel, then use a stiff brush to remove any excess powder. Another method is to mix 4 tablespoons of any good dishwashing liquid, 1 tablespoon methylated spirits and 1 teaspoon eucalyptus. Put the solution into a clean bottle for storage. Add a few drops to 1 litre (2 pints) of warm water, wring out a rough towel in it then rub the article all over. Particularly dirty areas, such as seamed edges, might need a brush rather than the towel to get them clean. For articles that are just grubby from handling, smother them with talcum powder, leave overnight inside a pillow slip, then brush the powder off with a rough, dry towel.

TRANSFERS – CLOTHING

Transfers which have been put onto clothing with an adhesive can sometimes be removed by saturating the back of the transfer with methylated spirits, then putting a wet towel over the area and holding a hot iron over it. Quickly, while it is still hot, try to lift the transfer around the edges and gently peel off. The success of the treatment depends on the adhesive used and the fabric to which it is adhered.

UMBRELLAS

An old umbrella frame can be used for garden decoration by stripping the cover from it, painting the frame to prevent rust, then planting the open umbrella into a large pot of soil, or in the garden. Grow ivy or a flowering creeper beside it and trail the runners up over the frame. This makes a spectacular display.

Another use for an old umbrella is to turn it into a useful clothes-dryer. Remove the fabric, paint the frame with a good enamel paint to stop it rusting, and suspend it by the handle. It can be used over the bath. It is also excellent for hanging under a verandah or a tree. You will be amazed at the extra hanging space your old umbrella will provide. When not in use it can be folded and stored away.

VALUABLES

Make sure important items are valued regularly. It is a good idea to have either photographs or sketches of everything that is of any value. This makes life easier in case of burglary, not only for regaining possession of the valuables, but also for claiming insurance.

VARNISH

To clean varnish, rub with equal parts of raw linseed oil and kerosene.

VASES

Crystal vases can be washed in warm soapy water with a little cloudy ammonia. Shake vigorously and rinse thoroughly with clean, warm water.

Pottery vases should be sealed on the inside with bees wax before using. Melt the wax and coat the inside of the vase using a small brush or pour some wax in and swirl it around, making sure the interior is fully coated.

VEIL

For a veil made of cotton, a weak solution of bleach and water will remove the age marks. Put a tablespoon of bleach into a cup, then fill the cup with cold water. Dip a cotton bud into the solution, and with a towel held under the stain, dab the rust marks. Once the marks are removed, rinse the solution out of the fabric.

If the veil is old, the removal of the rust marks could alter the even look of whiteness. If so, it will be necessary to dip the whole veil into an increased amount of the solution to achieve an even look. Rinse well, drip dry away from direct sunlight. Use a light homemade starch, or a spray starch, and iron with a tea towel over the veil so the iron does not catch and tear the net.

Before packing away, make sure the veil is clean. Pack in plenty of acid-free tissue paper in a cardboard box with some Epsom Salts sprinkled in the bottom of the box but not touching the veil. If the veil needs stiffening use Arabic gum water. Another method is to iron the veil with waxed paper. Avoid tearing a veil with the point of the iron by covering it with a cloth before ironing.

VEIL – NYLON

Put ¼ cup of cream of tartar and ¼ cup of bicarbonate of soda (baking soda) into a bucket with enough warm water to cover the veil. Soak the veil in this solution for about an hour. It may take longer, depending upon how yellowed the nylon has become. Rinse in warm water and dry away from direct sunlight. Don't forget to test a small corner first to see how the treatment will react on the fabric.

VELLUM

Vellum used to be made with calfskin and the best cleaning agent was benzine. Vellum has been replaced with synthetics or coated papers and benzine (probably because of its lead content) is no longer on the market. Shellite (naphtha) is the next best alternative. To remove ink from vellum, put a little shellite (naphtha) on to a cottonwool ball and dab gently. Change the cottonwool ball frequently to be sure that the stain being removed is not transferred back to the vellum.

VELOUR

The easiest and cheapest method of cleaning padded velour is to smother it with a mixture of 4 tablespoons powdered borax, 4 tablespoons salt, and 4 tablespoons shellite (naphtha). Rub the powder into the nap of the velour, leave overnight, then rub all over with a clean, rough towel. Brush or vacuum the remaining powder off. Any residual stains can be sprayed with carpet stain remover, following the instructions on the container.

VELVET

For jewellery boxes or picture frames covered with velvet, use a carpet cleaning powder to remove dirty marks, or simply freshen by rubbing with nylon net rolled into a ball to lift dust. Washable velvet with candle wax spilt on it, can be put into a plastic bag in the freezer for about an hour for the wax to become hard and brittle. The wax can then be lifted off with fingernails, or a plastic spatula. Any residual stain can be sponged with eucalyptus oil on a clean cloth. Use warm, soapy water to sponge the eucalyptus oil from the velvet. If the velvet cannot be put into the freezer put ice blocks into a plastic bag and put the bag on top of the wax to achieve the hard brittleness.

A good general cleaner for velvet is to mix together 4 cups of powdered borax, 4 cups of salt, and 4 cups of either shellite (naphtha) or dry-cleaning fluid. Store the mixture in a glass jar with a firm-fitting lid. When required for cleaning, sprinkle over the velvet. Lightly spread the powder so the area to be cleaned is evenly covered. Leave for a few hours, then use a rough towel to rub all over the velvet. Brush or vacuum any residual powder away. Layer the powder more thickly over areas that are more soiled than others, or repeat the treatment on those areas.

Velvet is a fabric that attracts dust, so curtains should be brushed and vacuumed regularly. Once every six months should be sufficient. Soiled edges, usually from hands pulling the curtains across, can be sprayed with carpet stain remover, following the instructions on the container. When the curtains need to be cleaned all over, dry cleaning is best because dry cleaners have the facilities to handle large, heavy items.

VENEER

Furniture with a wood veneer sometimes develops mould spots. Before doing anything check with a specialist cabinet-maker. Maybe the veneer is lifting slightly, allowing moisture or condensation to get under the veneer. For surface mould, put a little antiseptic disinfectant on a soft cloth and rub the mould. For veneer that is ridged, use antiseptic disinfectant on a soft toothbrush. Leave to dry and make sure all the mould is eradicated before polishing.

VENETIAN BLINDS

The tapes of venetian blinds can be scrubbed with any good detergent and a dash of bleach. Its a tedious job, particularly as you either have to climb a ladder, or take the blinds down. It is easier, and less time consuming, to brush the tapes to get rid of any dust, then paint them with shoe colour. There are various brands on the market, used predominantly to colour fabric shoes.

Match the shoe colour to the colour of the tapes, or even change it to suit the decor of the room. It will still be necessary to climb the ladder, but not as time consuming, or as messy, as soap and water scrubbing.

VERTICAL BLIND – GENERAL

A weak solution of bleach will remove the marks from vertical blinds. Use about 1 part bleach to 3 parts warm water. Because the vertical blinds are a woven fabric, it is a good idea to use a soft brush, or even an old tooth brush, so the solution gets in behind the weave.

VERTICAL BLIND – GREASE

To remove fat, or grease marks, from vertical blinds, I suggest very hot water with any good detergent and about 2 tablespoons of household detergent in the water. Use a soft brush to be sure of removing the grease from the weave of the fabric.

VINEGAR

White vinegar is a good substitute for fabric softener but don't use it for nappies because the acid could burn tender skin. Some people use vinegar (about 1 cupful) as a toilet bowl cleaner. Brick fireplaces can be cleaned with undiluted white vinegar on a cloth wrung out in hot water.

VINYL

Both vinyl and leather need to be heated with hot water before attempting to remove ballpoint pen marks. Wring out a cloth in very hot water and let the cloth sit on the stain for a couple of minutes. Remove the cloth and immediately, while the vinyl is still hot, rub the mark with pen remover on a soft cloth. Depending on the ink in the pen, some marks wil simply disappear, while others may change colour. With the marks that change colour, rub them immediately with methylated spirits, then sponge over with warm water and a little shampoo.

Furniture covered with vinyl sometimes absorbs colour from clothing that is almost impossible to remove. The vinyl stretches when it is sat upon and body heat opens the vinyl pores like the skin on a hot day. By the time a stain is noticed, the vinyl has become taut and trapped the stain. It is therefore necessary to apply hot towels to open the vinyl and expose the stain for treatment. It is always best to first try hot, soapy water before using chemical cleaners. Use pure soap, not detergent. Next, try hot water and shampoo. Only if those don't work should chemical cleaners be tried, and it is essential to test on a small inconspicuous area to see how any treatment will affect the fabric or the colour.

Leather look–alike, usually vinyl furniture, is best cleaned regularly with hot, soapy water. Wring out a cloth in the water, and rub firmly, paying particular attention to any badly soiled areas. The regularity of cleaning depends on the amount of use the furniture gets. The best cleaner is probably wool wash, made by mixing together 4 cups pure soap flakes, 1 cup methylated spirits and 50 millilitres (2 fl oz) eucalyptus oil. Store the mixture in an airtight jar

and use about 2 tablespoons to ½ bucket of water. When the furniture is clean and thoroughly dry, apply a good vinyl polish. I use commercial wax paste, but apply sparingly and use a clean, dry towel to buff up and remove excess polish before sitting on it.

The reason vinyl hardens, or withers, particularly where hand contact occurs, is because body oils and perspiration cause a chemical reaction with the synthetic material. Pure soap, such as pure soap flakes or laundry soap and warm water should be sufficient to keep the vinyl clean. The chemical reaction which hardens the vinyl is not reversible but can be helped by a light application of commercial wax paste. Apply it with a soft cloth and buff up with a dry towel. Test first on a small area to be sure the product suits your particular vinyl. Commercial cleaners are good for the doors and dashboards of cars but should not be used until the vinyl has been cleaned. When vinyl is very dirty, clean with hot water and wool wash. Be sure the vinyl is completely dry before applying a polish.

To clean mildew from vinyl, put 1 teaspoon of dishwashing liquid into half a bucket of very hot water. Add a dash of antiseptic disinfectant to the water, then wring out a towel in the mixture, hold the towel over the vinyl for about 30 seconds, then rub well. It may be necessary to use a soft brush as well as the towel. This method is not likely to remove any colour but it is always wise to test on an inconspicuous area first. Vinyl repair kits are available at motor accessories shops. Most will carry at least three types and the choice depends on the repair which needs to be done.

A scratch in vinyl can be made less noticeable by using a matching felt-tip pen colour. Carefully fill in the scratch and remember it is always best to use a lighter colour and apply two or three coats than to fill in with a dark colour which will make the scratch more obvious. When the scratch is satisfactorily covered, spray with any good vinyl polish.

VOMIT

The smell of vomit in a car, if it is not removed, will very likely outlast the life of the car. Remove solids from the vomit with a plastic spatula, then sponge the soiled area with warm water and wool wash. Any areas of the car that have been soiled should, if possible, be removed so the under surfaces can be cleaned. Mats can be lifted and the back of them scrubbed. The floor under the mats should be washed and allowed to dry. Before putting the completely dry mats back, smother the floor with powdered borax. After three weeks, vacuum the borax away. Seats should be taken out if possible, cleaned underneath and allowed to dry out in the air. Smother with borax to absorb any lingering odour. On other places in the car, pay particular attention to seams and grooves in the upholstery. Use an old toothbrush, or a soft nailbrush, to scrub seams and grooves. If the upholstery is fabric, mix together 4 tablespoons of salt, 4 tablespoons borax and 4 tablespoons of shellite (naphtha). Sprinkle it over the offending area, and if necessary, cover the mixture with a towel so the car can still be used, and vacuum the mixture off after two days.

There are two possibilities for removing the stain from the carpet. First, dampen the stain, cover it with borax powder, and leave for 12 hours, vacuum off and repeat if necessary. The second method is to dampen the stain, cover it with denture powder. Leave for about 20 minutes. Remove excess

powder, then sponge with warm water and a little nappy-soaking powder. Don't forget to work from the outside edge of the stain towards the centre and mop up residual moisture with a thick towel.

VOMIT – ON CLOTHING

Dampen the stain, then cover it with denture powder. Leave it for about 20 minutes then wash the garment with a small amount of oxygen bleach washing powder or nappy-soaking powder in lukewarm water. Turn it inside out to dry, but not in direct sunlight.

WALLPAPER

Washable wallpaper can be cleaned with warm water and a little cloudy ammonia. Nonwashable wallpaper poses a problem, particularly grease stains. Make a paste of talcum powder with very little water, allow to dry on the stain then brush off with a soft cloth. Bread will also clean wallpaper. It must be two days old. Remove all the dust from the wallpaper first, then hold the bread in the hand and wipe lightly over, changing the bread as its surface becomes dirty. Vinyl wallpaper can be cleaned with white vinegar on a cloth wrung out in warm water.

WALLPAPER – WATER STAIN

Make a paste with starch and white vinegar. It needs to be about the consistency of thick cream. Spread the paste over the line of the stain and when it dries, brush it off. If it looks like fading the stain, if might be worth repeating but don't waste too much time on what is probably a fruitless task. It is better to paste a matching piece over the stain. When patching wallpaper, don't cut across the paper, use a ragged tear. It makes the patch less noticeable.

WALLS

Painted walls or ceilings that have been stained by smoke or gas heaters frequently resist all cleaning methods and have to be repainted. It is no good just covering the stains with a coat of paint because the stains will bleed through the new paint in no time at all. It is necessary to apply a sealant. Stain Seal is available at most paint and hardware stores.

During the winter months, condensation and dust gather on the walls, giving them a rather tired look. A bucket of hot soapy water, 8 tablespoons of powdered borax with 1 cup of cloudy ammonia will do wonders to brighten the walls. To remove the grease around the stove mix together ½ cup of cloudy ammonia and ¼ cup each of vinegar and washing soda in 5 litres (1 gallon) of warm water. Wear rubber gloves to wash walls with this solution. For crayon on walls, rub with dry steel wool, then sponge with eucalyptus oil.

Ballpoint pen marks can usually be removed with pen remover. Put pen remover onto a cottonwool pad, dab the marks then sponge any residual with a cloth wrung out in warm soapy water.

Painted walls that are very dirty are best cleaned with sugar soap that is sold at hardware stores or paint shops. Follow the instructions on the container. For painted walls that need only a general clean, very hot water and washing soda, or even very hot water and wool wash should

be sufficient. Whichever method of cleaning is used, be sure to cover the floors with plastic to catch the drips. I prefer to put plastic down, then cover the plastic with an old sheet so the drips don't form puddles on the plastic.

WALNUT – FURNITURE

Use a cotton bud dipped in methylated spirits to rub along any scratch mark to get rid of the polish. Then dip a cotton bud in iodine diluted 50 per cent with water, to colour the scratched walnut table. Once the scratch is coloured to your satisfaction, polish over it.

WATER

On leather, whether it is a shoe or handbag, try wiping over a water stain with a soft cloth and a little brown vinegar, or equal parts of cloudy ammonia and milk rubbed on with a soft cloth will sometimes remove the stain.

On fabric: If colours are light, a weak solution of vinegar and water can sometimes remove water stains. Or try a hot cloth wrung out in a solution of cloudy ammonia and water.

On wood furniture, water marks can sometimes be removed by rubbing the area with a little cigarette ash mixed with water. Be sure to rub with the grain of the wood or, put some Brasso on a soft cloth again rubbing with the grain of the wood.

WATER – DISCOLOURED

Discolouration of the town water supply can usually be remedied by fitting filters to the taps. A reader once told me that she made her own filtration system by putting a loose wad of cottonwool around the tap, covering the cottonwool with an open mesh nylon fabric, then securing it firmly to the tap with rubber bands. She did say that while it didn't look fantastic, it certainly saved her clothes from being stained.

WATER – STORM DAMAGE

Damage to upholstered furniture caused by storm or large spills can usually be treated without any water stain being left on the surface. The greatest problem from water-damaged upholstery is the smell. Dampness penetrates into the filling and springs, mould grows and the smell intensifies. It really is necessary to treat the unpleasant odour from the inside. It is not too great a task for a handyman or woman. The back and the bottom of chairs and couches are usually the last pieces to go on, so that is where to start. Use a screwdriver and an upholsterer's tack hammer as levers to carefully lift a corner of the back. Don't lift any more than is absolutely necessary to assess the damage. It may only need to be sponged out with antiseptic disinfectant to kill the mould, then dried, sprinkled with commerical odour neutraliser and the back tacked on again. For more extensive damage, some of the filling may need to be replaced. At this stage, most people might prefer to call a professional upholsterer. It is a good idea to get more than one quote, along with a guarantee for the work to be redone if the smell lingers on.

WEDDING

To restore a white leather wedding album that has yellowed, trea in the same way as shoes. First, wipe it over with methylated spirits on a soft cloth to remove finger marks and dirt. Then use a good quality white leather shoe cleaner. If the yellowing is intense, use a white shoe colour change.

To keep an uniced wedding cake, wrap in two layers of brown paper, then store in a cardboard box in a cool dry place. Add some silica gel, (available from cake decorators) to the container, but be sure the silica gel does not touch the cake. For a wedding cake that is to be stored, before icing, paint the cake all over with egg white which has been lightly beaten with a fork. Let the egg white dry before icing the cake. This helps to keep the icing white. Wrap an iced cake in two or three layers of white paper and proceed the same as for an uniced cake. Another method is to put the cake into a freezer bag, pump all the air out, seal the bag and store in the freezer.

Stains on old satin wedding dresses should be entrusted only to a commercial cleaner who also re-dresses fabric. New satin fabric is usually made with synthetic fibre or a mix, and is probably washable. Check the label. If the satin is washable, rust marks can often be removed by covering them with a paste made with salt and lemon juice. Leave the paste on for about 12 hours before brushing off and sponging with a cloth dipped in a solution of one tablespoon bicarbonate of soda (baking soda) in half a cup if warm water or, use a rust remover.

The most important thing about storing a wedding dress is to make sure it is cleaned before storing. Dry cleaning by a specialist dry cleaner is best. The dress should then be wrapped in blue, acid-free tissue paper and stored in a cardboard box. Stuff the bodice and the sleeves with tissue paper so the dress is not packed into creases. Loose packing is preferable. Trimmings, particularly of gold colour, should be covered with tissue in such a way that the gold does not touch the white fabric. Epsom salts can be scattered in the bottom of the cardboard box to deter moths and silverfish, but don't let the salts touch the fabric of the dress.

For a very small make-up mark on a dry-cleanable wedding dress, first try talcum powder. Cover the mark with white talcum powder, cover the powder with a white tissue, wash your hands in very hot water, dry them, then with a thick towel covering the hand which is under the stain, press the other hand onto the top of the tissue. Hold it there for a few minutes before brushing off the powder. That may be all that is necessary to remove a small mark. The treatment can be repeated a couple of times and any residual mark can be lightly sponged with a cloth wrung out in lukewarm water with pure soap flakes dissolved in it. Pat dry with a clean towel.

Perspiration stains can oxidise and become rusty. Dampen the stained area and cover it with lots of cream of tartar. Leave for about 2 hours, then brush the cream of tartar off and use rust remover to remove the residual stain. Follow the instructions on the bottle, and don't forget to sponge the rust remover from the fabric with warm water and pure soap.

WEDDING VEIL

To store a wedding veil, do not fold, but roll in blue acid-free tissue paper and keep in a

cardboard box. Every few months it should be taken out and re-rolled the opposite way. Store away from light. To mend wedding veils, the old-fashioned way was to darn over small tears with hair. Another method is to dip a piece of veiling into thin raw starch, place it over the tear, then cover with a handkerchief and press on the wrong side with a warm iron when the starch is dry.

WEIGHT – TO PUT ON
This is the recipe that Martha Gardener used to give for people who wanted to gain weight, particularly after an illness. However, if someone has been ill, I suggest you show the recipe to your doctor and ask for an opinion before using it. Make up 5 tablespoons of sugar, 2 tablespoons powdered skim milk, 1 tablespoon nutritional chocolate food drink, 1 egg and 1 litre (2 pints) of milk. Beat it all together. This quantity will probably last for two or three days.

WHITEWASH
To whitewash wood, glass, or metal surfaces, either inside or outside, dissolve 1 kilogram (36 oz) salt in ¾ of a bucket of water. Start with hot water to quickly dissolve the salt, then add cold water. When the salt is dissolved, slowly add 5 kilograms (11 lbs) of lime, stirring continually until the mixture is smooth and creamy.

Whitewash was often applied with a piece of light canvas or cloth, but it can also be brushed on. Only mix as much as is needed at one time because whitewash should be applied immediately after mixing. About 2 tablespoons of alum added to the mix prevents rubbing.

To whitewash bricks or concrete, mix together 5 kilograms lime (11 lbs), 2.5 kilograms (5½ lbs) cement, and 500 grams (16 oz) of salt with enough water to make a thin mixture. It should be transparent when first applied. The ideal brush to whitewash any surface is a wide wallpapering paste brush.

WINDOW CLEANER
Use equal parts of kerosene, cloudy ammonia, methylated spirits and water. If kerosene does not mix well, a good shake before using is sufficient. After cleaning the windows, polish with a soft, dry cloth.

WINDOW CLEANER – FOR SEASIDE HOMES
Mix together 4 dessertspoons of cornflour with ½ cup of cloudy ammonia and ½ cup of brown vinegar. Store it in a bottle with a childproof screwcap. Shake well before using and apply with a slightly dampened sponge. Rub over with scrunched up newspaper to complete the window cleaning.

WINDOW CLEANER – GLORIA'S
Into a 750 millilitre (26 fl oz) bottle with a screw cap put ½ cup each of methylated spirits and cloudy ammonia. Add ¼ cup of washing-up liquid, then fill the bottle with cold water and label it. Shake the bottle before use and add about 2 tablespoons of the mixture to ¼ of a bucket of hot

water and use a window sponge to clean the windows. While the windows are still wet with the mixture, hose it off to prevent streaking. If that is not convenient, use scrunched-up newspaper to dry the windows.

WINDOWS – STEAMED

The problem is caused by insufficient ventilation. If it is not possible to have a window open, then you really need an exhaust fan, preferably in the kitchen. Speak to your local hardware or electrical goods store about the cost of installing a suitable exhaust fan.

WINE STAINS

Fresh wine stains on clothing or carpet can be treated immediately with soda water. Pour soda water onto the stain; mop up, working from the outside to the middle so as not to spread the stain. Repeat, if necessary. Wash or dry clean clothing as soon as possible after treating with soda water. For dry wine stains, dampen the stain then cover with a layer of powdered borax. Leave to dry, then brush off.

WOOD FURNITURE

Mix together equal quantities of linseed oil and turpentine and apply it, with a soft cloth, to the scratches. For very dark wood, old-fashioned shoe polish of a matching colour can be used. Match the colour to a lighter, rather than a darker shade. It is better to apply two or three coats rather than make it look too dark.

WOOD LICE

Wood lice, or slaters, gather and breed in damp dark places such as cellars, sheds and laundries. Chemists, nurserymen and hardware stores sell quassia chips that come from the bark of a tree, making it a completely natural product. Quassia chips are steeped in boiling water, strained, and the liquid used to spray areas where the insects are found. Particular attention should be given to all woodwork and the bottom of walls where they join with the floor. Regular spraying is a necessity.

WOOL ITCH

Wool that itches is usually woven, not knitted. However, wash the garments in homemade wool wash and rinse with a good fabric softener. If the garment continues to feel itchy, it may be due to a skin sensitivity, in which case, consult your doctor.

WOOL – KNITTING

To straighten wool before re-knitting, roll it around the ironing board, cover with a damp cloth and press. Another way is to roll into balls and put in a pressure cooker for two minutes, or microwave for 30 seconds.

WOOLLENS

At the end of winter, woollens which are being put away in drawers for the duration of the hotter months should be washed in wool wash, using the no rinse method. To be sure the drawers are free of silverfish eggs, just waiting to be hatched, use a hair dryer, turned to its hottest, to go round all the seams of the drawers. The drawers must be taken out to do this task because it is important to do the underside as well as the inside.

If you don't have a hair dryer, very hot water, then outside in the hot sun, will also cook the eggs and prevent them from hatching. Make sure the drawers are completely dry before putting the woollens in.

WOOLLENS – RE-SHAPING

It is sometimes possible to improve the look of woollen garments that have changed their shape in the wash. Dissolve 90 grams (about 3 tablespoons) Epsom salts in boiling water. Add sufficient cold water for the temperature to be lukewarm, and enough to cover the garment. Soak the garment in the solution for half an hour then squeeze out excess water. Lie it flat on a towel and push or stretch the garment to its correct size and shape. When almost dry, wring out a cloth in cold water, cover the garment with the cloth and iron. Leave it flat to dry and set.

WOOLLENS – SMELLY

Spray garments with a commerical odour neutraliser. Leave for about an hour, then wash in wool wash. Do not rinse. Roll in a towel and spin dry on the low cycle of the washing machine. Don't use the tumble dryer for woollens. Turn them inside out and lay them on a towel to dry flat. If there is any residual smell, spray again.

WOOLLENS STRETCHED

If a woollen jumper has been stretched, or simply knitted too big, try washing it by hand in lukewarm water with wool wash. Roll it in a towel and spin dry in the washing machine to get out as much water as possible. Don't tumble dry or it will become matted. Then lie it flat on a dry towel, pushing it back into shape, and leave to dry. If the jumper is too stretched, or big, for treatment to work, it would be better to undo it and start again. Another method is to simply undo the bands and re-knit to make them tighter. This method will achieve a blouson look that could be very attractive.

WOOLLENS – TO UNSHRINK

Dissolve about 3 tablespoons of Epsom salts in boiling water. Once the salts are dissolved, add enough cold water to cover the garment. The water should now be lukewarm. Put the garment into the water and leave it to soak for about half an hour. Empty the water from the container and squeeze (do not wring) the excess water from the wool. Put the garment flat on a towel, and push it gently to the correct size and shape. When almost dry, wring out a cloth in cold water,

cover the garment with the cloth, and press. Leave it flat to dry and set. And, please, never use boiling water on pure wool – I hate to think what it does to the wool.

WOOLLENS – WASHING

I think the best way to wash any woollen garment is with homemade wool wash. Always wash and rinse woollens in water of the same temperature. Do not soak woollen garments for more than 20 minutes. You can spin dry woollens in the washing machine, preferably rolled in a towel. Do not put woollens in the tumble dryer. Finish drying, with the garments turned inside out, away from direct sunlight. If you live in a district with hard water put 1 tablespoon of powdered borax in the wash water.

WOOLLENS – WHITTENING

It is sometimes possible to whiten cashmere or woollen garments that have discoloured because of age, improper storage or exposure to direct sunlight. One method is to soak the garments for about an hour in lukewarm water with 1 cup of bicarbonate of soda (baking soda), then hand wash in pure soap flakes. Always wash and rinse in water of the same temperature. Spin dry. Do not tumble dry. Complete drying as quickly as possible and away from direct sunlight, and with the garment turned inside out. Another method is to soak the garments for 10 minutes in 2 tablespoons of denture powder and lukewarm water, then rinse and soak, for 2 or 3 hours in lukewarm water and a little nappy-soaking powder, moving the garments about in the water every 15 minutes. Rinse in lukewarm water, roll in a clean towel to spin dry, then turn inside out to finish drying. Always dry away from direct sunlight and bear in mind that most knitted garments need to lie flat to dry. Never dry in front of a heater or any other direct heat. The manufacturers of nappy-soaking powder and denture powder do not recommend their product for woollens, but if a garment is unusable due to yellowing, it is certainly worth a try.

WOOLLEN UNDERBLANKET

A woollen underblanket should never be tumble dried. Spin dry, twice if necessary, then lay it flat, away from direct sunlight, to dry thoroughly. If the blanket has become hard because of incorrect drying, soak it in lukewarm water and 6 tablespoons of Epsom salts for about an hour, then spin it dry in the washing machine, once only, and spread it flat to dry. When it is almost dry, cover it with a sheet and iron over the sheet to flatten the matted areas.

WOOL MATTED

Garments made from wool, or a mixture of wool with another fibre, should not be tumble dried. With tumble drying there is always the risk of the wool becoming matted and shrinking. The only chance of reversing a matted look is to soak the garment for about twenty minutes in lukewarm water with 3 tablespoons of Epsom salts dissolved in the water. Remove the garment and squeeze the water from it. Do not wring. Then lie the garment flat on a thick towel and pull

it gently into shape and loosen the matted look. Change the towel from time to time, and turn the garment over. When almost dry, put a tea towel over it and press to set the shape.

WOOL WASH RECIPE

The old-fashioned wool wash recipe is made by mixing together four cups of pure soap flakes, 1 cup methylated spirits and 50 millilitres (2 fl oz) of eucalyptus. The mixture will look like mashed potatoes. Put it into a jar with a tight-fitting lid. Use about 2 tablespoons of the wool wash mixture to a bucket of water. When washing woollens, it is not necessary to rinse. This method of washing woollens without rinsing is particulary good when woollen clothing is being put away during the summer months because it helps deter insects and silverfish

YELLOWING – COTTON AND SYNTHETICS

For garments of cotton, or synthetic fibre, which have yellowed, mix together in a 750 millilitre (26 fl oz) bottle with a screw-top, ¼ cup of methylated spirits, ¼ cup washing-up liquid, 1 tablespoon ammonia, 1 teaspoon eucalyptus, 1 dessertspoon citric acid, and 3 cups of cold water. Soak the garments overnight in ½ bucket of cold water with a quarter cup of the mixture. Next day, wash in warm water with pure soap flakes.

YELLOWING – WOOL

Woollen garments that have yellowed can be put into ½ bucket of lukewarm water with 2 teaspoons of cream of tartar and one tablespoon of citric acid. Leave for ½ hour, then hand wash with wool wash. Do not dry woollen garments in a tumble dryer. Turn inside out to dry, and do not dry in direct sunlight.

ZINC

To clean zinc, rub with a mixture of salt and lemon juice. Alternatively, cut a lemon in half, dip it in salt and rub the zinc. White vinegar mixed with salt also cleans zinc. Rinse well after cleaning, then buff up with a soft dry cloth.

ZINC CREAM

Zinc cream can usually be removed from washable surfaces with wool wash. Put the wool mix onto a clean cloth, wrung out in hot water and dab the zinc cream, changing the cloth as necessary to prevent spreading the stain. Work from the outside edge to the centre of the stain.

For heavy zinc cream staining on fabric, put eucalyptus oil onto a cloth and remove the stain by working from the outside edge to the centre. When the excess is removed, regardless of the fabric, wash completely, or sponge, with wool wash and rinse well. For light staining from zinc cream, washing, or sponging with wool wash should be sufficient.

ZIPPER – STUCK

If a zip fastener becomes stuck, talcum powder liberally sprinkled over the teeth of the zipper often help to free it. Zippers sometimes stick because of fabric from inside the hem folding back into the zip. Try to jiggle it loose rather than cut, and when free, stitch the hem back so that it does not catch again.

NOTES